First published 2014.

Written and published by Neil Warburton.

Photos have been credited where photographers are known, if you have not been credited please contact for inclusion in any possible future re-prints.

Printed and bound in the UK by
Inky Little Fingers
Unit A3-A5
Churcham Business Park
Churcham
Gloucester
GL2 8AX
www.inkylittlefingers.co.uk

Orders/Info: neilkor@yahoo.com

ISBN: 978-0-9931049-0-9

A catalogue record for this book is available from the British Library.

THE DIRECTOR'S CUT
(FEATURING EXCLUSIVE EXTRAS)

Best Wishes,
Neil Whatson

FOREWORD
by Peter Innes

Without Kevin's at-times fucking annoying contrariness, no "Don't Stand Me Down", no "One Day I'm Going To Soar", no "My Beauty"; without Jimmy's beyond the call of duty, broad-shouldered loyalty, no Dexys. Without "Because of You", no "A Million Miles Away"; without the hard-training self-discipline of Dexys Midnight Runners II, no "Goody Two Shoes". Without the sweet voice and funky bass of Pete Williams, the one-of-a-kind supportive, reliable genius of Mick Talbot, without Billy, Al Archer, Micky B, Helen, JB, Lucy, Stoker, …no collective us, we, together, where we are, today.

Jim had been more than kind to me, a stranger, on a project I worked up in the 90s. We share the pain of supporting Aberdeen FC through thick and (mostly) thin… at sun-drenched Easter Road May 3rd 1980, it was Hibs 0 The Dons 5, Aberdeen champions and fittingly, the glorious "Geno" was the UK's number one. It fits.

I'm privileged to feel that I've slowly become a tiny part of this nuclear family – it's good, it's fulfilling, to be part of something this special, this brotherhood – thank you guys, my great friends, from the bottom of my heart, for accepting me, for looking after me. Even in the fallow years, when we relied on the old vinyls, copy-of-copy-of-copy tapes, and Neil's keep the dream alive manifesto that was "Keep on Running", simplistically a fanzine but, in reality a defiant gesture of faith, a refusal to let this good thing die. A hard road at times for sure... but what better time than Rowland's remarkable resurrection of 2012 to celebrate this unique experience we have shared? Keep On Running, indeed – thanks Neil.

The original 'Inky' copy of 'KOR' before I changed them

It was like this...

I remember picking up a copy of Record Collector magazine (it must've been early '95), I turned to the Fanzine Reviews section - Madness, Adam and The Ants, Duran Duran etc... "No Dexys," I thought! After seeing this it was on my mind for a while to start a Dexys fanzine (I'd already built up a huge collection of press cuttings etc over the years). Anyway, it didn't happen for a while, then one day when visiting my Nan there was an old type-writer outside her house, which had been thrown out by a neighbour for the scrap man (not many people had computers in '95, including me!). "I can try and do it now," I thought. I rather hastily put the first issue together and after all the adverts went out, the response I got was quite overwhelming, interest from all over the world. My thoughts that I was the ONLY Dexys fan in this whole wide world were soon diminished!

The first few issues were a bit of a 'Cut and Paste' job, although a friend sometimes helped me on his computer with designs etc. I later totally re-designed the first four issues (although the content remained the same) after getting my own computer! I think Keep On Running really got started on Issue 4, when I managed to contact Andy Leek (Piano 79/80), he agreed to do an interview with me in a cafe in Wolverhampton, drinking tea! What else!? Andy then got me back in touch with Kevin Rowland, who remembered me as "a serious lookin' kid!" (Kevin lived in the same road as me at the time of 'Geno') and we ended up meeting in Brighton in 1997. I later had a phone call from Al Archer (proper name Kevin, but only room for one Kevin in Dexys! As Kevin 'Billy the boy' Adams later found out!). Then Big Jimmy Paterson contacted me, later on I even got to interview the legendary Geno Washington in his hotel room.

Issue 15, April 2000 was to be the last issue of 'KOR', this was mainly due to me working in Holland and not having the time to work on it. 'KOR' signed off by organising a Dexys fan convention in Birmingham in September of that year - 'Breakin Down the Walls...', this was a first meeting (for most) of wild hearted outsiders! The event included a showing of rare Dexys TV appearances and promo videos, along with music from the soul throughout the day. But I think most of all, it was about like-minded people meeting up for the first time and reminiscing and sharing their tales. "There's Pete Williams at the bar" says my good Dexys brother Vincent Cain, then Kevin Rowland's brother Pete (RIP) arrives in the afternoon and later shares some great stories that I can't really share here! But don't say that you hate dogs to Big Jim!

'Breakin Down the Walls...' Birmingham, 2000

Following that there was a second convention 'The Gathering' in 2004 (organised by John Salsbury, Nicola Cooke and Ian Jennings), which saw Archie Brown (The Bureau) perform an acoustic set from a selection of The Bureau back catalogue and songs he's recorded with his other band Archie Brown and The Young Bucks. Micky Billingham (Dexys keyboards 81-83) then took to the keyboards as he sang his own, very touching, treatment of, believe it or not, George Formby's 'Leaning On A Lamp Post', followed by some of the old Dexys classics (that's when he could remember the notes and what key they were in, well it had been some twenty-years since he last performed them!). In an unplanned climax to the evening Archie Brown and Micky Billingham performed together for the first time ever! There was also a guest vocal performance by Dexys fan Vincent Cain! Who can now add that he's performed with Micky Billingham to his CV!

Micky Billingham and Archie Brown perform at 'The Gathering 2004'

The Bureau re-formed briefly for live shows in 2005, this coincided with their debut album from 1981 being re-released in a 2-disc set featuring bonus tracks and a stunning live disc. A long-awaited completely new album was released in 2008 titled '...and another thing'. The Bureau disbanded shortly afterwards and the band GI Blythe were born with original Dexys brass men Geoff Blythe and Big Jim, joined by Archie Brown on vocals (album 'Lost in Space' released 2011). Kevin Archer's band The Blue Ox Babes also seen their album from 1988 'Apples And Oranges' finally released on CD in 2009 with bonus tracks. Pete Williams (Dexys and The Bureau) is still going strong as a solo-artist to this day (album 'See' released 2011), that's when he's not too busy with Dexys! A new album from Pete Williams is due to be released late 2014.

Dexys Midnight Runners reformed in 2003 and played to packed venues up and down the UK. The line up included original Dexys man Pete Williams on co-vocals and Mick Talbot on keyboards. Of the twenty-date 'To Stop The Burning' tour, I went to ten shows, but I know a man who went to all! Unfortunately nothing materialised after this, apart from a Greatest Hits package that included new tracks 'Manhood' and 'My Life In England'. A promo only CD of 'Manhood' gave fans hope of an official single release, but nothing followed and copies of the promo CD were soon selling on Ebay in the region of twenty pound. In the same year Dexys were awarded the long overdue Classic Songwriter award in Q magazine.

The year 2010 marked the 30th Anniversary of Dexys debut LP 'Searching For The Young Soul Rebels'. To celebrate this an event was held in Birmingham (organised by Ian Jennings, Stuart Cranston and Clive Gray). I was given the job as chauffeur for the day and my first job was picking up Anthony O' Shaughnessy (front cover 'Searching' LP) from Birmingham airport (where I amused him by holding up a 2-foot sized cardboard poster of his image on the 'Searching' LP at the arrivals lounge, I did have some strange looks!). Then I picked up Big Jimmy Paterson and his wife Sandra, along with Paolo Hewitt from Birmingham New Street Station and driving them to their hotel.
I HAD BIG JIMMY'S TROMBONE IN MY CAR!

Stuart Cranston, Neil Warburton and Gemma Sizer (who kept the poster as a souvenir)

It was a fantastic evening that included very rare photos of Dexys shown at the event by Mike Laye (one of Dexys early photographers). Music critic Gavin Martin interviewed Anthony O' Shaughnessy, along with original runners – Big Jim Paterson, Pete Williams, Geoff Blythe, Steve Spooner and Pete Saunders. Music critic Paolo Hewitt told his own Dexys story and the night was capped off with a live performance by Stone Foundation, who were joined on stage for the finale by Big Jim and Geoff Blythe to perform two tracks from Dexys debut LP - 'I Couldn't Help If I Tried' and 'Tell Me When My Light Turns Green'. The crowd that packed this sweaty club, wanted more. They had just witnessed these two guys performing on stage together for the first time in thirty years!

Original Dexys men – Geoff Blythe, Steve Spooner and Big Jimmy Paterson joined by Anthony O' Shaughnessy at the 30th Anniversary

Dexys run back to glory days

Original Dexys brass section members "Big" Jim Paterson and Geoff Blythe take to the stage with Stone Foundation at The Flapper and Firkin pub

Musicians mark anniversary of classic first LP

Original members of hit 1980s group Dexys Midnight Runners reunited on their old Birmingham stomping ground for a 30th anniversary celebration of classic album Searching for the Young Soul Rebels.

Five members of the original 10-man line-up behind the record, released in July 1980, gathered for the event at The Flapper and Firkin near the National Indoor Arena – some meeting for the first time in more than 15 years.

And two members of the brass section, Geoff Blythe and "Big" Jim Paterson even performed songs from the album with Midlands band Stone Foundation including, I Couldn't Help It If I Tried and Tell Me When My Light Turns Green.

The band members were brought together by fan Ian Jennings, from Yorkshire.

Frontman Kevin Rowland was missing but fans did not seem to mind and packed in to the venue to hear those members who did turn up speak, illustrated by photos from their heyday.

After speculation going on for over ten years, Dexys finally returned with a new album in 2012. The 'Midnight Runners' had gone, they would simply be now known as 'Dexys'. "It's the same, but different." says Rowland. The new album was released in June titled 'One Day I'm Going To Soar' (ironically released on what would have been my Mum's birthday), and entered the Radio 1 chart at Number 13 and the HMV chart at Number 3. It's already being regarded by some music critics as "The album of the century," let alone the year! Prior to this in May, Dexys embarked on a short UK tour performing the new album in it's entirety along with a few old favourites. The shows went down a storm and received critical acclaim across the board.

Kevin and Big Jimmy even gatecrashed the Queens Jubilee celebrations when they appeared on BBC Breakfast TV with Bill Turnbull!

In September, Dexys went on an eleven date tour of the UK with sold out shows at London Barbican and Edinburgh Queen's Hall, they also took in the home town of Birmingham along the route and ironically ended in Oxford on my birthday! And yes, I was there!

In November 2012 Dexys played at The Harvest Festival in Australia, much to the delight of long-term Dexys follower – Andy 'The Kiwi' Purcell. Andy, who was born in Birmingham and now living in New Zealand, had flew over from New Zealand for the 2003 tour and followed them up and down the country for three weeks, taking in eleven shows. This time he only had to take the short three-hour flight across the Tasman Sea to see his beloved Dexys in Australia. Andy takes up the story - "I loved 'Searching For The Young Soul Rebels' and when I came on my own to Birmingham in 1981 Dexys had split up. The Bureau was around, that's how I met Pete Williams at The Brum Beat Christmas office party, I've known Pete since then. In May 1982 Dexys were due to play their first gig in months, so I went to Newcastle in May '82 for the Radio One weekend. The first night was The Boomtown Rats, I kipped in the park that night, then Dexys were there the next night. It was the first time ever that 'Come On Eileen' was played. Then in 2003 I was away from the family for exactly three weeks. I met fellow fan Ian Jennings for the first time ever at Newcastle train station on November 2nd, saw the last eleven shows of the tour, eleven weren't enough. Nine years later Pete Williams messages me to say they were going to Australia. I wasn't keen on a festival. Then Madeleine Hyland's dad told me that a show may be on the cards. I was there. It's a three hour flight to Sydney, I haven't been to Australia since I was 18-years old. The show at The Enmore Theatre was nine years to the day

Andy with Kevin in 2012 and inset with Kevin in 1982

of the Dublin gig. I had a few Guinness with Maddy's dad before the show, he flew over there too. Pete invited me backstage after the show, so great to catch up with Lucy, Mick Talbot and Pete again. The festival performance two days later was brilliant too. Later in April 2013 the family did the tourist thing in London and Paris etc. And yes I took my four kids to see Dexys at The Duke Of York's Theatre in London. I couldn't have been prouder. They loved it. Pete came and said "Hi" to the family after the show. I went to the show the next night on my own. A beer with Pete and Lucy etc afterwards. God I love and miss 'em all."

Towards the end of 2012 Dexys were awarded the Q magazine 'Q Icon' award, and the award was presented to them by, none other than, Geno Washington! It was the first time that Kevin had met Geno in person and when he was asked how he was feeling afterwards, he replied *"Good, especially having it presented to us by Geno Washington, just amazing. I saw him when I was a kid, a young teenager, and all these years later he gives us this award, it's amazing."*

The touring continued through 2013, with an amazing nine night residency in London's West End at the famous Duke Of York's Theatre. I went to two of these shows, and later in the year I went to shows in Dublin and Belfast before flying over to Holland to see them perform at The Parkpop Festival in The Hague and then onto The Melkweg in Amsterdam the following day. Whilst in Ireland I had the pleasure of being in the company of 'Searching For The Young Soul Rebels' cover star – Anthony O' Shaughnessy. Anthony became myself and fellow Dexy's fan Ann-Marie McKenzie's tour-guide. The first thing Anthony did when we arrived in Belfast from Dublin on that Friday morning was to point me out where the nearest Wetherspoons pub was! Anthony had some business to sort out, so I went to Wetherspoons alone at about 11am, only to find out that they don't serve alcohol until 12pm! (What's that all about!?)

Anthony meets me later in the afternoon (after I'd had a few pints and a lovely Irish stew!) and we head off to meet Ann-Marie and then to find a pub near to the venue. We find McHugh's Bar, which is right opposite the venue where Dexys were playing. Luckily it was a nice sunny evening as we spent most of the time standing outside the front, as we could hear Dexys rehearsing and we even heard Maddie singing 'Geno'! We went over to the venue just before opening time, as we couldn't see many people hanging about, only to find that a large queue had already formed around the corner! The venue was open-seating and Ann-Marie was quite worried that we wouldn't get front row seats, but as soon as the doors opened Ann-Marie ran past everyone dragging myself and Anthony in hand as we stormed to the front, the fight for front-row seats was quite comical, but yes we did manage to get them, much to the delight of Ann-Marie! I was wearing my 'LOVE YA LUCY! XXX' t-shirt (which I had previously unveiled a few weeks earlier at one of the London shows), and it was so hot in this packed Belfast venue that during the final encore I decided to strip off my shirt, as I duly

Kevin with Geno Washington

went topless at the front of the stage and threw my shirt towards Lucy, much to the amusement of Lucy and Kevin! (Although I was told that apparently Pete Williams said "Not that fuckin' shirt again!"). Of all the twenty shows I have attended Belfast was definitely the highlight, the crowd were on fire. On the following day Anthony takes us to the actual street where the photo of 'Searching For The Young Soul Rebels' was taken in Cranbrook Gardens in Belfast during the troubles of 1971. Anthony tells me that he never returned there until 1980 when the local press discovered that he was the cover star.

In September of 2013 Kevin Rowland was awarded an Honorary Degree of Doctor of Letters in Wolverhampton, so he's now known as Dr Rowland!

The touring continued through 2014 and Dexys even made a debut appearance at Glastonbury! At the time of this publication going to print in October of 2014 Dexys have just released a live album of the show at the Duke Of York's Theatre, combined with a DVD film documentary titled Nowhere Is Home, featuring the live performance in full. In July the film Nowhere Is Home was shown simultaneously at an amazing thirty-seven Vue Cinemas across the UK! Those who attended received a free limited-edition 7" vinyl single of live versions of 'Nowhere Is Home' and 'I Love You (Listen To This)'. At the time of going to print the album has just entered the Radio 1 UK charts at Number 38.

Kevin and Dexys are most definitely SOARING.

Neil *"The serious lookin' kid"* Warburton, October 2014.

I would firstly like to thank my good Dexys brother Peter Innes, without his assistance, guidance and continued support this would not have been possible, he was my Big Jim. Special thanks to all those who have contributed new and exclusive features especially Dexys men - Geoff 'JB' Blythe, Big Jimmy Paterson, Steve Shaw, Paul Speare and Kevin Archer. Thanks to Yasmin Saleh for her amazing contribution. Thanks to Eddie Blower for sharing his 'Dance Stance' story. Anthony O' Shaughnessy, Gavin Martin, Andy Keys Clark and Colin Hall for all contributing. Thanks to those who gave me permission to re-produce their stories – Paolo Hewitt, David Innes and Ian Jennings. Thanks to Clive Gray, Andy Purcell and Carbie Warbie for allowing me to share their excellent photos. Thanks to Sandra Paterson and all of the Koast Train Radio crew for their support. Finally, thanks to all those who have contributed to Keep On Running over the years, without all your support and contributions this would not have been possible.

R.E.S.P.E.C.T. x

Top – Ann-Marie with Anthony in Cranbrook Gardens. Above – myself with Lucy Morgan.

Please take into account whilst reading through Keep On Running that the original fanzines were written between 1995-2000, my views and that of others (including group members) may have changed since then. Keep On Running is totally unofficial and does not represent Dexys or Dexys Midnight Runners in any way.

METROPOLIS MUSIC BY ARRANGEMENT WITH THE AGENCY PRESENT

Dexys

PERFORMING THEIR ENTIRE NEW ALBUM 'ONE DAY I'M GOING TO SOAR' AND A FEW OLD FAVOURITES

SEPTEMBER 2012

TUE	11	CAMBRIDGE CORN EXCHANGE	01223 357 851
WED	12	BIRMINGHAM SYMPHONY HALL	0121 780 3333
THU	13	SOUTHAMPTON GUILDHALL	02380 632 601
SUN	16	LONDON BARBICAN	020 7638 8891
MON	17	GATESHEAD SAGE	0191 443 4661
TUE	18	EDINBURGH QUEEN'S HALL	08444 999 990
THU	20	BRIGHTON DOME	01273 709 709
FRI	21	MANCHESTER BRIDGEWATER HALL	0844 907 9000
SAT	22	BRISTOL COLSTON HALL	0117 922 3686
MON	24	LIVERPOOL PHILHARMONIC	0151 709 3789
TUE	25	OXFORD NEW THEATRE	0844 847 1585

BOOK ONLINE: GIGSANDTOURS.COM / 24 HOUR TICKET HOTLINE: 0844 811 0051

THE NEW ALBUM OUT JUNE 4TH

Dexys 2012
(L-R) Lucy Morgan, Mick Talbot, Kevin Rowland, Madeleine Hyland,
Jim Paterson and Pete Williams

Photos: Carbie Warbie

Soaring back to greatness

POP

DEXYS
Duke of York's Theatre, WC2
★★★★★

RICK PEARSON

FOR many people, Dexys Midnight Runners (now called simply Dexys) are the novelty rockers who gave the world Come On Eileen. Actually, their musical contribution is much richer and more complicated, taking in three great albums, 30-odd members, half a ton of cocaine and, ultimately, redemption.

Last year's album One Day I'm Going to Soar – the Birmingham band's first in 27 years – was a triumph; last night's show – the first of nine at the Duke of York's – was even better.

Never knowingly understated, frontman Kevin Rowland took the stage dressed in a fedora, clown trousers and a jacket straight out of Del Boy's wardrobe. His voice was equally striking – part Elvis Costello, part Swiss yodeller. Behind him, Jim Paterson's trombone playing cued applause from the crowd; Pete Williams provided backing vocals and appeared later dressed as a policeman for reasons unclear. And Madeleine Hyland thrilled as Rowland's mistreated muse.

Among the many highlights were the smouldering R'n'B of She Got a Wiggle, the full-blooded duet Incapable of Love, the anti-marital anthem Free, and Rowland's invitation on Nowhere Is Home to "take your Irish stereotype and shove it up your arse". Best of all, no matter how desolate the sentiments were – and, at times, Rowland seemed almost inconsolable – the overall effect was impossibly uplifting.

Encore followed encore as Dexys treated the crowd to the highlights of their early career including a rousing version of Geno and – thank the Lord – no Come On Eileen.

There will be other gigs this year but few as big-hearted, bizarre or downright brilliant as this.
■ *Sporadic dates until April 27 (0844 871 7623, atgtickets.com)*

The Wanderer returns in style as Dexys show off new album

Dexys, Birmingham Symphony Hall, by Stuart Filmer

By rights, this should have been a concert to celebrate Dexys nomination for a Mercury Prize.

That Dexys was overlooked in yesterday's nominations for the 2012 music competition was a surprise. The band's comeback album, One Day I'm Going to Soar, has been one of the most lauded of the year.

Last night, Birmingham's Symphony Hall was treated to a theatrical presentation of the album, a story of self-doubt, identity and an inability to love.

And there were some treats too, including an eight-minute version of Come on Eileen and a wonderful finale of What's She Like, the stand-out song from the last album Don't Stand Me Down, released in 1985.

This is no greatest hits tour, however, with Dexys leaving out standards like Geno in the second half of the show in favour of more obscure album tracks from the past.

The emphasis of the tour is very much on the new album, which features actress Madeleine Hyland as the love interest as the new songs are threaded into a narrative, which is by turns profound, hilarious, and heart-wrenchingly sad.

Rowland and Hyland last night milked the drama of that narrative to the full, he posturing and pouting and she teasing and ultimately running from the stage in a dramatic love-tiff tantrum.

One Day I'm Going to Soar is a truly remarkable work. The soul-filled She Got a Wiggle was a highlight despite a technical error with a projector screen. Incapable of Love was full of energy and humour.

But Rowland's strength was, and continues to be, his distinctive and powerful voice, which only appears to be improving with age. And that came into its own on ballads like Nowhere is Home and It's OK John Joe.

The self-styled Wanderer returned to his West Midland roots in style. And the rapturous and emotional reception he and the band received proves the enduring appeal of Dexys despite their 27-year break.

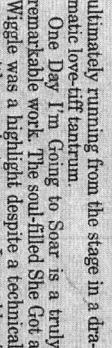

Rowlands and co-band founder Pete Williams

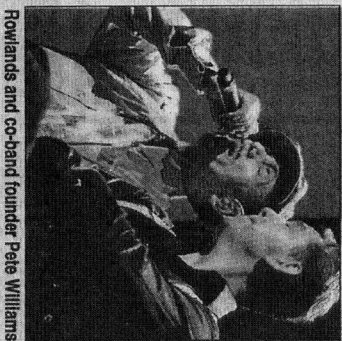

On a hot night in July 78 two men, Kevin Rowland and Al Archer left their low-profile Birmingham hide-out to round up a firm of boys. Fed up with petty spoils from their previous team – a small-time new wave group – and disillusioned by the lack of response from the major fences, they knew this one was going to the big one and if they were going to have it off they would have to be eight handed... with the hardest hitting men in town.

First stop was a rundown nightclub on the edge of town, well known for it's clientele of hard rock villains from the last generation. The band were in full swing as the two men strolled in. They were a mean bunch of smash and grab artists thumping away and rolling over on the floor, as if expecting a punk revival – all apart from the drummer Andy Growcott who was exceptional and was recruited immediately.

A week later young Pete Saunders armed with a Hammond organ was instated. His only form was having played with a local pop group. The following day tenor sax player JB was kidnapped from the late great "Geno Washington and the Ram Jam Band." Then there were five.

The rest of the team took a bit longer to recruit and some of the boys got impatient. Rowland and Archer assured them that this sound was the big one and was well worth waiting for. The boys cooled down and consoled themselves by listening to records of Cliff Bennett, Zoot Money, Sam and Dave, James Brown and Aretha Franklin etc...

Soon after a young bass driver by the name of Pete Williams walked into the hide-out carrying his tool under one arm and the complete Stax collection under the other. Disillusioned with new musak, he put his soul records on the table and shouted "I want to do something as good as these – only better." The boys knew exactly what he meant and welcomed him with open arms.

The team was completed by the inclusion of Steve "Babyface" Spooner, the alto, who got the word from a local snout and Big Jimmy Paterson who had been laying low in the north of Scotland. He got wind of a big one going off in the Midlands, grabbed his trombone and jumped on the next train. The firm was complete – now for the caper...

'Keep On Running' ran from 1995-2000. What follows are the highlights, known here as 'The Director's Cut'...

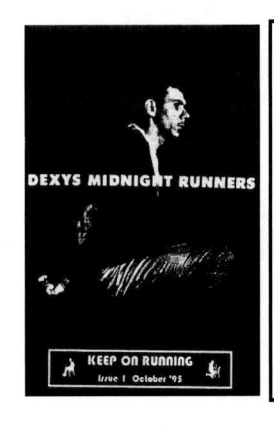

KEEP ON RUNNING
ISSUE 1 OCTOBER 1995

"I'll only ask you once more
You only want to believe
This man is looking for someone to hold him down
He doesn't quite ever understand the meaning
Never heard about, can't think about..."

DANCE STANCE (No. 40, January 1980)

My DEXY History
you don't mind if I get personal...

I was about nine-years old when I brought my first record (I'm now twenty-three), and to this day I'm pretty sure that the first record I brought was (yes, you've guessed it) 'Geno', what else!?

I have never stopped playing it to this day. I remember thinking at the time how individual it seemed to sound with other music that was around at the time. I knew that I had just purchased a truly precious possession (even without the picture sleeve), which I later got. Do you remember how difficult it used to be to get picture sleeves? I had to buy 'There There My Dear' twice (but it was well worth it). I think that if I won the lottery I would just go out and buy every single Dexy record in the shops (a million times over), to get them back to where they belong.

Anyway, just after I had purchased 'Geno', a few days later they were on Top Of The Pops, I watched this with my parents and when Dexys came on I could not believe it when my Mother turned round to me, looking very surprised, and said something like – "He only lives up the road", 'up the road' did not mean about two mile away or something, it actually meant about ten doors away. I could not believe it, here I am, just brought my first record and I'm told that the lead singer lives up the road.

So, as you can probably guess, the next morning I'm knocking his door, holding my copy of 'Geno' tightly to me. What I was dreading happened – no bloody answer, I walked home with my head down – there's always tomorrow I thought. When I did finally get round to seeing him they had just released 'There There My Dear' and they were on Tiswas on the Saturday morning performing this, I went round his house that very evening and he was in. I could not believe it when he opened the door, I said something like (all of a panic) - "Can I have your autograph please, I seen you on Tiswas this morning," he seemed quite pleased that I had seen him on the TV that morning and invited me into his house. There was a girl sitting down in there who looked the spitting image of Eileen in the video (maybe it was), I remember thinking how nice she looked! Anyway, he asked me where I lived and so on, not knowing to me beforehand, I had actually seen Kevin walking down the road on numerous occasions. Kevin signed 'Geno' for me and also gave me a very nice signed photo – which is now framed.

From that day on Kevin always acknowledged me (remember the thumb routine Kev?). I remember the one time when I was returning from swimming with the school and Kevin was sitting at the window in a cafe, he stuck his thumb up to me and nodded his head, my friends could not believe it - "God, you know Kevin Rowland."

I visited his house three or four times after this, the one time was with my cousin whose sister was very bad in hospital, Kevin signed a photo for her – 'To Helen, Get well soon – Kevin Rowland'. My cousin proudly displayed this at her hospital bedside. When she was better and it was time for her to leave the hospital, the nurses asked if they could keep the photo at the hospital to cheer up the other children, how could she refuse, we'll probably never know who has got that photo now.

Anyway, just after the release of 'Liars A To E' I see that Kevin's house is up for sale, it nearly brought tears to my eyes (don't laugh, I was only about nine). I tried on numerous occasions to see him before he moved on, but with no luck. So that was the last I got to see of Kevin, I remember thinking that maybe someone like Adam Ant would move in next (how silly can you get!).

I was too young to go to any concerts and the next time I get any where near to him is about seven years later – and then I missed him! It's the day of the launch of his solo career and the release of 'Walk Away', which is available as a limited edition 12" gate-fold biography. So I go into Birmingham in the afternoon and see a signed copy of the limited edition. I enquire - "How come this is signed?", he replies "Oh, he came in this morning, we didn't even know that he was coming in." I'm sure that you can understand my anguish that after about seven years I had just missed him by about two hours (ah well, that's life). I was still very pleased though to get that limited edition and signed as well, but meeting him again after all those years would have been a bit special.

So I suppose, as you all are, that we are all hoping and eagerly awaiting that Dexys comeback. Our hopes were raised a few years ago with that stunning Saturday Zoo TV appearance. I think that Kevin was having a few problems with getting the right record contract, yet at the same time they were getting excellent coverage in the music press etc, one report saying 'You must have record companies queueing all down your road'. There may have been enough interest but unfortunately nothing was to follow. I'm sure you know what these record companies are like, and I don't think they like Kevin's attitude too much. They're more bothered about what the individual is like rather than the music – idiots. No wander there's been so much crap in the charts for the past five or so years.

From now on Dexy's Midnight Runners will not take part in any interviews with the New Musical Express, Melody Maker, Sounds, Record Mirror or any other music papers.

Instead of filling these pages with the usual boring LP adverts, we have decided to use the space to accommodate our own essays which will state our point of view. These essays will appear regularly as we have strong views on several subjects and feel it is important we are understood.

We are doing this because we are totally disillusioned with the music press. We have attempted at least one interview with each of the papers but have never been represented properly. Instead these "journalists" conduct their own two hour schoolboy analyses which always reflect their own, oh so predictable, personalities.

Though some descriptions of us have intended favour, we have found them so persistently inaccurate, patronising and standardised, that it is obvious to us that these "writers" are so out of touch, they should be frightened. They are probably not. Instead they try to cover their total lack of understanding behind a haze of academic insincerity.

We won't compromise ourselves by talking to the dishonest, hippy press. We are worth much more than that.

dexys midnight runners

searching for the young soul rebels   dexys midnight runners

The KILLJOYS are from Birmingham. Lee Wood saw them live at a club in March (a small town near Kings Lynn) in June 1977 and their energy and enthusiasm was fantastic. The conviction with which singer Kevin Rowland put over the songs was incredible. It was difficult to decide how to get this energy and enthusiasm onto record. Many top bands had tried in the past but never had anyone been able to put onto tape the complete rawness of a live gig. Never had the studio engineer seen anything like it, the producer and the whole band 'pogoing' around the studio in an effort to produce the atmosphere of a live gig. In some way that can never be explained (a one in a thousand chance) everything clicked the atmosphere was electric - JOHNNY WON'T GET TO HEAVEN/ NAIVE were the result of this 'legendary session' - Two incredibly powerful tracks that are both becoming 'punk classics' in fact NAIVE is so powerful that many people including John Peel remarked on it's power, John Peel on his Radio programme stated that all the dials on the studio equipment reached bursting point from the very first note of the track and didn't budge at all until the very last note, near the end the song builds to a complete frenzy that has been known to destroy not so hard wearing stereo's.

The Killjoys have now unfortunately split up but two bands have been formed out of the remnants. Kevin Rowland has formed a nine peice band with brass along the lines of 'Geno Washington' and guitarists Mark Phillips and Ghislaine Weston are forming a band more along the lines of the Killjoys.

Tracks recorded that have never seen the light of day include RECOGNITION recorded on the same session as Johnny/Naive and DEFINITLY DOWN ON THE FARM and an untitled track, both recorded in London in mid 1978. Both produced by Lee Wood but not for Raw, the tracks were recorded to interest major record companies into signing the band. I can tell you that both tracks are even better than Johnny Won't Get to Heaven/ Naive but unfortunatly will probably never see the light of day.

1977 was an incredible year for great singles on independant labels and the Killjoys was certainly one of the best singles of the year.

Kevin Rowland   : Lead Vocals
Mark Phillips   : Lead Guitar
Ghislaine Weston : Bass Guitar
Heather Tonge   : Harmony Vocals
Joe 45   : Drums

Killjoy Kevin is having fun at last

by JOHN HESS

KEVIN ROWLAND was 22, had worked at 40 different jobs since leaving school, then decided rock music was the best road to success.

He put a classified advertisement in the Evening Mail 18 months ago looking for musicians to form a new band.

It heralded the birth of the Killjoys, today one of the most exciting local new groups.

No one is more surprised at the Oldbury-based outfit's success than lead singer Kevin.

Now major recording companies are vying with each other to sign up the band.

They were featured in a live session of John Peel's radio show and are now set for a week-long booking at a Paris night club.

Yet it is less than a year since their live debut—bewildered and with a drummer they persuaded to stand in minutes before getting on stage.

It was a meeting with the boss of Cambridge-based Raw Records after an early London gig, that secured their first recording deal.

The result was "Johnny Won't Go To Heaven," their debut single. Penned by 24-year-old Kevin, it sold more than 20,000 copies, a tremendous sale for a relatively unknown band. Then the Killjoys started dozens of London club bookings.

The present line-up includes guitarist Mark Phillips, aged 20, from Edgbaston, who answered Kevin's advert, and 19-year-old Ghislaine Weston, from Hollywood, Birmingham.

Drummer Bob Peach, 21, and guitarist Keith Rimell, 20, complete the band.

Kevin lives in Apollo Road, Oldbury, and writes all the material, but he's the first to admit The Killjoys jumped on the punk rock bandwagon. Now he is set on a new direction in rock music and stage presentation.

"We want to bring some fun and colour back to the music scene," he told me. "The audiences are now fed up with the black leather scruffiness that's been the fashion. They want a change—there's going to be one heck of a reaction against punk."

Killjoy's lead singer Kevin Rowland with Ghislaine Weston belting out their own distinctive style of pop.

KILLJOYS

KEEP ON RUNNING
ISSUE 2 JANUARY 1996

"Back in 68 in a sweaty club
Before Jimmy's machine and the rocksteady rub
On a night when flowers didn't suit my shoes
After a week of flunkin' and bunkin' school
The lowest head in the crowd that night..."

GENO (No.1, March 1980)

DEXY HISTORY

As we all know, Dexys have had quite a few turbulent times in the past, what with Kevin's ever changing music directions and images. It was always too easy for Kevin to stay with the same sound/image, he would always jump five stepping stones rather than taking a nice and easy step onto the next one. But wasn't this one of the reasons which made Dexys stand out from any other groups, the thought that you would never know what they would come up with next, what a perfectionist he was – whatever he was doing at the time, he always had an idea of how he could improve something and take it a stage further and better. Who else would have the nerve to hi-jack the master tapes for their debut LP from their record company so that they could get a better deal? Or change from the tramp look to well dressed businessmen?

Dexys also had many personnel changes over the years, this mainly due to the pressure they were receiving from Rowland as he strived for perfection. Many could not handle this and took the easy option out. One of the first Dexys to leave was Andy Leek back in 1980, whose departure caused rather a lot of unrest in the camp at the time. His reason for leaving was that he hated the commercialism of it all and he wanted to pursue a solo career. His debut single titled *Move On In Your Maserati* received rave reviews but unfortunately did not get anywhere. Andy is still performing now.

DEXY DOES A RUNNER

ANDY LEAK, keyboards player with Dexy's Midnight Runners, has quit the group . . . the same week as the group's single 'Geno' hit the top of the charts.
Andy Leak, who gave his reason for leaving as "really hating being famous all of a sudden," will have his own solo single out on Target Records in a few weeks.
"This time I'll go about it in a totally different way," he said. "There was no ill feeling with the rest of the group at all, I just didn't like all the attention.
"Just because I've been on 'Top Of The Pops' doesn't mean I should get any more respect. I didn't want people asking for my autograph all the time."
And he added: "My old man has been a window cleaner for the best part of his life and he deserves more respect than me. I'm just a person like anybody else."
Leak joined Dexy's Midnight Runners about six months ago, after the previous organist had left, and shortly after the band clinched a major record company deal. Now he plans to start again with the single 'Move On In Your Maserati'.
"It's a sort of goodbye to the band," he said. "Then I plan to form my own group where I can get my views across. I've got too much to say, and that was difficult with the number of people in Dexy's."
There's still been no statement from the rest of the group about a replacement, but Andy denied that it would be "worth a fortune" to anybody.
"I never made any money from the band, and I'm still in debt to the Social Security," he said.

DEXYS SPLIT UP AFTER DIRECTION ROW

This was the big one, which shocked the music world at the time and all Dexy fans thought 'Well that's it, no more Dexy'. How wrong we were (thank God, or Kevin should I say), so all split leaving just Kevin and Big Jim to sort it out. Various reasons were mentioned for the split, the main reason seemed to be that most of the group did not agree with the release of *Keep It Part 2*. Other reasons included that Kevin wanted to make some type of film and then blow up the houses of parliament.

Dexy's split up after 'direction' row

Dexy's Midnight Runners, the controversial Birmingham band with an Oldbury lead singer have split up.

Rows about the future of the band — which reached the top of the charts with its first single Geno" — have resulted in four members leaving.

Andy Grocott, Steve Spooner, Pete Williams and Jeff Blythe are now planning to form their own band — while front-man Kevin Rowlands, from Apollo Road, Oldbury, Al Archer and Jim Paterson continue under the old name, and search for replacement members.

A spokesman for the band's record company EMI said: "The band couldnot agree on future plans, and four members left. The details of the argument are being kept among band-members."

Before the split the band recorded a new single, Keep It, a remake of a track on their hit album, which will be released on November 17.

Kevin Rowlands

So the ex-Dexy members went off to start their own group, all apart from Al Archer who wanted to do his own thing. The Bureau were formed with Archie Brown on vocals and also playing for them was Mick Talbot (later 'Style Council'). Their first release was *Only For Sheep* which still had that very distinctive Dexy sound. The follow up single was a classic – *Let Him Have It*, a protest song about the hanging of Derek Bentley, with some hard-hitting lyrics – *'There goes Bentley, legs swinging just above the ground, his hands tied behind his back and nothing to see – no, someone here is going to pay for this – too bad that you're the only one who's old enough now'*. An album release followed which is really quite good, *Looking For Excitement* probably being my favourite track. Unfortunately no success followed in England, this was probably due to the fact that they were really cast as Dexy outcasts, had they been a completely new group I think it may have been a different story. They were quite popular over in Australia though.

The Bureau

Another band was also later formed called These Tender Virtues (pictured right), led by Pete Williams. A seven-track LP was released titled *The Continuing Saga...*, this had more of an Irishy sound with banjo and electric organ.

So while the ex-Dexys were trying to hit the heights again, Kevin Rowland had assembled a new group of lads and were soon back in the charts with *Show Me*. Unfortunately the Dexys of '81 never managed to release an LP. This period seen some of the most powerful Dexys songs ever, these included *Plan B* and *Liars A To E*. Kevin says to this day that the Dexys of '81 were one of the strongest.

TOO-RYE-AY

This was the most successful Dexy period and *Come On Eileen* was the best selling single of '82. Through this period Kevin took to hiring session players. The main nucleus was Rowland, Billy Adams, Seb Shelton, Steve Brennan and Helen O'Hara. Seb later left and once again there were many different reasons being mentioned, but we wont go into that. Seb has since been managing Julian Cope and remembers his Dexy times with some admiration - "No matter how much any of us moaned, we knew it was the best band we could ever have played in. That's why I stopped drumming after I left. Every old Dexy you meet is proud to have been part of it." After all the successes of '82 and '83 it was a further two years before we would see Dexys again.

> IT COULD be 1850, the Victorian brogues of the band looking more at home in the countryside of a Hardy novel, than in the dingy light of one of London's college bars. And yet *These Tender Virtues* shine through.
>
> Leading light Pete Williams started on the soul trail back in 1979, when he was recruited to the ranks of those minstrels of intense emotion Dexy's Midnight Runners to play bass. After doing a runner to set up the Bureau with four other ex-Dex members, he's now keeping the passion precious with soul brothers Ian, Mac, Fred and Brett.
>
> With banjo and electric organ resplendent, he captures the feeling and melancholy that makes soul. 'Waltz No 1' has a fairground hurdy-gurdy lilt to it, then there's the almost military backing to 'A Polish Prayer', a soulful rendition of 'Waltzing Matilda' and 'The Bottle' — a possible single.
>
> It has to be said though, the Dexy influence runs deep — and an excellent influence it is to be sure. Kevin Rowland without the lisp, but the mannerisms and manic gesturing are still there.

DON'T STAND ME DOWN

1985 and Dexys were back, though nobody would recognise them with straight hair and suits (the Ivy League look). Kevin refused to release a single despite pressure from the record company and some group members, so the LP *Don't Stand Me Down* was released with no single promotion. Even with no Dexys for two years and a new image the LP still reached Number 6, even though it did not stay in the charts for too long. This was mainly due to bad reviews and the LP had a really personal feel to it which many people could not associate with. Needless to say it is now regarded as one of the greatest 'lost' LPs of all time, ten years after release. Billy Adams and Helen O'Hara were the main nucleus of Dexys at this time. A single was later released from *Don't Stand Me Down*, an edited version of *This Is What She's Like*, it did not chart.

THE WANDERER

1988 and Kevin is on the solo path. Helen and Billy depart, Helen was last seen on violin for Tanita Tikaram. The debut solo single *Walk Away* is released, soon followed by the LP *The Wanderer*. No success came, *Tonight* and *Young Man* were released from the LP. *Tonight* was a classic with Rowland having his usual swipe at the middle classes – '*Well I spent this afternoon in a charabanc with some middle class bitch, been no where man*'.

MANHOOD

"*I'm trying hard to be a man – I sometimes wander if I can.*" This is what we hear as Dexys re-form in '93 and appear on Jonathan Ross TV show Saturday Zoo. Billy Adams is back along with good old Jimmy Paterson, who lends a hand at vocals (stick to the trombone Jim!). Dexys perform two songs *Manhood* and *If I Ever* with Kevin now in a cowboy outfit. Dexys appeared in the music papers etc and got some excellent write ups, but after this there was nothing. It was heard that the great Al Archer had also teamed up with Kevin once more, what a line-up that would have been – Kevin Rowland, Billy Adams, Jim Paterson and Al Archer – formidable (and still possible?).

LET'S SORT IT OUT KEV

SINGLE OF THE WEEK

KEVIN ROWLAND: Tonight
(Phonogram)
I like this. I like this a lot. Despite *NME's* recent savaging of Rowland's 'The Wanderer' LP, and Rowland-bashing in general, this sounds like a man in mighty fine form. Very classy pop, with a cunning lyric. Deceptively simple and quite wonderful. It made me want to go out and shop-lift Rowland's entire back catalogue. I don't want to read another word against him, but doubtless I will. Like Poor Johnny Thunders, Rowland is a much punctured, music press dartboard.

DEXY'S MIDNIGHT RUNNERS
RADIO ONE SESSIONS: NIGHT TRACKS
Windsong CDNT009
8 tks/33 mins/CD only

"KNOWLEDGE of beauty is these days rare."

Let's get this straight from the start. Some dolt recently had the temerity to suggest the biggest bunch of blithering idiots ever to con their way onto the hit parade are the heirs apparent to Rowland's crown. Lies, children, lies. Dexy's were an inferno, Dodgy are a... barbeque. On a rainy day.

Where does one begin to describe their legacy? Ah, yes. The end. "Don't Stand Me Down". The best album ever made by anyone ever and it's pistols at dawn if you dare disagree. Proof that truth and beauty need not be diametrically opposed. Commercial suicide, but "compromise is the devil talking."

Most bands drift into the music business bereft of vision or purpose, making the twin betrayal of their talent and ideals inevitable. Not Dexy's. When Rowland sang "I'll Show You", his paean to the diaspora, the destitute "coulda been contenders" battered into submission by the slings and arrows of outrageous fortune, you could tell he was determined not to share their fate, never to allow the insolent flame of his creativity to be snuffed out. To keep striving.

Dexy's were marvellously, heroically myopic, positively Calvinist in their pursuit of perfection – "I'll punish my body until I believe in my soul" – and blessed with the unshakeable conviction their chosen path was the right one. Who else would have had the courage, the faith to steal the master tapes of their first album to negotiate a better deal?

"Sessions" comprises songs which mostly ended up on "Too Rye Aye", justifiably considered to be the runt of the litter. But – wait for it – even at their weakest, they were Herculean. "Give me a record that cries pure and true/No, not those guitars, they're too noisy and cruel" ("Let's Make This Precious". Quite). This, remember, was where they began to wander into wonder, penning longer, more ambitious songs ("Until I Believe In My Soul"), the springboard to "Don't Stand..."

In retrospect, however, perhaps it was a little laboured, overworked, a casualty of their rigorous regime (though still a revelation compared to anything their contemporaries produced); the versions here – rougher, rawer, purer – are undeniably superior, stimulating as an adrenalin injection.

Two years ago, a reformation was promised. The band gave interviews, appeared on television airing new material, dispatched demo tapes to the fortunate few. Then, sadly... nothing.

Lord knows we need someone who can burn this brightly now.

JAMIE T CONWAY

KEEP ON RUNNING
ISSUE 3 APRIL 1996

"Dear Robin, hope you don't mind me writing
It's just that there's more than one thing
I need to ask you
If you're so anti-fashion why not wear flares
Instead of dressing down all the same..."

THERE THERE MY DEAR (No. 7, July 1980)

Reminisce Part One
by Adie Nunn (age 18), Aberdeen

Ah, the wonders of second-hand records. I had a bit of money to spare and decided to find something cheap. Obviously a CD was out of the question, unless I was going to buy a single, so a used record was my only choice. There were knackered Beatles LPs going for about twenty-pound each, even though they were scratched to pieces and the sleeves torn. Eventually I came across 'The Very Best Of Dexys Midnight Runners', I'll have this I thought. I recognised a couple of the song titles; *Geno* and *Come On Eileen* were songs I'd always seemed to have known, like half the Madness back catalogue, the Human League's *Don't You Want Me*, Pink Floyd's *Another Brick In The Wall*, practically every Kinks release from the '60s... in other words, catchy, classic songs that won't leave your head, and continue to haunt you wherever you go. There was no price on the record, so I asked at the counter and managed to get it for the measly sum of six-pound. Not bad for a four-year old record in mint condition.

I played it as soon as I got home, already knowing I'd made a very good purchase. Normally I'd be doing something else when a record or CD is playing – I'd be reading, writing, mucking about on the computer – but this time I just sat on my bed, jaw to the floor. Six quid for THIS! Most of the tracks were instant hits for me, especially *Show Me, Plan B, The Celtic Soul Brothers* and the songs I'd previously known, but because the record only ever left the deck when it was time to turn it over, the songs grew on me even more.

At the time I was studying for my final exams in 6th year. OK, I sat three exams and failed two of them, gaining a much worse grade than expected in the only one I passed, but I'd like to think it was Dexys that pulled me through a hellish period of studying, hours on end. It was practically the only album I listened to. If it was anything different I would have probably gone insane. It was also the album that helped me live through the post-exam stress.

Anyway, I wasn't to be fooled. I knew from past experience with these compilation albums that 'The Very Best Of' was not the best the band had produced. It wasn't long before the other albums were in my possession, as well as a few singles and bits off television. Only recently I saw a clip of the 'Eileen' promo, and strangely enough it seems I've always known that as well. My youngest brother, age seven, has now christened 'Eileen' as his favourite song. He used to come into my room whenever I played it (which was often), and leave as soon as it finished. He'd listen to me attempt to re-create the song on my PC, recognising it when I played only a few seconds. This is good because his favourite used to be Whigfield's 'Saturday Night' (which I never owned!). Now he wants to buy a Dexys tape himself, and can recognise the band from photos – I've probably scarred the child for life.

Thanks to Dexys, and a bit of help from The Commitments, I've got into soul music. Geno Washington played a gig (an acoustic set) in Aberdeen in October. I couldn't go because my money was rather on the short side, and it's still annoying that I missed him. Dexys and people like Aretha Franklin, James Brown, Wilson Pickett etc have shown me how bland the so-called soul/R&B bands are today. You just need to look at the American Billboard chart to see how dull everything is. These are songs that won't be remembered in six months time, let alone twenty years. They aren't singing from the soul, they (Mariah Carey, Janet Jackson, TLC, Boys II Men, M People, and all the other talentless chancers) are singing because they know these are the type of songs, watered-down rubbish that appeals to a vast audience, that can make them a quick buck and get them on MTV and Top Of The Pops. It's too depressing to think about. If this isn't proof that we NEED another band like Dexys, who could combine soul music with pop, folk and all sorts, then I don't know what is. There was never a band like them and there's never been anyone since.

Dexys have fuelled my already existent desire to form a band. The major problem is that I have little talent in playing guitar, and so far the best song I have written sounds like The Buzzcocks on extremely bad acid. To further rub salt in the wound, the only other 'musicians' round here are into house music (and nothing else) or long-haired, greasy American bands (and nothing else). And most of them are older than me and wouldn't take me seriously, or want to be bossed around by a GIRL. Ooh, perish the thought!

Whenever I get disillusioned I'll go to the student union and hang around until the last song is played, which is always on a good day, *Come On Eileen*. Then I'll go home, at 2am, and listen to *Searching For The Young Soul Rebels*, trying to play along on guitar. After that I'll just fall asleep on the floor and dream of the day I get out of this hell-hole college and find people enthusiastic enough to form a band unlike anyone else in the charts. I'll get there in the end. Now where did I put that guitar...

POLL RESULTS

Best Single -
THERE THERE MY DEAR
2. Geno
3. Dance Stance
   Plan B
   Show Me

Best B-Side -
BREAKING DOWN THE WALLS OF HEARTACHE

Best Single sleeve -
THERE THERE MY DEAR

Best Album-
SEARCHING FOR THE YOUNG SOUL REBELS

Best Album track -
Tell Me When My Light Turns Green
Seven Days Too Long
Until I Believe In My Soul
This Is What She's Like

Best Album sleeve -
SEARCHING FOR THE YOUNG SOUL REBELS

Best Image -
Mean Streets/New York Dockers

> **KEEP ON RUNNING**
> *ISSUE 4 JULY 1996*
>
> *"From now on I'll only read books*
> *That shows the worst of my looks*
> *No time to find the time to rewrite mine*
> *I could show it to you if nothing better to do*
> *But there's no point it doesn't look like you..."*
>
> **KEEP IT PART TWO (November 1980)**

Reminisce Part Two
by John McKelvie, Wishaw, Scotland

May I reminisce...? Can I get personal...?
Everyone has a story to tell and here's mine:
My own Dexys story goes back to about 1980 I think. I remember seeing them on Top Of The Pops and they just looked so different from anything else around; others in school were into Madness, Adam And The Ants, The Jam, Des O'Connor or whatever. I was thirteen and they were one of those bands that no-one else I knew was interested in and in a way I was kinda glad; that way I'd get to explore this band myself without anyone else telling me what they represent or that it wasn't hip or whatever.

When I got the 'Rebels' album I thought 'YESSSS!', this really is something here – music that may actually mean something and not just concocted together haphazardly by a group's manager, image consultant, PR guru or whoever. Anyway I think I heard *The Teams That Meet In Caffs* on the radio soon after and that clinched it for me. It was and still is just so inspirational... everything that I believe Dexys stand for and are passionate about is encapsulated in there... their finest four minutes. If any song was to make me a Dexys disciple then this was it. The horns are on fire, the hammon organ agonisingly splendid and the pace and feeling would bring Moses down from the mount.

So I guess then I was a fan of the Midnight Runners although it was to be 1985 before I saw them in concert (Edinburgh Playhouse and Dominion London). At the Edinburgh show a girl next to me appealed for quiet by a rather loud 'SHHHH' at a particular point just as Kev had done at The Old Vic in '81, although by slightly different means.

Now we awaited their next caper; I'm not superstitious in any way but sometimes you do wander... for most of '84 and up until summer '85 I was desperately awaiting news of their next album. The Dexys Circle newsletter were saying that it was due for release late '84 then early '85 but come summer no definite release date was fixed. I'd even heard that Kevin would spend an entire day in the studio just looking for the exact piece of tape he wanted to work on; another story was that the album was delayed as Kevin wanted the maroon border on the cover to match exactly the shade of his tie on the album cover!! So I went to work in the USA with Camp America in June '85 still waiting on it's release. After I'd finished I went backpacking from New York up to Buffalo then onto Niagara and Toronto. On my way back I stopped into a record store in Buffalo as I usually can't resist. I was browsing through some magazines and seeing what, if any, Dexys records they had when, after a few minutes, I thought that the voice I heard on the song they were playing in-store was familiar, although the song certainly wasn't. After another couple of minutes I was convinced that it was Signor Carlo Rolan on vocals, so I asked them what they were playing. Turned out it was an advance promo cassette of *Don't Stand Me Down* – it was still another month away from even a UK release. I almost shouted in celebration and couldn't wait to hear it. I arranged to get a copy of the tape if I gave them an interview tape of Kevin I had with me in return. Turned out the woman in the store was a big Dexys fan but didn't really know too much about them and there wasn't much to go on in the American press. I was delighted to give her a good background on the band; how they formed, line-up changes, confrontations with the British press, legendary snatchings of master-tapes etc.

My walkman was doing overtime from that point on and I was delighted with the new work. They promised to return my tape but it took about six months before they did. I'm glad they did because they also sent me, by way of thanks, a US promo LP of *Don't Stand Me Down* and a promo sampler containing *This Is What She's Like* edit and full length version as well as *One Of Those Things*.

I for one believe that a band gets the fans they deserve and for Dexys fans to be still passionate about the whole thing is indicative of the energy, feeling and commitment created and transmitted between the grooves of their records.

Will Kevin/Dexys ever record again? Will Scotland win Euro '96? Will Michael and LaToya Jackson finally be found out to be one and the same person...?

I know which I'd bet on.

dexys midnight runners
searching for the young soul rebels

FIRST ALBUM

EXCLUSIVE ANDY LEEK INTERVIEW

Andy Leek was the young Dexy who had fame and fortune at his fingertips as keyboard player with Dexys Midnight Runners. Yet when 'Geno' was sitting comfortably in the Number 1 position he decided to quit. I caught up with the short distance runner in a bar in Wolverhampton where I discover what went wrong and what he's been upto since his departure from Dexys. I also discover that it's no myth that Dexy men prefer tea to anything else!

How did you get into the music business and how did you get to join Dexys?
I was born into a family where I had two older brothers and sisters. All the four kids all played the piano so I was bound to grow up musically. I just grew up writing songs from when I was very little. Then I think it was probably punk that got me started in a band, probably a bit like Kevin actually, I was in a couple of punk bands and things like that. Then a guy named Roy Williams, who used to manage this club in Wolverhampton, he phoned me up and said there was a group called Dexys who needed a keyboard player. He didn't tell me anything about them or anything. I went along to an audition and they asked me to join and that was it. I think there was only five of them at the time – Kevin Rowland, Kevin Archer, Jimmy Paterson, Steve Spooner and Pete Williams. Then they needed a drummer, I can't remember who the drummer was at the time, but he left or something and a friend of mine at the time joined – Andy Growcott. I said that I know this drummer and that's how I got into them really. I went to the audition and they just seemed like dead good y'know, because I'd never been in a band that was really cool before (laughs).

And there's never been one since?
There's never been one since (laughs), well I've been on my own since. But that was the only thing I wanted to do, play keyboards and sing. So that's how I got into the music business really – I was just made for it.

33

So what went wrong? *Geno* **was at Number 1 and then you quit – what's the reason behind this?**
Well, I think there was various reasons. I always felt out of place because I'd been writing songs all my life and they weren't doing any of my songs, so that was frustrating for me – just being the keyboard player and playing somebody else's songs, although I liked all the songs that we were doing, but I wanted to write some and I think eventually that would have happened. At the time I also found that some of the band members, one in particular, I really didn't get on with and in Dexys we kind of like had this pseudo image of being really tough guys and I'm not a tough guy – I'm a sensitive person, probably the opposite really. People would do things like... y'know there'd be like fights within the group, it was just too much for me to bare that was. I thought people should respect each other a bit more and I got in a few fights with people in the group, one in particular and I just couldn't stand it any more, so I just said either he's going to leave or I'm going to leave. At the time there was so much happening to the group and they were all like freaked out by the success and somebody leaving didn't really seem like a big deal to them, because they were all on cloud nine. I know later that they regretted me leaving, but at the time there were so many things happening and they just got their old keyboard player back – Pete Saunders. I played on half the tracks on *Searching For The Young Soul Rebels* and they never credited me. I played on *Yorkshire, Geno, Burn It Down, Tell Me When My Light Turns Green*, I played on *Walls Of Heartache* as well, I think that was it.
Have you seen the sleeve-notes for the Radio 1 Sessions?
No, I did play on some of them – what does it say?
For *Tell Me When My Light Turns Green* **all Kevin's wrote is "This version is improved by Andy Leek's keyboard playing."**
Ah well, thank you Kevin, very nice (laughs). Yeah, I know he rated me and everything, we were really good friends actually. I probably got on better with him than most of the rest of the group, but it didn't work out and I was only very young and you get easily thrown by things at that age. But as I say, I always really wanted to be in my own band and be the singer anyway. So that was another thing that kind of made me leave, but really it was like... having people attack me in the group – sometimes that was just too much, I just couldn't put up with that. People would like have fights on the bus and things... y'know it was like I wasn't into it... all this kind of gang thing. They dropped that soon after, they all got much more friendly y'know – should've hung around for the friendly phase (laughs).

When you left Dexys the main reason seemed to be that you hated the commercialism of it all and actually being famous?
I think it's a very false situation, everyone probably needs a hero and something to aspire to. Pop Stars are so over admired for doing something which is really quite easy and I found that very lopsided to me, that all I'd done was joined this group, played keyboards, and then suddenly there were all these people worshipping us. It was a great group y'know, but it just seemed so false and I don't know why but it just turned me off – I didn't like that. I'm not saying I wouldn't ever want to be famous, but being famous for something that deserves some merit I wouldn't mind, but just playing the keyboards on a record seemed to me so trivial to have everybody screaming and shouting after you. Also within the group people started to think that they were so fuckin' important and that really

pissed me off as well. They didn't have a perspective on it, probably Kevin did but a lot of the others didn't, they started walkin' around thinking they were it y'know and I hated that.

You later went solo – is this not still the same thing?
Then people would have been raving about me, although they didn't, would have been raving about me for something that I'd done myself and a bit more important written the song, sung it and played the instruments on it. But I mean yeah, it would've been almost the same thing I guess, in a way. I'm a musician and songwriter, I can't do anything else, so I don't have any choice but to do that. That wasn't the main reason I left Dexys though – all that fame stuff, that was just something else that irritated me.

And I suppose being on your own you would have the final say more?
Yeah that's right, I would have the final say and I could control everything more. That will always be my ambition anyway because I can sing y'know (laughs), I don't want to be just like keyboard player – although I don't mind doing that as well.

Did you later have any regrets about leaving Dexys? Especially with the success they later achieved.
I did have regrets for sure because I would have liked to have been part of all the success, but most of the members that were in the group when I was all got fired and left anyway. I experienced my own joy in the music business that I might never have achieved if I'd stayed. For instance a few years later I would a song for Frida – Frida being the girl singer with Abba, that was called *Twist In The Dark* and was a hit in Europe. I was in various other bands like The Blue Ox Babes – which I couldn't have been in otherwise. Eventually I had my own record out on CD, which I might never have done if I'd stayed... so yeah I had some regrets about it, but not that much really. I don't know if I might have been one of the people who were fired anyway (laughs).

Andy Leek (far-left) back in 1980 with (L-R) Al Archer, Kevin Rowland, Jim Paterson, Steve Spooner, Andy Growcott, Pete Williams and Geoff Blythe

Was it that they were fired or did they quit?
I don't really know, I remember The Bureau and I knew all of them and they asked me to join that group. I didn't join that group because my whole feeling is that Kevin was the most talented person in Dexys and he was Dexys. A lot of the people who joined The Bureau... y'know I don't want to sound too scathing, but I don't rate any of those people at all – I just didn't rate them at all or the group, I thought they were a joke and without Kevin all those people were nothing. Kevin was the one that was inspiring and got the vision and the talent to me, him and Kevin Archer and probably Jimmy Paterson as well. I didn't rate any of those people in The Bureau anyway and I don't know whether they were fired or they quit, but knowing Kevin I would think they were fired (laughs). I mean why would they quit because they'd got everything with Kevin and when they left they had nothing really – just one record and that was it.

Did the success that Dexys later achieved surprise you at all?
No, what surprised me was that they didn't carry on more and have more success. Maybe if he'd stuck with the 'Too Rye Ay' image a bit longer... but then that's the nature of him isn't it. It's kind of like the Bowie thing isn't it – changing with every record, he started all that didn't he – although he did it in a very weird way.

What have you been up to over the past ten or so years?
The two main things I've been up to is making two albums. The first album which was called 'Say Something', I recorded in 1989 and that was with George Martin. How that came about was I'd been knocking on record company doors for about four years or even more. I supported a group called Mr Mister who were an American band, they had a hit with a song called *Broken Wings* I think it was. I supported them at The Marquee and a girl from Record Mirror did a review of the gig, she didn't like Mr Mister but she was really into me. After this review that she wrote of the gig, Atlantic Records contacted her and tried to contact me. For some reason they just read about me and said let's hear some of his stuff. They heard some of my stuff – they really liked it and they sent me to a company called Hit And Run Music. They managed all of Atlantic Records big acts like Phil Collins, they did a deal with Atlantic Records and they started managing me. Then it came to the time of like who's going to produce your first album? Now that you've got a record deal and worldwide and everything. I didn't know anything about famous producers or anything, I'd always been a bit suspicious of them in fact. I was always into The Beatles as a kid and I said George Martin would be good as a joke, a sort of off-the-cuff statement, and they said - "Well we can send him a tape of your stuff" and low and behold he actually came back. He said "Oh I love this, I want to produce his album," to like have him produce your first album is like quite a coup, bit of a stunner and everybody sort of fell off their chairs sort of thing. Then I did an album with him for Atlantic Records and the trouble with it was... I mean the music was largely how I wanted it, except a bit over-produced which is what you'd expect with George Martin, a few too many strings and brass sections for me... but I still thought it was good. But they spent so much money on the production that they didn't really spend any promoting it, so I'd got a great album but people really didn't get to hear about it very much. I never did a tour, never made a video, they never advertised it and you'd think they would have gone to town with all of that. But because I think I was signed to the company in New York

and I was only sort of licensed out to another company – WEA, who'd already turned me down previously, so they weren't that enthusiastic about me in England. A lot of the promotion was in America and it's such a big place that I just got lost y'know, but it still sold over 50,000 copies. So after that wasn't a big hit and they'd spent so much money making it – paid for the orchestras and god knows what, they didn't want to make another album with me because I was sort of so much in debt to them. Then trying to get another record deal proved like virtually impossible. People would say to me – "Well you made an album with George Martin and with Atlantic Records and you had this big management company and you didn't get anywhere, so obviously you're destined not to get anywhere and what can we do that was different to them?" So that was the sort of thing that the record companies were saying to me. So I sort of gave up to be honest – I gave up being in the music business at all. I started studying classical music at Cardiff University, how to write for orchestras and all this kind of stuff. That was good actually – it got me sort of out of being depressed about not getting anywhere, it was something else to do in music that was kind of like enjoyable in a completely different way. So having played by ear all my life I sort of learned to appreciate the likes of Beethoven, Liszt and all those sort of guys, which I'm quite still into. Then I had a manager who was taking my tapes around Germany and there was this producer over there called Gunter Kuch, no ones heard of him over here but he's had a lot of hits over in Germany and Europe. He latched on to me and he really loved my stuff, he paid himself for me to go over to Germany at various times to record an album over there. It's him that got me the record deal with Polydor and that's how I got my new single out in January this year, which is the first thing I've had released for about six years. The first release since 'Say Something'.

Did you have any singles released from 'Say Something'?
Yeah, I had two singles released from it – 'Please Please' the first track and 'Holdin Onto you' the second track. They both got into the Top 50 or something, not good enough to be a hit but made an impression sort of thing. They didn't get into the Top 10 or anything – if they had have done then I would have probably carried on with Atlantic Records. The album 'Say Something' got to like Number 60 and I was on a few TV programmes like – 'This Morning', 'James Whale Show', 'Music Box', 'The Late Show', I did a few TV and things. On the TV programmes it was a bit crap because I never had a band, it was just me on the piano playing to people, it's sort of hard to impress people like that nowadays. Everyone is so into beat and the beat of a song now. Girls are like wearing tight dresses and shaking all their stuff y'know, and just a singer songwriter sitting at a piano is like very rare now and probably not entertaining enough any more, although some people still do well that way. My new record is called 'All Around The World' and that's just been released all around Germany, so I'm hoping that something will come of that, if not anyway it's just nice to have something else released.

Andy Leek with George Martin

Any plans for an album release?
I've made an album, recorded twelve tracks and I suppose it will depend on what happens with the singles. There's going to be a second single released called 'Forgotten People' and I think it will depend on what happens to them whether the album's released. I've got a feeling though that they will release it – especially now they've paid for it, I'm hoping they will anyway.

Throughout 'Say Something' it would appear that the world situation quite upsets you throughout the LP – especially during 'All Day Long' and this is evident again with your forthcoming single 'Forgotten People'. Do you think about this a lot?
It's kind of hard to talk about myself like that, y'know about my own songs, in a way, because they just come out. People have pointed this out to me before, that I do seem to write about things in the world that I don't think are right. 'Forgotten People' is about homelessness and it's about a story of some people I knew in London. The husband had got a job and it was OK, and they'd got a little kid and I knew them quite well. Then he became an alcoholic and lost his job and she ended up... well I saw her begging outside a tube station and that's what I wrote the song about. On 'All Day Long' it's like... I was just wandering how did the world that could be so great end up with so much shit y'know, how come so many things seem to go wrong, how come there's so much hatred and crime and war. Everybody's asked these questions and I never come up with an answer, all I can do is hope that thing's get better. Which is what the song 'Please Please' was about – I was just hoping... y'know perhaps if people could just smile a bit more, that'd be a start. There's so many wars isn't there, it's never stopped. People always think well there was World War One and then World War Two, but in fact war has just never stopped – it's just carrying on all the time and it's probably down to greed and politics. The people fighting the wars often don't want anything to do with it, they just want a normal life. I mean surely there's got to be enough for everybody. Why everything's like this... who knows? Perhaps one day there'll be a better day, it probably won't come from writing songs though.

I found 'Say Something' to be a very individual yet very commercial LP, I could not really see any influences in there – are you influenced by anybody?
I think I do have influences, but I know what you mean, my voice doesn't really sound like many other people, although people sometimes say that I sound like Mick Hucknall nowadays – I suppose that's gotta be good in a way. Influences... well I was always into The Beatles, which is a real cliché now because everybody's into the fuckin' Beatles, it was a real retro thing with them. I was always into Bob Dylan, but I don't think you can hear his influence. I was certainly into Dexys, maybe a bit of Paul Simon as well. I think those people I've mentioned are the only ones that I can think have really influenced me. I've always just been on my own street if you like, I just do what I want to do. I've never really thought about copying anybody or trying to be a particular way, like Dexys were stuck into soul then folk. That's never been it for me – it just comes out, done whatever I wanted. That's why I think, in a way, the LP 'Say Something' it's got no one particular direction either, a lot of the songs are very different to each other. It's the same with my new LP as well – just got my own direction and there's lot's of different types of songs on it.

How do you approach writing a song?
I don't think I really approach it, it just comes to me. Often in the middle of the night, when I'm just half asleep or I might be just fooling around on the piano and I'll start singing something and just think 'oh that's good' and that's it y'know. I don't really set out ever to write a song and the ones I have set out to write have never really worked out very good. It's just a feeling isn't it, it's a feeling inside, maybe it comes from something that effects you emotionally, that's how it would start for me, especially the love songs. You start with a feeling and just try to express it.

I was reading that the group 'Pulp' write the music first and add the words afterwards – I cannot understand that.
I can't understand that, but apparently Abba used to do it that way as well. I've always written both things together, I have written some songs where someone's give me the lyrics – I have done that – it's quite an obvious way of doing things sometimes. I think Kevin and Kevin Archer went that way a bit as well, Kevin would write some lyrics and Kevin Archer would make them into a tune. As for the other way around, I can't imagine how that would quite work somehow – a bit difficult really.

What do you think of the current music scene with the likes of 'Oasis' and 'Pulp'?
I guess I've enjoyed some things by Oasis and certainly by Pulp. To be honest I don't really pay that much attention to the music scene now, I'm a bit of a loner, I've never paid attention to the music scene at any point. I'm more likely to listen to classical music right now or old records by Bob Dylan or something – that's what I like – the greats. In fact I like Oasis, they're alright and Pulp are quite good fun, but I'd never buy an LP by them. In fact I wouldn't buy an LP by anybody really, if Dexys did another album I'd buy that though, I'd pick that one up, that'd be alright.

What hopes do you have for the future?
I'd like to have some success – that'd be great, but as long as I can sing to people and get paid for it... that's almost good enough. I think fame definitely brings it's own problems, that's for sure, ask Kevin about that one, or anybody who's ever been famous. People think oh being famous must be so great, but it's got a negative side to it as well. People always expect certain things when they meet you – they expect you to be a God or something – instead of just a normal guy, and that can be hard. For myself really I just want a peaceful life and good living. I'm pretty contented, I'm alright, I think I've become philosophical enough that whatever happens now – I'm gonna be alright.

Andy Leek's other hopes for the future are that his latest single reaches Number 1 and that he gets to play at Wembley (The Arena, not the Conference Centre!).
He also hopes to win the lottery next Saturday and then retire.
Andy Leek is just a normal guy, Kevin Rowland is just a normal guy (although we all think otherwise), Elvis Presley was just a normal guy, but...
"Everyone needs a hero and something to aspire to"

KEEP ON RUNNING
ISSUE 5 OCTOBER 1996

"You've always been searching for something

But everything seems so-so-so

Tightly close your eyes

Hold out your hand

We'll make a stand..."

PLAN B (No. 58, March 1981)

Reminisce Part Three
by Daryl Easlea, Newcastle Under Lyme

Monday Nights, 1980; Graham and I after school had the 'Monday Night Binge', a weekly chance for chat, sometimes have a beer, watch 'Not The Nine O' Clock News', and importantly, listen to records, Madness, Beatles, Jam etc. *Searching For The Young Soul Rebels* arrived (on the day Renee Roberts was killed in Coronation Street): We'd loved *Dance Stance*, thought *Geno* was pop, and *There There My Dear* was incredible. At fifteen, had heard nothing quite like it, listened to the album four times end to end, the last time in darkness – Everything would be different after this...

Keep It Part Two, possibly the most astonishing thing committed to vinyl, the split, the purchase of The Bureau singles (we knew we shouldn't but...), *Plan B*, The Projected Passion Revue at Chelmsford Odeon – there were only about fifty in the audience, Annelese Jesperson? Meeting them afterwards: *Show Me,* Top Of The Pops, Bournemouth Guest House, July 1981, delaying going out until after the performance: *Your Own* becoming *Liars A To E*, the beauty, the regime; final Projected Passion, the programme, I had to buy or hear all the records listed... what were the DT's? *Celtic Soul Brothers*, who was Giorgio Kilkenny? *Hey Where Are You Going With That Suitcase* mutating into *Too Rye Ay*, *Eileen*, The Bridge concerts in Shaftsbury Ave, complete sell out, No Jimmy, watch for future members of Status Quo and Queen, (I'm on the video – I told so many, could they care?), *Merry Xmas Everybody* on Xmas TV show, The Brothers Just?

The silence, The rumours, a glimpse of a sleeve with London bridges, a year later, the greatest album they ever made: I was managing my own record shop by then, everyone laughed, I knew. Quoting it extensively; Graham had drifted from Dexys by now, my Wife to be understood every nuance; it was OK, it was alright, it was OK.

The decline, Park St South at The Dominion, there was only about fifty in the audience, Kevin and Billy at new heights of reportee – ('I've just been to the circus', 'What? Lions and tigers?' 'No, Piccadilly Circus'), Brush Strokes, my wedding, The Wanderer, Showaddywaddy meets the pub singer, The Blue Ox Babes, the disappearance, the

rumours, 'Something Beginning With O', Q, The Radio One Sessions CD (replacing a very worn out cassette), this fanzine, the hope of return, the greatest group ever, the deepest vision, the spirit of the Monday Night Binge remains -
Everything was different and will always be after this.

ALBUMS

In one week in July, 1982, Mercury Records released two of the greatest long-players ever. HARRY ADAMS gets all misty-eyed over DEXYS MIDNIGHT RUNNERS, while PAUL LESTER comes over all peculiar about ABC

DEXYS MIDNIGHT RUNNERS
TOO-RYE-AY
Mercury (18 tks/73 mins)

"THE Italians have a word for it."
"What word – what is it?"
"A thunderbolt or something."
"What, you mean the Italian word for thunderbolt?"
"Yeah, something like that."

Kevin Rowland never stopped searching for that word. Elsewhere, he'd describe it as "that burning feeling". On "Let's Makes This Precious", he'd had it up to here with guitars, thinking perhaps that the feeling would identify itself if he removed the things obscuring it. No joy, however. The search continued.

The reissue of "Too-Rye-Ay" (newly remastered with eight extra tracks, including ferocious live renderings of "Respect" and "Jackie Wilson Said") serves to remind us that things could have never been any other way. That a man so brave should have channelled such raw humanity into three of the greatest soul albums ever made is something for which we should all feel privileged. Bravery, of course, is a term you hear bandied all the time. Jarvis was "brave" the other week. Greg Dulli was "brave" when he smashed a chair over someone for "disrespecting a woman". Mmm. Perhaps.

Well, I'm currently listening to "I'll Show You", where Kevin Rowland – fired by a stampede of trumpets and Northern Soul pianos – is shrieking a roll-call of society outcasts: *"Alcoholics, child-molesters, nervous wrecks and prima donnas, petty thieves, hard drug pursuers. Lonely tramps, awkward misfits, anyone of these . . ."* See, it might have just been his Catholic upbringing, but Kevin believed in redemption for *anyone who wanted it*:

"It's so hard," he continues, *"to picture dirty tramps as young boys. But if you see a man crying, hold his hand, he's my friend."*

That's bravery.

People used to go on about Kevin Rowland being a stroppy git. But Kevin was merely intolerant of idiots; people who desire the rewards but shy away from the effort. That was a mentality Kevin could never understand: in the build-up to "Too-Rye-Ay", Kevin introduced the band to a strict regime of abstinence: that eight trained musicians went circuit training every morning and then took to wearing torn dungarees at the behest of a musically illiterate 28-year-old from Wolverhampton, gives you some idea of the faith that Kevin Rowland could instil. The Dexys of "Celtic Soul Brothers" and "Plan B" sound *immutable*, harnessing the titanic uplift of every great Otis Redding/Van Morrison/Jimmy Ruffin record and spinning pure synergy from it.

So much of "Too-Rye-Ay" is distinguished not by its allegiances but by what it defies. "Soon", an confession-booth cry for purification, once again sees Kevin looking beyond Catholicism for deliverance (*"Take these ridiculous moods all away"*). On "Old", he's railing against the disrespect that young people have for their elders. He knows some of you are laughing (*"If these words sound corny, switch this off. I don't care"*) but the ferocious ire that propels the song into such a wounded crescendo of horns is too real to disregard. Remember that burning feeling.

"Too-Rye-Ay" doesn't so much end as crumble beneath a landslide of libido. After the wracked, purgative gospel of "Until I Believe In My Soul", the manic adrenalin riot of "Come On Eileen" rampages in to remind us why the Dexys succeeded in catapulting all these complicated emotions to the top of the charts. Because they had tunes to die for. Being the kind of band that could significantly change your life was, I guess, just a bonus.

The Rendezvous Cafe, Birmingham
Wednesday 6th August 1.00 am

Present: A few taxi drivers, a drunken middle-aged man, a reluctant tea sales-lady and most of Dexy's Midnight Runners.

We want to explain ourselves as best we can.

We formed two years ago because we were tired of unemotional insincere music. We were genuinely inspired (too mild a word) by some records from the sixties. These have been well highlighted in pages like these, so we won't go into that.

We see things from a different angle to the original soul artists, so it's natural that we should sound, look and feel very different.

We don't consider ourselves to be musicians. Fortunately JB and Big Jimmy have a strong musical knowledge and are usually around to help the rest of us. The group is made up of stylists and technicians, with the style constantly feeding the technique.

We came together as people because we had a lot in common. Frustration, intense emotion, confusion, but most of all a new soul vision. An intense vision that encompassed the above feelings, but with enough warmth and passion to be soulful. We all share a lack of confidence and a total disinterest in insensitive people.

We believe soul is honesty and our music is honest, therefore we are asking our audience for an honest approach when listening to our records or watching our live shows, because at some shows we've been quickly disillusioned by ecstatic audiences who think they are encouraging us when we have done no more than walk out onto the stage. Thanks but no thanks. We just need an honest "credit where due" approach. We need to summon up our own passion from our own pain and to be given the freedom to work it up to a more intense level. Please try and understand that soul can't exist amid rowdy celebrations in the way that rock and roll can.

Recently we've been asked some very confusing questions about a hunt for young soul rebels. We'd like to clarify the situation. Searching for the Young Soul Rebels is the title of our LP and we have already found the soul rebels; they made the record. We're very suspicious of cults, and while quite a few of us believe clothing to be a very important way of expressing ourselves, we are far from flattered by people dressing up like us. Why don't they dress up like themselves? Goodnight

the midnight runners

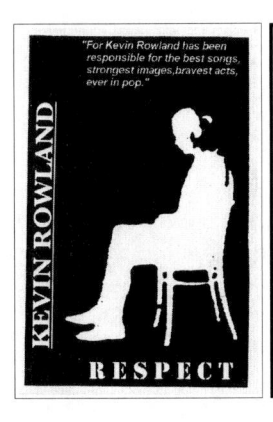

KEEP ON RUNNING
ISSUE 6 JANUARY 1997

"Show me them now
Those wild little boys
The ones that spelled trouble
And stole all their toys
Young boys with contempt..."

SHOW ME (No. 16, July 1981)

"For Kevin Rowland has been responsible for the best songs, strongest images, bravest acts, ever in pop."

KEVIN ROWLAND — RESPECT

Dear Neil,

Andy Leeks interview, though interesting, was a bit of a joke to me. I would like it pointed out that Andy joined our group at the end of December '79 and left less than six months later, <u>not when 'Geno' was Number 1</u> but when it was <u>Number 33</u>, having just risen from 37 or 38 it didn't look at that point like it was going to set the world alight. He left suddenly giving me no reason and no time to find a replacement. A month later we had to read newspaper reports of Andy walking out on a Number 1 selling group because he 'didn't like the false way we were reacting to our success', <u>he didn't see our success</u>, he left when the single was stuck at 33. I was pissed off because most of us had worked hard for two years and here was somebody who'd been in the group less than six months and hadn't been through all the hard times with us, grabbing all the glory and implying we were phoney in the process.

He didn't play on half of 'Searching For The Young Soul Rebels', it was recorded after he left. He played on one single – 'Geno' and consequently the B-side 'Breaking Down The Walls Of Heartache', and the other track we recorded at that time – 'Yorkshire', 'Geno' and 'Yorkshire' were included on the LP. He didn't play on 'Burn It Down' or 'Tell Me When My Light Turns Green' like he claimed in your interview. I suppose we didn't credit him for the two tracks he did play on because it didn't occur to us. We were so angry at the way he left and subsequently used us. He didn't speak kindly of us at that time and got loads of national press by doing so, to promote his own record. The whole episode sullied our success.

I like Andy and during the short time he was with us he and I seemed to get on quite well. I have seen him recently and enjoyed it but his memory is a bit skewiff.

All the best Neil,
Take Care,
Kevin Rowland

I would like it to be known that prior to my interview with Andy Leek that I did ask him when he left Dexys, as there were so many different stories going around at the time. Andy informed me that Geno had been Number 1 for about two weeks before he left. Thanks Kevin for putting the record straight.

KEVIN ROWLAND
THE EARLY YEARS

John Francis Rowland emigrated to England from his home in Co. Mayo in 1939. He arrived with little money, but a lot of ambition. He started work in the building trade as a carpenter, he was later to gain respect as a master builder and become a successful businessman with his own contracting company.

In 1940 he met Maureen Teresa Browne at a dance in Preston, Lancashire. Although they had never previously known each other they discovered they were born and raised only a few miles apart.

Maureen had come to England at the age of 15. She would have liked to have developed her childhood interests in music and literature, but times did not permit. It was Maureen who was to give Kevin and the rest of the family their knowledge of beauty.

John and Maureen married in 1945 and within 18 months produced the first of five children. Kevin was the fourth born, with two older brothers, an older and younger sister. The Rowlands wanted the best for their children, including the benefits of education. Kevin didn't adapt as well as his brothers and sisters as regards education, but eventually equalled their achievements as well as finding his own fulfilment through music.
The chain goes on...
Billy Adams

An early shot of the family in Ireland when I was about 2. Sitting on the wall (left-right): Peter, Sharon, John. I'm the one at the bottom.

"I was born in Wolverhampton in '53, just before the family moved to Ireland. My Dad's building business had just gone bust and he'd totally run out of money. I was born at 6 in the morning, at 2 in the afternoon two men from the electric shop arrived to take the cooker away.

I remember Ireland being green fields and me fighting with friends all the time. I remember leaving to come to England, getting on the boat at Dublin for a 12-hour journey to Liverpool. I was 4 at the time but my Dad kept telling me to say I was 3 as then he wouldn't have to pay for me. I insisted I was 4, so he had to.

I remember arriving at Wolverhampton at about 6 0'Clock in the morning. The house was dark and pretty grotty and a horrible place, and my Mother kept saying 'you were born here', us three brothers would sleep in one bed. We started off poor but gradually my Dad's business took off again and by the time I left home we lived in a big detached house in Kenton.

When I was a little kid 9, 10, whatever, I always thought it'd be really great to do a job like my Dad and his friends did – physical, manual work, out in the fresh air, it'd be brilliant y'know.

The teachers at school used to say 'Oh work hard and you can get a job in an office', y'know that'd be useless, and I really believed that. I thought it'd be great to go out, drive your lorry, have your dinner in a cafe, this sounds great. It was only when I came to be 15, or whatever, and left school and started to do those jobs that I realised the contempt you get treated with. The way you're expected to look up to very stupid people with 5 O'Levels. I always thought it'd be the other way round, that they'd look up to the manual workers for being strong and good and everything. What was more alarming was the way the workers accepted it and had no self-respect. I don't think it's there fault; it's impossible in that situation. It made me more and more bitter. I had to do something about it; if I'd carried on I'd have got real mad about it.

When I was about 21, 22 I got this job as a sales rep selling mats. Suit, company car – Ford Escort Estate, brand new one. I was very successful at it too. Actually I nearly got married at the time too. I thought, well this is it, I've got the car, I've got the house, I've had my fling, I've got this girl – she was called Heather, and if she died I'd feel sorry, maybe I love her? Perhaps we should get married? For some reason we didn't. I think it was because I started getting involved in groups."

(as told by Kevin Rowland, actual source unknown)

THE EARLY YEARS

KEVIN ROWLAND AGE 8

A HEAVY METAL HIT BY POP STAR KEVIN

POP star Kevin Roland's smash-hit landed him with a nine-month suspended jail sentence yesterday.

For the leader of Dexy's Midnight Runners made it with a length of scaffolding.

And a member of a rival rock band was on the receiving end, a court heard.

Roland, 27, who was also fined £250 with £100 costs, admitted assaulting Malcolm Ball of the Birmingham group, Troops.

The singers clashed when the Runners, who topped the charts last year with Gino, were filming in Birmingham, the city's Crown Court was told.

Six youths, including two from Troops, started swopping insults with Roland, said Mr Granville Styler, prosecuting.

Lashed

He added: "They told him his group was terrible and he replied: 'So is yours.'"

Finally Roland, of Oldbury, West Midlands, was cornered and lashed out with a 5ft. scaffold pole.

Mr. Brian Escott-Cox, QC, defending, said: "Like the Bible story, the enemy, though, more numerous, were scattered."

Roland caught up with

By JOHN SCOTT

Ball when he fell over a bollard said Mr. Escott-Cox.

He added: "What started as self-defence went beyond that in the heat of the moment."

Roland, who is currently involved in a contract row with pop giants EMI, said after the case: "A lot of people resent the Runners."

Kevin Roland ... angry after rival knocked the Midnight Runners

Singer pays rates at twelfth hour

Dexy's Midnight Runners lead singer, Kevin Rowland, saved himself from prison for the second time this year by paying off Sandwell at arrears at "the last minute."

The pop star, whose group topped the charts for weeks earlier this year, was due to appear before Warley magistrates for the second time over outstanding rates.

He was to face a council warrant committing him to prison for failing to pay £66.98 in rates on his Apollo Road home.

But rating officer, Mr. Val Rago, was told at Warley Magistrates Court that Mr. Rowland had now paid up to the police.

Mr. Rago said after the hearing: "The £66.98 was for rates up to September. Mr. rowland is now in the clear."

Early this year Warley magistrates approved a warrant committing Mr. Rowland to prison for £240 in rate arrears. He paid up as the police went to arrest him.

Mr. Rowland was said today to be on tour with his group.

THE SUN, Saturday, March 24, 1990

DEXY DID A MIDNIGHT RUNNER, SAY THE COPS

£20 restaurant row

By NEIL SYSON

DEXY'S Midnight Runners star Kevin Rowland is to appear in court — accused of doing a midnight runner from a restaurant.

Kevin, the pop group's leader, and two mates allegedly legged it from a trendy all-night cafe after a £20.85 breakfast.

But they were arrested at 4.50am. A fourth man stayed behind at Harry's All Night Cafe in London's Soho — because he was too drunk.

Kevin, 36, of Cricklewood, North London, and his pals were stopped by police 200 yards away.

Kevin said last night: "Yes, we did a runner for a laugh, just like we used to when we were kids. It was a bit silly."

Dexy's star on assault charge

KEVIN ROLANDS, lead singer of the Sandwell pop group Dexy's Midnight Runners, has appeared in court on an assault charge.

The 26-year-old, who lives at Appollo Road, Oldbury, is also accused of possessing an offensive weapon — an iron bar.

Rolands (pictured), was remanded on bail when he appeared before Birmingham magistrates.

The leader of the chart-topping band was arrested after a late-night disturbance near Newhall Street, Birmingham, on Saturday.

Filming

It is understood the group, who shot to No. 1 with their hit Geno, were involved in filming for the release of a new single.

Rolands, was charged with assaulting a youth and causing actual bodily harm.

BLOODIED: Rowland

Brawling Dexy star is fined

POP STAR Kevin Rowland was back in the dock yesterday — after a "friendly" punch-up with a mate.

Police arrested bloodied Rowland – lead singer with Dexy's Midnight Runners – after a drunken brawl with pal David Philips.

Passers-by screamed as the pair swung punches at each other in London's Soho Square in the early hours, Marlborough Street Court heard.

Rowland, 36, was fined £50 with £25 costs after telling magistrates: "It was just a friendly fight."

The singer, of Cricklewood, and Philips, 27, of Putney, admitted threatening behaviour.

In April Rowland appeared in the same dock after leaving a restaurant without paying.

You can't hide, Kev

KEVIN Rowland might have grown an extremely silly beard and sideburns — but he can't hide from us! We snapped the reclusive Dexy's Midnight Runners Star celebrating the success of his latest single, Because Of You, at London's Limelight Club.

AUGUST 7, 1990

Dexy star fought his pal

FORMER Midland rock star Kevin Rowland of Dexy's Midnight Runners was arrested by police after a fight left him bloodied and bruised, a court heard.

Police stepped in when Rowland and a friend, David Phillips, were seen fighting in the early hours of the morning in a London park, Marlborough Street court was told.

Wolverhampton-born Rowland (36), of Fordwych Road, Cricklewood, and Phillips (27), a self-employed builder, of Santos Road, Putney, admitted using threatening words and behaviour in Soho Square on Sunday.

Both were fined £50 with £25 costs along with Laurence Coles (39), of Cornwall Crescent, Notting Hill, who admitted a similar charge.

Phillips said: "Yes, it's right that I was fighting with Kevin, but nobody could have been distressed because it was early in the morning and there was no one else there."

Kevin . . . "bit silly"

but let's face it, we all do mad things when we have had a few.

"It was a boys' night out. I was celebrating reforming Dexy's."

Harry's waiter Jason McNamara said: "They were obnoxious."

Dexy's — famous for hits Come On Eileen, Jackie Wilson Said, Geno, and the theme to TV's Brush Strokes — are reforming after splitting up in 1985.

A Scotland Yard spokesman said: "Three men have been charged with making off without payment."

Pop star hit rival with bar

Odbury pop star Kevin Roland beat a rival musician with a five-foot iron bar in a late night city centre clash, Birmingham Crown Court heard today.

Roland, leader of Dexy's Midnight Runners, was filming a video for a single when a street slanging match broke out with members from another group, The Troops.

Police stopped the pop group punch-up, but Roland, aged 27, followed several youths through the city centre into Temple Row West, the court was told.

One of the youths, Mr. Malcolm Ball, ran into a bollard and fell to the ground as he tried to escape, said Mr. Granville Styler, prosecuting.

As he lay in the road Roland hit him with a five-foot scaffolding pole he had picked up in the chase, Mr. Styler claimed.

Mr. Ball escaped with bruising when the fight was broken up by a passing policeman.

Roland, of Apollo Road, Oldbury, pleaded guilty to assault occasioning bodily harm. He denied carrying an offensive weapon in public.

He was sentenced to nine months imprisonment, suspended for two years, and fined £250.

The court was told that Roland, who sprang to fame last year with the No. 1 hit, "Geno," had been trying to film down-and-outs in the city for the group's single, "There, There, My Dear," which later reached No. 7 in the charts.

Mr. Brian Escott Cox, defending, said: "I submit that this was a case that he was subjected to taunts such as, 'Oh, look, there's Kevin Roland, the pop star who will not talk to us now.'"

After the trial Roland, his black hair tied in a bun, said: "A lot of groups resent us because of our puritanical zest."

DAILY MIRROR, Thursday, April 19, 1990 — PAGE 17

DEXY STAR FINED FOR DOING RUNNER

By MIRROR REPORTER

He didn't pay £20 cafe bill

DEXY'S Midnight Runners star Kevin Rowland lived up to his band's name... when he took to his heels without paying a restaurant bill.

The singer and three pals had been on an all-night booze binge before eating breakfast in a Soho cafe, a court heard yesterday.

But when Rowland, 36, and two of his party did a runner "as a joke", the friend left behind could not afford the £20 bill.

Staff at Harry's Bar called police, who arrested Rowland and his mates in the street.

After being fined £30 and ordered to pay £20 costs by London's Marlborough Street magistrates, the angry star stormed: "It was a bit of a joke.

"What sort of country is it that takes you to court for egg on toast? I mean, there's a big case on next – hamburger and chips!"

Rowland, of Hampstead, North London, admitted dishonestly making off from the bar without paying his bill.

The star – whose band split up in 1985 after hits like Come On Eileen and Geno – told the court he had been out celebrating the re-forming of Dexy's Midnight Runners.

He admitted: "Yes, we did make off without paying, but it was a joke. I use the cafe on a regular basis, the staff know me. So it was ridiculous to say we were trying to get away without paying."

JOKER: Rowland

Lawrence Coles, 20, of Hounslow, and Pany Louki, 38, of Chiswick, West London, also pleaded guilty and were fined £30. A fourth man, who denies the offence, will be tried in May.

Kevin's on the move, but not too far

Oldbury pop star Kevin Rowland, lead singer with former chart-topping Dexy's Midnight Runners, is selling his Oldbury house and moving... to Edgbaston.

Kevin, 27, says he already has someone interested in buying his Apollo Road house at Oldbury for an undisclosed amount.

Kevin shot to fame after moving to Apollo Road four years ago from the London area.

His group topped the charts for several weeks with the hit record "Geno" and are at present back in the charts at No. 24 with their latest number "Show Me".

Relaxing at his Apollo Road terraced house after an extensive European tour Kevin said: "I now want to live closer to Birmingham and I have a house in mind at Edgbaston. I already have someone interested in buying my Oldbury house although contracts have not yet been signed."

Kevin Rowland

---

18 EVENING MAIL, THURSDAY, APRIL 19, 1990

Dexy's 'runner' puts him in court

SINGING star Kevin Rowland, lead singer with the defunct Midland band Dexy's Midnight Runners, has been fined after "doing a runner" from a restaurant.

The Wolverhampton-born pop star, whose hits include Come on Eileen, Jackie Wilson Says, Geno and the theme tune to television's Brush Strokes, said he and two friends ran off without paying for the meal at a London restaurant as a joke.

Rowland told Marlborough Street Court in London: "I know the staff and they know me, it was ridiculous to say we were trying to get away without paying.

"It was the last one to the door who would pay the bill," he added.

The court heard the men were arrested near the restaurant.

Rowland (36), of Fordwych Road, Cricklewood, London, was fined £30 after admitting dishonestly making off from Harry's Bar without paying for a £20.85 bill.

The prosecution claimed Rowland was celebrating with friends after the reforming of the group.

Earlier, as he glanced at details of the singer's previous criminal record the magistrate, Mr John Nichols, said: "It doesn't make pretty reading, but broadly speaking, they are very old matters."

Also fined £30 after admitting the same charge were Lawrence Coles (30), a plasterer, from Hounslow, Middlesex and Pany Louki (38), a carpenter, from Chiswick, west London.

All three were also ordered to pay £20 costs plus £7 compensation each.

Terence Wheeler (38), an unemployed plumber of Kenton, Middlesex, denied the same charge and was bailed for trial.

FANS LAY SIEGE TO THE WRONG HOUSE

Oldbury housewife Mrs. Jaswant Sunnerd has found herself running an unofficial fan club after moving into a pop star's former home.

Fans of Dexy's Midnight Runners lead singer Kevin Rowlands swamped the house in Apollo Road with telephone calls, unaware that the star had moved to Edgbaston.

Girls even turned-up on the doorstep waiting for autographs and Mrs. Sunnerd and her foundry worker husband, Pal (30), soon got fed up.

Mr. Rowlands had not left a forwarding address and Mrs. Sunnerd had trouble at times persuading the young fans he no longer lives there.

She said: "Some of them thought we were only joking. We had eight calls in one day and one girl got quite upset and phoned several times as well as turning up at the door.

"I listened to them all, but my husband got a bit annoyed after a while."

The couple, who have three young children, moved from Handsworth into their new home just before Christmas and the calls began almost immediately.

But the trouble should have ended now—because the singer's brother has left a forwarding address in Edgbaston.

Mrs. Sunnerd said: "We knew he was in the pop business, but we didn't realise he was so popular. It was strange having all those people calling for him."

Kevin, lead singer with the former chart-topping band, sold his house six months after putting it on the market.

Mrs Jaswant Sunnerd answers a phone call meant for pop star Kevin Rowlands.

Kevin Rowlands

Reminisce Part Four
(My Nights With Kevin)
by Rona Topaz

It was 23rd May 1983, the nation was watching the Motown 25th Anniversary programme on which Michael Jackson made dancing history. BUT a few thousand of us youngsters had flocked to The Beacon Theatre in New York City, to witness Dexys first concert since having the all important chart hit – Come On Eileen – of course!

I was a budding songwriter and was anxious for constructive feedback from people I admired. After explaining this to a nice gent from Dexys production company, he said 'yes, you can go backstage and speak to Kevin Rowland and Billy Adams'. But at the stage door I was stopped by someone demanding to know the name of the person I had spoken to... I couldn't remember. I begged Helen O'Hara to assist me, she didn't want to get involved. C'est La Vie – there's always after the show.

The concert was outstanding of course, if anything, far too short. The audience was rowdy, abusive and typically American. I tried several times to get Kevin's attention – as a fan might do, he was oblivious. I had never witnessed a more intense passionate performance from any artist, before or since. I also noticed radical re-arrangements of album tracks, artists tended not to do that – they usually reproduce their songs note for note. This was a brave, risk-taking thing to do thought I.

I was one of only four fans waiting at the stage door. We waited for two hours, courtesy of a local resident visiting Kevin backstage, named Yoko Ono. I thought it strange that she would be curious about Dexys – she had more taste than I had ever given her credit for! When Dexys left the building, the four of us spoke to Kevin. Eventually the other fans left, as did the other band members, and Kevin and I were left alone. I was anxious to pick his brains on my lyrics, and generally ask his advice on how to obtain a recording deal. He was very confused as to why his opinion meant so much to me. He was and is a great believer in the power of self-belief, and could not understand my dependence on his feedback. We fell into a conversation on how his band started – how he took over his brother's band before striking out on his own. I talked about my own disfunctional, abusive background. Kevin had returned home to his family before forming Dexys with Al Archer. I didn't have that option, it simply was not a choice in my case. When I made Kevin aware of this fact, he seemed at a loss for words, or further advice. Without warning, he reached into his wallet and peeled off the top note, the last thing I was ready to accept was money – whatever the sum! I argued and he argued, it was a battle of wills, eventually Kevin won out - "I'm perfectly aware of the fact that you weren't asking me for money – take it anyway" he said, gently but very firmly – I succumbed.

I used the money only for things in Dexys name. I travelled to Philadelphia to see the band the next day, if possible, they were even better. I waited afterwards, this time with many other 'groupies'! I was so touched, so overwhelmed by Kevins gesture, I couldn't stop talking about it. During this time he managed to converse with a few other fans, as well as nurture and encourage me as an artist. He talked of 'taking some strength and finding the confidence and determination necessary to affect a positive change in ones life'. He inspired me more than any other person I've ever known, he also thought I was getting slightly carried away by his behaviour, and shook me a bit, telling me to come to my senses and not to be so silly and obsessive!!

The encounters with Kevin had a profound affect on me, and my life altered radically for the better. I still haven't paid him back, but I will one day – soon!!

KEEP ON RUNNING
ISSUE 7 APRIL 1997

"Nobody tells you, you end up knowing
Bad habits - you should sleep alone
Open to suggestions, is that the way you feel?
Because you're the voice of experience
Every word you choose is sweet stolen info..."

LIARS A TO E (November 1981)

KEVIN ROWLAND

KEVIN ROWLAND / DEXYS MIDNIGHT RUNNERS

I'M REALLY PLEASED TO SAY THAT I'VE SIGNED TO CREATION AND I'M EXCITED ABOUT STARTING WORK SOON. I WILL TRY TO BE WORTHY OF THE FAITH SHOWN IN ME.

THE FIRST THING I INTEND TO DO IS START WORK ON A SOLO RECORD CALLED 'MY BEAUTY' MADE UP OF ALL BEAUTIFUL SONGS THAT I HAVE HEARD THROUGHOUT MY LIFE AND THAT HAVE TOUCHED ME IN THE MOST POWERFUL WAY, OFTEN WHEN I WAS SAD. OVER THE LAST FEW YEARS THESE SONGS RESURFACED IN MY CONSCIOUSNESS AND HELPED ME WITH WHERE I'M GOING. MOSTLY I DIDN'T BUY THESE RECORDS WHEN THEY WERE OUT BUT THEY GOT INTO ME AND HAVE LIVED IN ME AND WHEN I NEEDED THEM THEY WERE THERE GUIDING ME AND EXPRESSING FOR ME WHAT I COULDN'T MYSELF, THEY HAD ALWAYS BEEN THERE I JUST DIDN'T NOTICE THEM. IT'S NOT ABOUT AUTHENTICITY OF ORIGINAL RECORDINGS OR ARRANGEMENTS, OR ANYTHING LIKE THAT, BECAUSE I OWN MY EXPERIENCE OF THESE SONGS - WHAT THEY MEAN TO ME, AND THAT'S WHAT I WANT TO EXPRESS HERE, WHAT I UNDERSTAND TO BE REAL BEAUTY, MY BEAUTY.

FOLLOWING THAT, BIG JIM PATTERSON AND I INTEND TO START WORK ON RECORDING THE NEW DEXYS ALBUM.

BEFORE ANY OF THIS 'DON'T STAND ME DOWN' WILL BE COMING OUT ON CREATION IN MARCH WITH A NEW SLEEVE AND TWO EXTRA TRACKS; 'REMINISCE PART 1 ' AND 'THE WAY YOU LOOK TONIGHT' . I'M REALLY PLEASED ABOUT THAT.

MOST OF ALL I NEED TO SAY THAT 'DON'T STAND ME DOWN ' WAS/IS IMPORTANT FOR ME BECAUSE IT CAME AFTER THE 'TOO RYE AY' RECORD. I EXPERIENCED HOLLOW SUCCESS WITH 'COME ON EILEEN' AND 'TOO RYE AY',THE MUSICAL SOUND OF WHICH, FOLKY FIDDLE AND TEXTURE, MIXED WITH TAMLA TYPE SOUL, CAME FROM KEVIN ARCHER AND NOT ME AS I CLAIMED. THE IDEA AND SOUND WAS HIS , I STOLE IT FROM HIM HURTING KEVIN ARCHER DEEPLY IN THE PROCESS. I CONNED PEOPLE ALL OVER THE WORLD FROM THE PEOPLE CLOSE TO ME AND THE PEOPLE I WORKED WITH, TO THE FANS, TO THE RADIO AND TV PROGRAMMERS, AND I MADE A LOT OF MONEY. TO EVERYBODY I CONNED I'M SORRY , TO MY BEAUTIFUL FRIEND KEVIN ARCHER I LOVE YOU, I'M SORRY I HURT YOU. I WAS JEALOUS OF YOU AND YOUR TALENT, YOU DESERVED BETTER, I HOPE YOU GET WHAT YOU DESERVE.

APPROPRIATELY I FELT LIKE A TOTAL FRAUD, AND UNWORTHY AND UNABLE TO DEAL WITH THE ACCLAIM THAT CAME MY WAY.

BEST WISHES,

KEVIN ROWLAND.

CREATION RECORDS.

Special thanks to Steven Jones who sent this in over the Atlantic from San Francisco

Return of the Genius?

Search for the Not-So-Young-Anymore Soul Rebel: Kevin Rowland, then (L) and now.

POSSIBLY the best news in years has come across the Atlantic with the word that Kevin Rowland, former leader of the inimitable Dexy's Midnight Runners, has signed a new recording contract with Creation Records (the very-hot label which gave us Oasis, among others). Since Dexy's last record (1985's simply excellent *Don't Stand Me Down*) Rowland has been missing in action, as befitting his very-odd self and rumored personal troubles. The numerous former members of the Liverpool-born band have scattered (one has been for many years a member of Black '47).

Dexy's were always way better than the one U.S. hit single they are remembered for — 1983's 'Come on Eileen.' Rowland's take on Van Morrison-style blue-eyed soul was simply outstanding. By the time he got to *Don't Stand Me Down*, an album initially misunderstood by many critics but eventually revered among the best of the eighties, Dexy's dictatorial Rowland had run out of bandmates.

Neither Creation nor Rowland will say what their partnership will entail, but the rumor is a long-overdue solo album (a dozen years in the making). Hopefully, they'll also get 'round to a CD re-release of the classic Dexy's albums, from *Geno* to *Too-Rye-Aye* to *Don't Stand me Down*. (Incidentally, a very difficult-to-find CD copy of that last album has surfaced in the jukebox at the Lexington Avenue bar Rocky Sullivan's. If you come across a copy of the same in a used music shop buy it immediately. Otherwise, go to Sullivan's and play 'Just One of Those Things,' an amazing song which finds Rowland mumbling about Northern Ireland, to the tune of Warren Zevon's 'Werewolves of London.' You shouldn't be disappointed.)

IRISH VOICE, Wed., Nov. 13, – Tues., Nov. 19, 1996

...es decided t.
...nship wasn't suitable.
Go! Discs project also fell by the wayside.

Many people who have met Rowland in the past ten years agree the music he is working up in demo form is astonishing, and that Rowland's famous intensity is undimmed.

As *NME* went to press, it w... not possible to contact Arch... ...o was last seen with the

The Wonder Scruff

Ah, the '80s – a decade rife with musical embarrassments, save for the dungaree-clad, maverick genius of Kevin Rowland and **DEXYS MIDNIGHT RUNNERS**. As the band prepares for a rebirth in the '90s, TERRY STAUNTON recalls their turbulent career...

Happily, they drew the line at workman's bum-cleavage...

SHARLEEN SPITERI of TEXAS on the records that make her go, 'Yee-hah, the 'noo!'

DEXYS MIDNIGHT RUNNERS
"GENO" (Late Night Feelings single)
"THE one record I always adored at school discos, it was always full-on. You've got to go with it because Kevin Rowland definitely believed it. I'm dying to hear his new records, too. He was the original soul boy. I've got some tapes of rare Dexy's stuff which I put on when I go on long journeys and I end up singing the whole way. The only trouble is that you do kangaroo braking in the car because you want to tap your foot. You want to watch that."

"I've been searching for the young soul rebels/I've been searching for them everywhere/I can't find them anywhere/ Where've you hidden them?"
— There There My Dear – Dexys Midnight Runners, 1980

KEVIN ROWLAND has always been a man with a mission, a man on a relentless quest for all that's honest, true and pure in music. A surly upstart to some, but a committed, awe-inspiring visionary to many more.

As the '70s came to an end and the rage of punk gave way to disillusionment, as the melting pot of 2-Tone attempted to politicise British youth, and as the likes of Duran Duran threw shapes in the mirror, Kevin Rowland scowled at the world around him and took solace in the healing power of sweet soul music.

He'd tried his hand at punk, as guitarist with Birmingham's Killjoys, releasing one single ('Johnny Won't Get To Heaven') and then vanishing. But with fellow Killjoy Kevin Archer, Rowland put together the prototype of what was to become one of the most lauded, most misunderstood groups of the '80s. Dexys Midnight Runners were the most uncompromising kids on the block, refusing to fit into any kind of "new wave" pigeonhole, playing the music they loved: Stax, Motown, Atlantic – grubby, sweaty, dirt-under-the-fingernails soul music.

They had two Number One hits, released three brilliant albums,

played classic gigs, underwent numerous line-up changes and put many noses out of joint. It's now eight years since Kevin Rowland's name has graced a record – but that looks set to change, with Rowland now being courted by Creation Records.

So, what was all the fuss about? Let's get this straight from the start...

DEXYS FIRST surfaced in late 1979, the opening act on a 2-Tone package tour with The Specials and The Selecter.

> "In the old days, I think we were obsessional. Believe me, we took it to ridiculous extremes."
> — Kevin Rowland, 1993

Rowland declined offers to sign for the label, opting instead for the EMI-distributed Oddball, run by former Clash manager Bernie Rhodes.

The band's debut 45, 'Dance Stance', appeared in February 1980, supported by a gruelling seven-week tour which gave the public their first glimpse of Dexys strong visual image – woolly hats, white T-shirts, donkey jackets and leather coats, influenced by such films as *Mean Streets* and *On The Waterfront*.

'Dance Stance' was a sonic assault of Stax brass and a taut rhythm section which screamed "Soul!" Rowland's lyrics were an articulate response to rash generalisations and prejudices about Ireland, allegedly inspired by

hearing another member of the band tell an Irish joke. The single scraped into the charts at Number 40.

Rowland was formulating a soul masterplan: "I'd like to see the charts filled with soul, loads of feeling everywhere," he enthused. "Other people can have their musical choice and exist, but soul hasn't been around at all. I really believe that rock'n'roll music is a spent creative force."

The follow-up single, 'Geno', was a gorgeous, affectionate tribute to one of Rowland's favourite soul artists. Geno Washington. Surpassing all expectations, it went to Number One. But the music took second place in the summer of 1980, when the group hit the news after stealing the master tapes for their debut LP, 'Searching For The Young Soul Rebels'. Having lured producer Pete Wingfield out of the studio, the band made a quick getaway, holding the tapes to ransom until EMI agreed to renegotiate their contract.

At the same time, Rowland announced he would no longer be giving interviews, and that Dexys would be putting their point across in full-page ads, or "essays", in the NME and other titles. "We won't compromise ourselves by talking to the dishonest, hippy press," read a passage in the first essay. "We are worth much more than that."

WHAT APPEARED to be incredible arrogance on Rowland's part also alienated some of his money which are quite, quite nice...

We'll have to wait and see. What can Rowland deliver in 1996? Will the public clasp him to their bosom, or has he left it too long? And what on earth will he be wearing? No doubt about it – we should welcome the new soul vision. **VOX**

...uncertain an old schmo like that again? And isn't it a thrill to catch him banging away on form once more?

Ladies and gentlemen, a green light please, for the Celtic Soul brother.

THE BLUE OX BABES

in the view of Craig Stephen

The Blue Ox Babes may be of some interest to Dexys fans for they were formed by founder member Kevin Archer and also featured another ex-Dexy, Steve Wynne. In my view their two singles were as good as anything Rowland et al recorded.

The Blue Ox Babes are a bit of an anomaly. It's nearby impossible to locate any information on them at all. All those brilliant and informative reference books like The Great Rock And Roll Discography or Music Master omit them completely; two chaps who supply press cuttings on bands couldn't locate anything for me and even their former record company, Go! Discs were in the dark over this seemingly mysterious band.
The ignorance over them only detracts from their brilliance. The band only recorded two singles both of which were fantastic, Dexys type affairs. Somehow or another they never got round to releasing an album and they fizzled out rather prematurely in 1988. A definition of their sound would probably be best described as the coming together of Dexys and The Levellers.
That there is a strong resemblance to Dexys Midnight Runners is not surprising since it was Kevin Archer, once of the magnificent Birmingham band, who was the pioneering force behind the Babes. It has recently come to light that Kevin Rowland was not the creator of the famous folkie cum motown style that produced classics like *Come On Eileen* and *Jackie Wilson Said* but were the creation of Archer. The success Rowland had with those records he now admits were a "hollow success" and he has apologised to Archer for conning him in such a way.
Archers involvement in Dexys was, in the early days, as important as Rowlands. Along with Kevin he formed the Dexys punk forerunner The Killjoys in 1977. In the summer of 1978 the pair formed Dexys in Birmingham. Archer was the main guitarist and backing vocalist. He lasted until 1981 when there was a clear-out along with Mick Talbot, later of The Style Council.
In forming The Blue Ox Babes he took with him another former member of the band, Steve Wynne. Wynne's stay in the band was short lived. He was roped in as one of the replacements after the '81 clear-out but didn't last until the end of the year. He played bass on two singles 'Show Me' and 'Liars A To E'. The other members of The Blue Ox Babes were the beautiful Yasmin Saleh, Ian Pettitt, Pete Wain, Steve Shaw and Nick Smith.
The bands first single was *Apples And Oranges (The International Hope Campaign)* a four track EP. Three of the tracks were wondrous pop classics, the fourth a long beautiful instrumental. I bought this at a market stall in Aberdeen for the measly price of fifty pence. Needless to say it is one of the best bargains I have been lucky enough to get hold of. The follow up was *There's No Deceiving You*, a more moderate affair but another fine

pop song. It also included a fine cover of Al Green's soul classic *Take Me To The River*, which is infinitely better than Talking Heads pallid version. Neither of these charted, not even in the independent charts and they subsequently drifted into anonymity.
Archer has not been heard of since which is a great shame as the man obviously possesses a brilliant musical talent that has never been fully utilised.

(left) Archer and Rowland in 1980 and (right) Archer in 1988

Note: The first single was actually 'There's No Deceiving You', followed by 'Apples And Oranges'.

EXCLUSIVE GENO WASHINGTON INTERVIEW

The past two years have seen the great Geno comeback after a ten year silence – What have you been up to?
I had to go away and develop myself spiritually because Rock n' Roll can be very shallow at times, because I've been doing this for thirty years, it's not that I don't like it or I'm tired of it, but I wanted to find out a little bit more about me – what makes me tick.
I developed my spirituality so that I could be a better person, I went away to do that and I studied the art of hypnotism. I came back to England and I started doing the hypnotist shows around the country, I'm a trained hypnotherapist and I did the variety bout as well as singin' the blues. I have a band called The Blues Question and we done a lot of theatres, colleges and festivals on the outside and Europe and everything. I have The Ram Jam Band which, because I spent so much time with my hypnotherapist practice and shows and the blues, I hold the soul back for the crazy people who really want to get down and listen to some raw hardcore soul – then we show up with The Ram Jam Band and start kickin' it.

You recently performed with Van Morrison – How did that come about?
That was because I was doin' the blues with my guitarist Chris Staines and we'd go up and do some unplugged blues – just me and him. This started going down a storm and this guy had seen us in a theatre and he recommended it to the owners of the festival in Cork – Guinness. One of the kids used to see us at his local university and he goes - 'Right, I didn't even know he was in the country, that would be great – Geno Washington and Van Morrison – that would be a hell of a bill'. They put it on at midnight and the theatre was packed – it was beautiful, it was fun. I'd been to Ireland before, but I'd never been to Cork, and that was one of my dreams that on the Cork Jazz and Blues Festival that I would be able to get on there one day and do it for the joy, I got my dream come true – a chance to get up there and do some serious partying. It was good fun and me and Van hadn't seen each other for about twenty-six years, the last time me and Van had seen each other was at Sunderland University – that's when they had Johnny Dankworth, Cleo Laine and Geno Washington and The Ram Jam Band. That was a hell of a night – Party! Party! Party!

You've performed with many greats in the past – Which ones have you most enjoyed?
Van Morrison, Rod Stewart, Georgie Fame, Ron Wood, Charlie Watts, The Cream, The Move, The Action, King Crimson, Stones, Who, Hendrix. I've enjoyed them all, I've had a ball. Getting the chance to play with all these wonderful talents in the land has been fabulous.

Is there anybody who you would like to perform with?
I would like to perform with Tina Turner, that would be really good me and Tina on the stage doin' somethin' raunchy. I'd also like to do some blues with Clapton – that would be great. I'd like to do something with Little Richard – he's still my idol. I haven't worked with those guys and I'd like to do something with them. Bryan Ferry's not bad either – I like Bryan Ferry. I wouldn't mind doing something with INXS or U2 – I like a bit of rock myself – rock with some blues tint. But me and Tina up there would be pure joy, if me and Tina were together you'd have to call the fire department on our ass! Maybe one day it will come. I've just started recording again and it's going to be very blues influenced, very soul influenced at the same time, because whatever I do that soul influence is going to come in along with the blues influence and I like that. I'm ready to go back out there and start making records again. It's great and the concerts are goin' great, I'm popping up here, there and everywhere – I'm on a roll and I'm very happy with my life now.

You've been mentioning a lot recently about all the hard times you went through when you were younger – Was it really that bad?
It was extremely bad, it's like I ask you to do me a favour and you might print this or you might not print this – it doesn't bother me because I truly mean it from the heart. It taught me a new ass – I mean, I was out there, didn't know where to turn and basically would do a lot of things that Kevin Rowland went through and he's going through now. Fortunately for me, I fell in love with my wife of twenty-eight years and she's been a great help to me. She stopped me from going all the way, where I would actually have gone – become a dope freak, an alcoholic from the injustice of the business. As a young guy you don't know about these things, there's a lot of phoney, back-stabbing type people out there, out to rip you off. You come a long way with these people and you develop a trust for them and everything, and then they turn on you and you find they never fuckin' liked your ass. It's a hate trip, that's why I had to disappear for a while to develop my spirituality because it was killing me, it was getting on me real bad and I had depression, thought about suicide and things. This is real bad for me because I'm a happy, jolly type person, partay, scrape me off the ceiling, I love life. This new thing that comes in – it goes along with success – you must pay for it. You don't know about these things when you're very young and you can go off the deep end.

You're now playing the more upper class type clubs like Ronnie Scotts – Do you prefer these to the normal live venue?
I'd rather play at these places because when I come in I have my own audience, they are there for me and I know they're there for me. They know I'm going to entertain them and I'm going to entertain them, no gimmicks, just old fashioned entertainment – what blues and soul

stand for. I'll take the place and turn it into the Mardi Gras, they know they're going to come and see me at the end of the night and everyone's going to be standing up – it's gonna be like you went to the Mardi Gras. People like to go to a happy party, I sell the feel good factor, it's no use me getting around it, Geno Washington is in business because I make you forget your problems and start feeling good – that's what I stand for. I pick my ground and when I appear you're not just coming to listen to the music or see me singing or dance, you're coming for the feel good factor – you want to let it hang, you want to be out there doin' your thing – you want to invite your mates and shit to watch something different – that's kickin'. Which is what Kevin's trying to do – re-group and come out with something kickin' – not just doing exactly what people expect from Dexys Midnight Runners. That's why he's got all these fuckin' problems – he don't want that shit. You start getting problems when you wanna start changing, you want to be more creative, you want to change a direction. It's like eating chicken every mother fuckin' day – pretty soon you'll strangle someone if they just mention chicken. It's like there's got to be more to me than eating mother fuckin' chicken everyday. I enjoy what I do now because I've become like a cork now, I deal in the feel good factor and it does me very good. This is the 90s and a lot of people are down, miserable, pissed off, stressed out – so I stepped into the market and you come and see me and you're going to feel good. It's hard for a person to kick you in the ass when they're having fun – so there's never any violence. I can go and it's going to be like a party, I won't be just standing there and I won't know anybody, nobody talks to me and things, hey, everybody's there for a good time, everyone wants to talk to one another. In the 80s I got them dancin' in the halls – that's not happened since the old Rock n' Roll days.

You really seem to be enjoying performing again?
Yeah, I'm home now, I've found myself and I'm going along quite peacefully, doing what I want to do and I realise how lucky I am. I'm making my own decisions now – I'm slow but show! I'm popping up everywhere... I thought that was very good – from at one time popping up nowhere and now I'm popping up everywhere. Everything is cool, I just decided that whatever I do there will be the feel good factor and I'm not going to try and hide it any more or disguise it, just tell the truth, it's gonna be a feel good factor. I'll rock ya anyway you wanna be rocked but you're gonna feel good when I rock ya.

You've released many albums from actual live shows – Is this to ensure that you get all the feeling over, rather than being stuck in a recording studio?
Yeah, that was so bad in a recording studio. They said "Let's just go for it live and then he's home – he's in control and the shit feels good – let's go with that, let's just leave him alone and see what comes up." And we'd do it and leave it alone and see what come up and the shit sold – so I got happy on that one.

Is it true that the Dexys single played a major part in you performing again in the 80s?
No, on purpose I stayed out until nine months after they'd had the hit. I was still doing my training with hypnotism and developing my spirituality. I came to England with a heavy metal band to keep my own identity. At the universities I went down a storm. A lot of

the places expected me to come out with the soul thing and the horns, they were saying shit like – "I'll see you never work again, you bastard."

What did you think of the 'Geno' single?
I didn't actually think... nothing. The good thing about it was that it made me laugh – there would be someone out in the audience at one of my shows, and all I'm going to do is get out there and do the feel good thing and hit that party streak and shit – get out there and start partying, it affected someone else – 'He wrote a song about this bastard!' It brought joy to me and it changed my thinking, at that point I was in the middle of my hypnotherapy training – which was self confidence and motivation, and I was heavily into that. It put in my mind 'hey, I must not be that bad, I must not be that fuckin' bad if this little kid went out and wrote this song about me, I must not be that bad, hey, I might be a cool mother fucker, shit, let me get myself together'. It forced me to get myself together quick because if people started to point me out and going – 'There he is, the legend, let's here him sing', and if I got on stage and sounded like shit and they'd go 'he's no fuckin' legend, listen to that load of shit'. So that got me to get my peckin' order right – gotta keep me chops up in case I run into these bad mother fuckers that go – 'Hey Geno, come over here and sing some of this'. I knew I had to keep my chops up now because I was in the spotlight because Dexys Midnight Runners made people start checking me out going – 'Yeah, well who the fuck is he?'.

Have you ever met Kevin?
No, I've been wanting to meet him and you tell him I want to meet him, I would truly like to meet him.

Kevin once said - "Geno Washington is the greatest soul singer that's ever lived."
Wow, that's just quite amazing, first time I've ever heard that and it makes me humble. I think that is one of the nicest things that someone has ever said about me. I'm thrilled and I would truly like to meet him more than ever now. I'm not just saying this because he said that but after every gig, every concert after Dexys for about two years I used to look in the audience and hope I'd see him or I'd hope he'd come back to the dressing room so that we could say hello and meet. I've come across his life and he's come across my life, I would really like to meet him and that's a wonderful thing that he said and I'm very grateful... beyond words... just unbelievable... fabulous... it's made my day.

Geno Washington is a truly extraordinary person and energy just flowed from this great man. It was a great experience for me meeting this legendary soul man and it seemed as if we had known each other for years, I even had one of his smokes!

'That man took the stage with his towel swingin high, this man was my bombers, my dexys, my high'

Reminisce Part Five
(from someone laying low in the North of Scotland)

It was April 1980, and not for the first time, Aberdeen were looking as if they might win the Scottish Premier League Championship. It had been a struggle since last January, but at last there was hope, even though all previous attempts had ended in failure. Was it likely to be any different this time? Were we destined to remain the wild-hearted outsiders? We were due to play Hibs at home on Wednesday evening. Earlier that day, on the van radio, I had heard for the very first time, the song that was to become our talisman during the last weeks of our unforgettable campaign. Geno.

That night, our hopes suffered a dent. Hibs, almost relegated, stole a point in a 1-1 draw. Whilst despairingly reading the match report in next day's papers, the song was playing on the radio. It's power struck me. Rasping brass, Kevin's impassioned vocal, the insistent bass... all conspired to give me inspiration (not academic, of course). We could still do it. The togetherness of Dexys, evident from the recording made me believe that if Aberdeen fans displayed the same "all for one, one for all" attitude, we were unstoppable. Two days later we won at Kilmarnock. Our nearest rivals, Celtic, tumbled 1-5 against Dundee. That night, in the local pub, the DJ played Geno at least three times. The place was jumping, GENO... GENO... GENO being chanted in unison by dozens as the place emptied at closing time.

An away midweek victory at shell-shocked Celtic followed and a 2-0 win at home to St Mirren left us clear at the top. Dexys were edging up the chart, our fates interlinked. If the Midnight Runners' team ethos that was evident in their appearances on TV at the time, Aberdeen fans replicated it in the third from last game against Dundee United on Tuesday 29th April, the day that Geno, our anthem, hit the number one spot. Aberdeen and the Runners ahead of the rest. That night at Tannadice Park, Aberdeen supporters showed a unity and single-mindedness that has rarely been seen since. Groups of fans were urging each other on to greater and greater vocal efforts to force the team towards the title. We only drew, but our destiny was in our own hands. We were that *"fighter that won..."*.

Saturday 3rd May dawned and we trekked in our thousands to Edinburgh to will the Reds to the victory that could seal the championship for us. No Aberdeen fan will ever forget that afternoon. A 5-0 triumph coupled with Celtic's draw with St Mirren gave us the League title for the first time in 25 years and the respect and self-belief we had been searching for. After the pitch invasion - *"the crowd they all hailed you and chanted your name"* - outpourings of emotion and much cheap champagne, the train journey home was to be endured, fortified only by one of the largest consignments of beer ever seen on a British Rail football special.

My lasting memory of that joyous trip is of carriageloads of delirious Dons, on the final thirty or so miles, bouncing on the seats, playing *air trombone* as Geno was sung from end to end time after time in a variety of keys and at ever-increasing volume.

One of the most powerful periods of my life, breaking down the walls of previous heartache. Without Dexys, I have to say it would probably still have happened, but the passion that Geno helped galvanise made it truly memorable for all concerned. And hey, wasn't Big Jimmy from Portsoy, and therefore one of *ours?*

David Innes

I just couldn't resist the temptation of including the following sketch in 'KOR'. It was expertly sketched on to the end of a letter that I recently received from Phill Sweet. Nice one Phill.

MEET IN CAFFS • DEXYS MIDNIGHT RUNNERS • THE TEAMS THAT

Are there any other artistic soul rebels out there!?

KEEP ON RUNNING
ISSUE 8 JULY 1997

"More please and thank you

Introducing the Celtic Soul Brothers

And featuring the strong devoted

Ladies and gentlemen would you now please take your leave..."

THE CELTIC SOUL BROTHERS (No. 45, March 1982)

As most of you know Dexys never had a Fan Club as such, but they did have an **Intense Emotions Circle**. If you were a member you got two newsletters (or thereabouts) per month. They also introduced a directory where kindred spirits could write and arrange to meet with each other. This was later disbanded as the **Intense Emotions Circle** changed to the *Dexys Midnight Runners Circle*, with the first of the new newsletters coming out in November '82. Kevin describing the change said - "*Intense Emotions just doesn't sound right any more; not in 1982. The directory I suppose was a good idea but would be unfeasible with a hopefully much larger membership. The new Circle will be value for money and should be entertaining for anybody interested in Dexys Midnight Runners.*"

As a new feature in KOR starting from this issue I will be including copies of the Circle Newsletters and also the letters that a member of KOR received from the circle.

Introduced by Clive Gray -

Can I reminisce for a while?

I can't remember exactly when it was but sometime between listening to The Jam or The Clash and going to Northern Soul All-Nighters I remember thinking there should be something more than this... *I dunno, music, films, something special perhaps*... it was then that I came across 'Dance Stance' and then 'Searching for the Young Soul Rebels'. Immediately, I sensed that I knew what Rowland was up to and that this music filled a void amongst all the power pop and ska of the early 80s. When 'Show Me' was released the enclosed essay insert mentioned Midnight Cowboy and Mean Streets as Kevin's favourite 'soul' films. At this time I had also been watching Mean Streets so I wrote to the band asking if they would like a copy of the video. I remember that I didn't even expect a reply but this actually started a series of correspondences between me and the band. Unfortunately, I didn't keep copies of my letters but what follows are the replies I received.

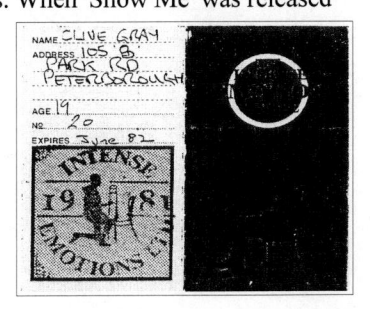

Dexys Midnight Runners

MAY 1st   Intense Emotions Circle,   Newsletter I.

Dexy's Midnight Runners Team is:

Seb Shelton	– Drums
Steve Wynne	– Bass Guitar
Big Jimmy Paterson	– Trombone
Micky Billingham	– Organ and Piano
Paul Speare	– Tenor Saxophone
Billy Adams	– Guitar
Brian Maurice	– Alto Saxophone
Kevin Rowland	– Singing
Paul Burton	– Manager
Pete Barrett	– Crafts and Design
Jenny Rogers	– Secretary

O.K. then, you've joined the Circle, let me tell you about it.

For almost a year now it's been pretty obvious that we should have some kind of organization that would at least supply information to anyone who took the trouble to write to us. But somehow, the idea of a fan club just didn't appeal. It seemed that every group had one and that each club was a very patronizing, self-promoting one way affair. The truth is we couldn't think of an alternative until now.

The idea came about one night, when a few of us were sitting around talking. Paul Speare said something about a network of letters, somebody else mentioned a Circle, then everybody started chipping in until we had the roughframework for the "Intense Emotions Circle". When we were happy with the ideas we contacted Jenny Rogers (whom I met at the Bristol date of last years "Straight to the Heart Revue") and talked her into being the secretary. The next thing was to convert 4, The Willows (our managers flat) into an office and away we go.

The first aim of the Circle is to supply information about the group, where we're going, what we're doing and why. If you need to know anything write to us, we'll always write back.

INTENSE EMOTIONS LTD. 4 The Willows, Four Oaks, Sutton Coldfield.

Also, we intend to make available our own range of good quality T-shirts, badges, photos etc. These will be all designed and sanctioned by us and sold at reasonable prices. By doing this we hope to eliminate the over-priced cash-in artists, who are currently selling things in our name.

The main aim of the Circle though, is to encourage an underground network of letters like no ones ever seen before. Do you like to get letters? I love them. Letters make you feel good, sad, tell you things you didn't know, its often easier to talk in a letter. One of the best things about Dexy's Midnight Runners for me is the way I've come into contact with so many kindred spirits, mostly through letters. You probably know already that the Circle directory will list everybodys name, address, phone number and age, and will be split into sub-divisions of areas and towns. You like the Midnight Runners, you might have other things in common, why not communicate, write, meet, find out. Not necessarily for pointless agreeing sessions, what about genuine encouragement, what about talk. Also we'd like suggestions, if you have any ideas for the Circle, please write them.

We've had alot of letters recently from people who held tickets for the "Projected Passion Revue" and didn't find out until the last moment that most of the dates were cancelled. Some had travelled long distances to find cancelled signs on theatre doors. I can only say that we're sorry for this and if we could have possibly done the shows we would have. The problem was due to lack of record company support, which we've now sorted out with the strong prospect of a new record company and release date of our next single ("Show Me") in late May. Of the three shows that we did salvage, Chelmsford, London and Birmingham, we were pleased with the performance and response. My verdict on the shows is Chelmsford: could have been better, London: great, Birmingham: nearly. It was so good for us to play live after looking forward to it for so long. The "Projected Passion Revue" is a format we'll definetly use again. We've put far too much effort, time and thought into it to let it go to waste. We'll stage the complete show in as many areas as possible as soon as we're properly organized.

Apart from launching the Circle, and re-scheduling the "Passion Revue", we've talked about the possibility of a short European tour, which should take us up to mid-summer, when the chances are our thoughts will turn to an L.P. It's funny, because after finishing "Searching for the Young Soul Rebels" and for quite a while afterwards, I felt (forgive me if I sound conceited) that the record was the best thing ever, and I personally would never be able to do anything better. It seemed such a complete statement. I really didn't want to make another L.P. Almost to the point where I was quite glad when four of the old group left, as the possibility then seemed more remote. It's only over the last few months through meeting the new members of the group and gradually assembling new ideas, that I can see past "Young Soul Rebels". The new L.P. will be better, it has to be. We'll re-write it, re-record it, wont release it until it is better. We're strong we have optimism through the new group. The new group: What can I say. I don't want to sound off like some musician on the radio telling how his reformed group is much better than the last one. Except with us it just happens to be true. Most of the new members have never played in groups before, and it shows. Untampered pure inspiration. We are spiritually more in-tune, we are stong, we're a group. The new L.P.? I can't wait.

Anyway, I'm sorry if I've gone on a bit. Finally to everybody who sent such encouraging letters over the last few months, thankyou, you've helped.

Sincerely

Kevin Rowland

Dexys Midnight Runners

Dear Clive

Thank's for writing, we're always glad to receive letters.

We havn't got a fan club in the traditional sense, but we do have a hopefully better alternative in "The Intense Emotions Circle". It costs three pounds for a year's membership for which you get a two monthly newsletter (which is written by one of the group), regular up to date photos, a membership card, discount on our mail order merchandizing, plus whatever else we can afford for three pounds.

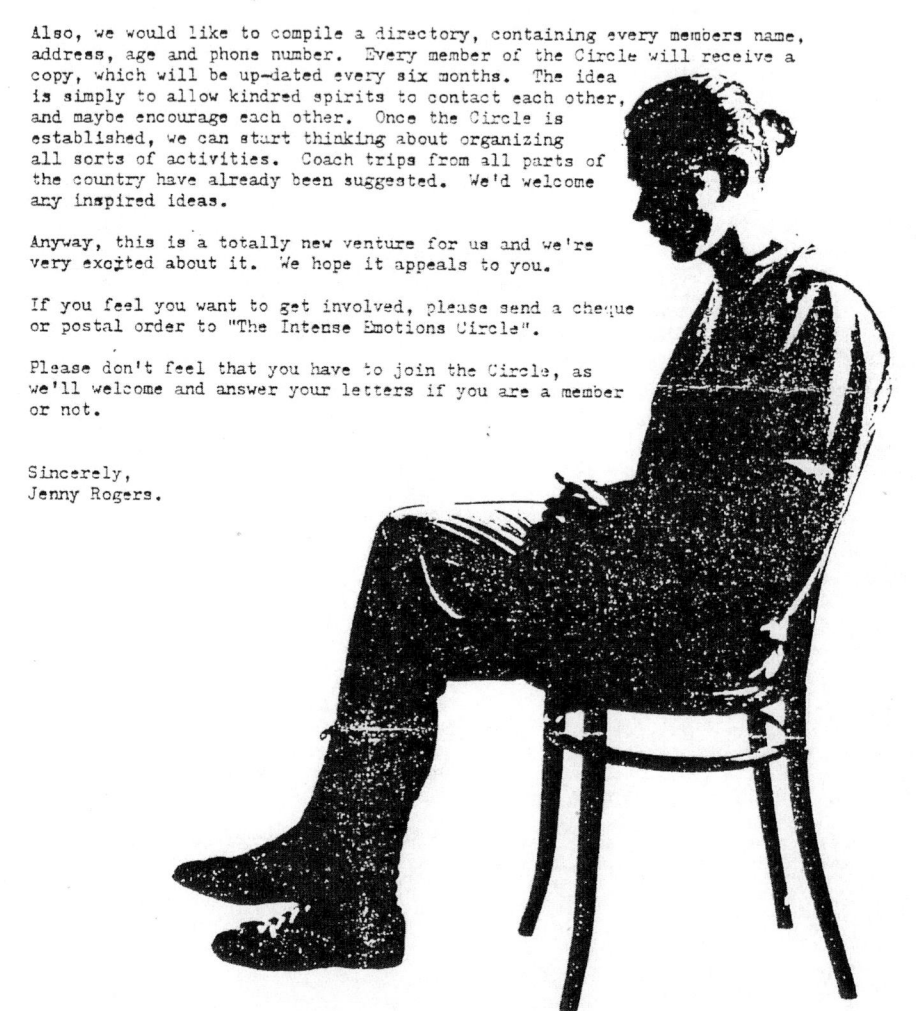

Also, we would like to compile a directory, containing every members name, address, age and phone number. Every member of the Circle will receive a copy, which will be up-dated every six months. The idea is simply to allow kindred spirits to contact each other, and maybe encourage each other. Once the Circle is established, we can start thinking about organizing all sorts of activities. Coach trips from all parts of the country have already been suggested. We'd welcome any inspired ideas.

Anyway, this is a totally new venture for us and we're very excited about it. We hope it appeals to you.

If you feel you want to get involved, please send a cheque or postal order to "The Intense Emotions Circle".

Please don't feel that you have to join the Circle, as we'll welcome and answer your letters if you are a member or not.

Sincerely,
Jenny Rogers.

INTENSE EMOTIONS LTD. 4 The Willows, Four Oaks, Sutton Coldfield.

Dexys Midnight Runners

Dear Readers

It's over six months now since our first communication when we stated that we wouldn't be doing any more interviews with the music papers and even now the bitching continues. Gallant reporters from all the papers never miss an opportunity to call us funny names or make snide remarks about our craft. The Musical Express (which, incidentally, we felt had more integrity than the other papers) seems intent on making Kevin this year's whipping boy. You won't do it chaps—he's stronger than you. Besides, the best thing you can do is ignore us then perhaps we'll go away . . . then again, perhaps not.

For those interested, some of the previous members of the group left suddenly after hatching a plot to throw Kevin out and still carry on under the same name. What happened was, Kevin discovered the scheme and asked the would-be overthrowers to leave. At the time of their exit the gentlemen were far from impressed with the group's future plans as well as with suggestions that they might learn new instruments. However, the main source of their heartache was the group's image and stance which they felt didn't particularly represent them anyway—a perfectly justifiable opinion since they were all initially recruited from very different walks of music. They now have their own group and we wish them the best of British (oh, and we don't mind you claiming credit for Kevin's ideas, honest chaps).

For totally different reasons Al Archer recently decided to leave. He had wanted to make a start on a project of his own for some time and felt that now was as good a time as any. He will be missed as a loyal friend most of all.

And there you have it.

Meanwhile Big Jimmy, Kevin and six new fusiliers have, for the last few months, been busily working on our next live venture, "The Midnight Runners Projected Passion Revue". More of that soon. Please don't expect this group to be exactly the same as the last one. It has to be better, otherwise there's no point.

Dexys Midnight Runners

We want to apologise to anybody who wrote to us over the last few months and hasn't received a reply. The delay was caused by our moving offices. We can now welcome letters at Intense Emotions Limited, 4 The Willows, Four Oaks, Sutton Coldfield, West Midlands.

I don't believe you really like Frank Sinatra...

With Kevin recording an LP of songs that have touched him throughout his life I thought now, *more than ever*, would be a good time to delve into the archives and have a look at the songs that have been covered by Dexys and Kevin in the past.

As an introduction in this issue, following is all the info on the original releases. We will be looking more in depth at a selection of the songs starting from the next issue.

COVERS (OFFICIAL RELEASES)

TITLE	WHERE?	ORIGINAL	YEAR	POS
Breaking Down The Walls Of Heartache	Geno B-side	Johnny Johnson & The Bandwagon	1968	4
Seven Days Too Long	Rebels track	Chuck Woods	1968	-
The Horse	There, There B-side	Cliff Nobles & Co	1968	-
One Way Love	Keep It Part 2 B-side	Cliff Bennett & The Rebel Rousers	1964	9
Soul Finger	Plan B B-side	The Bar Kays	1967	33
Jackie Wilson Said	45"	Van Morrison**	1972	-
TSOP	Jackie Wilson 12"	MFSB	1974	22
RESPECT	Let's Get This Straight 12"	Otis Redding**	1965	-
		Aretha Franklin	1967	10
Marguerita Time	What She's Like (double pack)	Status Quo	1983	3
Kathleen Mavourneen	Because Of You B-side	Frederick Crouch Marion Crawford	1837	-
The Way You Look Tonight	Walk Away 12"	The Lettermen	1961	36
		Denny Seyton & The Sabres	1964	48
		Edward Woodward	1971	42
Heartaches By The Number*	Wanderer track	Guy Mitchell	1959	5

COVERS (UNOFFICIAL, NOT COMMERCIALLY AVAILABLE)

TITLE	WHERE?	ORIGINAL	YEAR	POS
Big Time Operator	Live Show (79-80)	Zoot Money's Big Roll Band	1966	25
Hold On I'm Coming	Live Show (79-80)	Sam and Dave	1966	-
Merry Xmas Everybody	Xmas TV Show 82	Slade	1973	1
Can't Help Falling In Love With You	Live Show (1985)	Elvis Presley	1962	1
		Andy Williams	1970	3
		The Stylistics	1976	4
Something Old, Something New, Something Borrowed, Something Blue	Live Show (1985)	The Fantastics	1971	9
The More I See You*	TV Show 1988	Joy Marshall	1966	34
		Chris Montez	1966	3

MENTIONED IN PASSING

Michael	Geno	Geno Washington and the Ram Jam Band	1967	39
Tired Of Being Alone	RESPECT (Live)	Al Green	1971	4
Wedding Bell Blues	Reminisce Part 2	5th Dimension	1970	16
Lola	Reminisce Part 2	The Kinks	1970	2
I'll Say Forever My Love	Reminisce Part 2	Jimmy Ruffin	1970	7
Leaving On A Jet Plane	Reminisce Part 2	Peter, Paul & Mary	1970	2
Lean On Me	Plan B	Bill Withers	1972	18

"I heard that blind man, that man with the glasses on, I heard him singing, I didn't like the song y'understand but I did know what he meant about the higher ground..."

Higher Ground	Reminisce Part 1	Stevie Wonder	1973	29

---

*Kevin Rowland Solo
**Album Track

Researched for 'KOR' by David 'Ken Livingstone is, more than ever, a folk hero' **Innes**

like in the song, y'know the one about the donkey...

Then & Now...

With Don't Stand Me Down getting a Creation Records re-issue in 1997, 'KOR' looks back at the original reviews from 1985. ***Then...***

Taking the smooth..

1985: The new look of the Runners.

..with the rough

1983: The way they were.

BETCHA don't recognise the clean-cut pair at the top? No, they're not a bunch of bank clerks, it's fabulous Dexy's Midnight Runners, who've obviously cleaned up their act for their new single Don't Stand Me Down. That's Helen O'Hara and Kevin Rowland, more recognisable in the lower picture.

Dexys are back—with a passion

Kevin Rowlands: Back in business.

Would you buy a used record off this man? No, it's not a mate of Arthur Daley's, and it's not the new clerk at the listening bank.

It is in fact one Dexys Midnight Runner — the elusive Midland maestro Kevin Rowlands.

Kev has forsaken the gypsy locks which went with his top-selling *Come On Eileen* and the austere woolly cap that he wore with *Geno*.

Lilting mystery

It's no wonder that everyone has been looking for him for the last year or so — you wouldn't recognise him if you met him in the street.

The band's new album — *Don't Stand Me Down* — is terribly self-indulgent, but breaks from time to time into a lilting mystery reminiscent of Van Morrison.

Throughout, the missing Midnight Runner recalls past triumphs with vocal phrasing borrowed from the band's earlier songs.

I reckon he's on to a right earner.

PAUL COLE

KEVIN'S THE LEAGUE LEADER

THIS winter's thing could well be the "Ivy League" look if Dexys' Midnight Runners' Kevin Rowland has any say about it.

Kevin who made dungarees and the gypsy look popular in the summer of '82 with the No. 1 smash hit Come on Eileen has re-emerged with a new Dexy's and new album.

The dungarees and curls have been ditched and replaced by short, close-cropped hair, smart suits with raised edges on the seams, button down shirts and collegiate style ties.

"It's the Ivy League look" says Kevin. That's the term for the five or so top notch American colleges like Harvard and Yale.

Kevin denies that he's trying to start a fashion. "I've been wearing these clothes for a couple of years now only because I like them."

DEXYS STOOD UP?

AS *NME* went to press on Monday, a court battle was taking place in which producer Alan Winstanley sought to halt the release of Dexys Midnight Runners' forthcoming album 'Don't Stand Me Down'.

Contacted by this paper, Winstanley admitted that he was seeking an injunction but felt unable to comment on the case because of legal complications involved.

However, *NME* understands that the producer is unhappy with the album's inner-sleeve credits, which read "Produced by Kevin Rowland – Recorded by Alan Winstanley".

Story is that Winstanley was contracted to produce the album and agreed to do so on the understanding that it would be completed by 1 March, this year, at which point he was to commence work on the new Madness album.

The Dexy's, believing that their own album could be completed by this date, apparently agreed to Winstanley's terms. But time ran out while Winstanley and the band were still in New York readying the album for mixing. At which point, the producer flew back to the UK in order to get the Madness sessions underway, leaving Kevin Rowland to mix his own album tracks.

Winstanley now believes that even if he isn't listed as solo producer, he should at least receive a co-producer credit. But Rowland, for his part, apparently claims that as Winstanley didn't complete the album, he cannot receive any production credit. Hence the legal battle, which could see the album's release being deferred.

Roland, who as Carlo Rowlan regaled us with the high-quote *"I've no respect for anybody or anything"* in his first *NME* interview (12 January, 1980) has been involved in a fracas with a producer before.

In mid-1980, while working with producer Pete Wingfield and engineer Barry Hammond on the album 'In Search Of The Young Soul Rebels', the Dexys decided to snatch the completed tapes from Chipping Norton studio in order to hold EMI to ransom. Wingfield, who confirmed that at the time that he was convinced the group would have resorted to physical violence if he or anyone else had attempted to stop them.

That same week, the Dexys placed ads with all the main music papers in which they stated "Music Press writers... try to cover their total lack of understanding behind a haze of academic insincerity. We won't compromise ourselves by talking to a dishonest, hippy press." And now The Dexys, whose initial attempt to gain promotion for 'Don't Stand Down' by means of a highly touted *Tube* gig was sabotaged by a recent strike, could find their album in further trouble as a result of Winstanley's legal action.

There are some who might be quick to point out the folly of saddling the album with a decidedly dodgy release date – Friday the thirteenth!

Dexys Midnight Posers

We're the best band in the world and the rest are hopeless, says Kevin Rowland as Dexys Midnight Runners attack the charts again. Sharon Feinstein reports

DEXYS MIDNIGHT RUNNERS
Don't Stand Me Down
(Phonogram)

The latest Dexys image hits the street and the soundtrack to a collar and tie convention smacks onto a thousand turntables. Richard Lowe clutches his copy of 'Don't Stand Me Down' and waxes lyrical about sweat, emotion, torn dungarees and the young soul rebels.

They were so strong. Looking like extras from *Mean Streets*, the Midnight Runners burst out of their Midlands hideout at the turn of the decade to offer us their 'new soul vision' — piping hot Stax-style horns, intense emotion and a stunning LP, 'Searching For The Young Soul Rebels', which followed in the wake of the chart-topping 'Geno'.

A split in the ranks was only a minor hiccough — those numbers were soon

DEXYS MIDDAY STROLLERS

replaced and Kevin Rowland's 'Plan B' went into operation. The team was complete once again, "spiritually in tune", training and sweating together, perfecting their craft and blowing a storm on the Projected Passion Revue, one of the greatest live shows ever staged.

Striving to remain "wild-hearted outsiders", they shunned the "dishonest hippy press" and set themselves apart from their lacklustre contemporaries. Staunchly proud, theirs was an arrogance rooted in justified self-confidence rather than shallow conceit — they simply knew they were the best.

The Runners learned to swing and dabbled with jazz before delving into their mythical Celtic roots and donning dungarees for 'Too Rye Ay'. Another masterpiece, the horns blended with the fiddles, the folk with the soul, to create a fresh and unique sound. It was the perfect antidote to the empty gloss and glamour of 1982's sickly pop, and an emphatic comeback as 'Come On Eileen' swept to the top of the singles chart on both sides of the Atlantic.

Three years later, Kevin Rowland is back, with a revamped group sporting preppy executive tailoring, and a new LP that echoes but fails to rival the glorious Dexys of old.

The predominant sound of 'Don't Stand Me Down' is light, wistful, downbeat folk. The Van Morrison influence that emerged on 'Too Rye Ay' is clearly still important. However, Big Jim Paterson is back as a hired hand on two of the songs and the bliss and bluster of his trombone manages to beef up proceedings in places.

"You could say I'm a bitter man," declares Kevin in the 'The Occasional Flicker' and few would argue. In 'Tell Me What She's Like' he lists a host of *"scumbags"* who compare unfavourably with 'her': *"the kind that put creases in their old Levi's"*, *"the CND"*, the *"thick and ignorant"*, English upper classes and the *"newly wealthy peasants with their home bars and hi-fis"* . . .

Meanwhile in 'One Of Those Things' he dreads a tenuous parallel between the bland uniformity of the Radio 1 playlist and the blinkered dogmatism of the British *"socialista"*, whose ignorance of the Irish problem and lack of concern over the issue mystifies and angers this staunch republican.

Kevin's as angry as ever and also as irritating, particularly during the snippets of inane conversation between himself and guitarist Billy Adams, and the self-indulgence of 'Reminisce Part Two'.

Kevin Rowland does not make poor records. He is far too careful, takes too much pride in his work and is too talented for that.

'Don't Stand Me Down', however, is an awkward sidestep rather than the confident march forward we've come to expect.

But when the competition is 'The Riddle', 'Dream Into Action' or 'Youthquake', Dexys still have the strength and skill to set them a cut above the rest. ●

Stand and deliver

DEXYS MIDNIGHT RUNNERS
DON'T STAND ME DOWN — Mercury

COMPROMISE, as Kevin Rowland so sharply observes on the opening verse of this remarkable album, is the devil talking.

An artist, then, of extremes. A man who makes an art form out of overkill. A man of supreme arrogance. A man of *paranoia*? Such are the conflicts, the contradictions, the confusion of the tortured pop star. But compromise? *Never.*

And so. Gone are the dungarees, the gypsy scarves, the rebel posture, the need of a shave, the platoon of fiddles and the search for the young soul Ireland of "Too-Rye-Ay". Instead we have chartered accountants, button-down shirts, three-piece suits, Stock Exchange haircuts and hearts firmly pinned to sleeves. Yet these true confessions are laced with bizarre informal conversations, occasional bouts of restraint(!) and even — gasp — *humour*. This, surely, is a first.

We *also* have . . . quite the most challenging, absorbing, moving, uplifting and ultimately triumphant album of the year.

Being Kevin Rowland, of course, it's not *just* an album. It's a mood, an attitude, a complete scenario, a whole shooting party that extends well beyond image — and unlike "Too-Rye-Ay" the image appears to bear little relevance to the music. What the record does have is light and shade and depth and warmth and humanity. And where before Dexys have wasted a lot of breath *talking* about passion here they simply provide it . . . eat your hearts out Prefab Sprout. The closing track "The Waltz" — and it is just that — is both beautiful and poignant. A song, certainly, born of disillusion but resilient spirit . . .

"I've been to the promised land, I've been there/I've also been down to the bottom and looked up from despair".

The album ends with Rowland howling "Here's a protest, here's a protest" amid the bitter-sweetness; and sardonic references to British "greatness" suggest the theme of "The Waltz" may be obliquely political. Ah, word games, word games . . . they always were his forte.

Oddly enough some of the central themes of "Too-Rye-Ay" are explored more fully particularly in relation to nostalgia and childhood. One short track, "Reminisce Part Two", involves Rowland simply talking about a teenage romance in 1969 over an attractive piano/mandolin backing. "We decided to adopt a song that was current — she wanted it to be 'I'll Stay Forever My Love' by Jimmy Ruffin, I wanted it to be 'Lola' by The Kinks." Most people entrust this sort of information only to Mike Read and his "First Love" spot — Rowland puts it on a bloody record! With that sort of arrogance, how can he possibly fail?

Ireland, too, is a recurring topic. But this is not the romantic, tourist-eye view offered on the last album; Helen O'Hara's fiddle playing is more discreet and mournful. All these aspects make an important contribution to the elegaic "Knowledge Of Beauty" which Rowland sings, in classic Scott Walker style, of a sense of heritage re-discovered. It also enters into "One Of Those Things", in many ways the most successful track on the album, encompassing and binding all of the album's many qualities with its humour, its vigorous arrangement, its standard soul backdrop and a sarcastic lyrical shot at the uniformity of pop music. This, in turn, develops into a full-blooded blast at the current trendiness of obscure political causes while the doorstep problem of Ireland is steeped in general ignorance.

Following this, the Roxyesque love song "Listen To This" seems remarkably tame, but it's the only dull moment. For there is fire in the belly right from the opening cut, "The Occasional Flicker", which starts as a heart-wrenching personal soliloquy and drifts, almost imperceptibly, into a fierce rock 'n' roller before introducing the new Rowland self-mocking his image of martyrdom.

But if "The Occasional Flicker" displays an unexpected wryness, it's nothing on "This Is What She's Like", which parades a rare flair for outright comedy. Another spoken intro — a dialogue between Rowland and Billy Adams that could be a sketch from "Alas Smith And Jones" which continues its comic ways as the music blazes and the lyric adopts the pose of a Mike Leigh play.

Sour old Kevin Rowland has taken his mask off. The soul rebel in him has given us lots of driving sax; the Celtic soul brother in him has given us lots of evocative fiddle; the modern man in him has given us *piano* (Vincent Crane) and *steel guitar* (Tommy Evans). The combination is gripping.

He's not to be trusted with your life but he's worth a fiver of your money any day.

COLIN IRWIN

The messiahs of accountant chic . . .

TANGLED UP IN BLUE

DEXYS MIDNIGHT RUNNERS
Don't Stand Me Down (Mercury)

"No, I don't want sympathy, I just want somewhere for these six to go."

YOU'D THINK three years silence might have dimmed the man's burning rage, but no, Kevin Rowland is back with a resharpened axe to grind. Chapter three of the Dexys story unfolds with Rowland as self-obsessed, as unapologetically out to lunch as ever. If the quest for the Young Soul Rebels was a Stax-induced dream from a burgeoning obsessive and the follow up a mish-mash of Celtic gypsy romance dressed up in rags and tatters, what should we make of this weird, wilfully obscure landscape?

Don't Stand Me Down' arrives shrouded in contrivance, an advertising campaign and enigmatic sleeve featuring Rowland and chums looking for all the world like they were embraced for the shock of the new: only Kevin Rowland could make a record like this, as fussy, as unfocussed, as irritatingly compelling as this.

The Occasional Flicker opens proceedings with some kind of reiterated statement of intent; "*I was right the first time*", attests Rowland, still burning with conviction yet still having to convince himself over and over. Obsessive ambition holds court with undiminished self righteousness: "*You could say I'm a bitter man and once again, I think that's true, I still remain so until I know more than those that know more than I do.*"

Then 'This is What She's Like', certainly the single most bizarre escapade yet foisted on an unsuspecting public in the guise of a Dexys song. Prefaced by a staged and stilted conversation between Rowland and Billy Adams, the guitarist, the piece proper begins with a slow croon: "*Well, you know the kind of people that put creases in their old Levis?*" It goes on and on, taking in a few jibes at some of the singer's pet hates: "*Well, you know the English upper classes? Yes, and ignorant! You're familiar with the scum from Hampstead and Moseley, they're called the CND?*" A final vitriolic "*I don't really like these scumbags*" gives way to what sounds like an extended self-parody with Rowland and threatening to tell us what she's like but never actually getting round to it.

Side one ends with 'Knowledge Of Beauty' — the greatest song Van Morrison never wrote — a slow and stately homage to times past, which just about succeeds despite a tendency to lapse into contentious sentiment and a closing line that remarks "*My national pride is a personal pride.*" Rowland, as ever, going out of his way to rock the boat.

Side two's 'One Of Those Things' comes close to the unmitigated weirdness of 'This Is What She's Like' and again utilises Adams' voice to continually intrude on the music. Radio One and "*so called socialists*" are the strange bedfellows targeted here as the numbing blandness of chart pop is compared to the uniformity of most left wing posturing. From politics and received wisdom to 'Reminisce Part Two' is only a short step, herein out here recalls an old love affair conducted to the strains of various fondly remembered pop songs. 'Wedding Bell Blues', 'Lola', 'Leaving On A Jet Plane' and Jimmy Ruffin's 'I'll Say Forever My Love' are all namechecked in a rambling monologue which shares a name, but little else, with the Celtic daydreams of 'Reminisce Part One'.

The penultimate track, 'Listen To This' is the nearest we come to vintage Dexys of yore, as insistent horns blaze a trail through some stirring barrelhouse piano courtesy of Atomic Rooster refugee, Vincent Crane. And finally 'The Waltz' an evocative merging of the personal and the political which may, or may not, tie up all the loose ends that went before. Again there is a fitfully obtuse imagination at work here and what clues we are given are scattered willy-nilly over an allusive landscape. "*There's no beauty any more*", mourns Rowland at one point, a statement that is made all the more ironic by the introverted nature of all that's gone before. Where once there was a celebratory, striving appeal to Rowland's art, there now lies a fragmented, inward looking dourness about the music.

Throughout this minefield of buried clues and arid word play, there is a musical backdrop which manages to flow along in desperate sympathy with the lyrical indulgence. Shades of Springsteen, Dylan (circa 'Desire'), Lou Reed and the ghost of latter day Van Morrison flit through the whole album hinting at a certain inspiration and bankruptcy. We're left with Bowie-ish 'Still faint parting shot: "*Here is a protest*". Still clearly, still raging, he has tied himself, and this his eager listener, in knots. I'm not even sure if they're worth unravelling and therein lies the problem.

Sean O'Hagan

COME ON, DEXY!

No wonder they're looking so glum

DEXY'S Midnight Runners were licking their wounds last night after their long-awaited comeback turned into rock's biggest flop of the year.

Dexy's have spent more than £100,000 and three years of hard work attempting to follow-up their wonderful Come On Eileen which was the best selling single of 1982.

The band auditioned more than 100 musicians and finally unveiled their new album Don't Stand Me Down to a waiting world three weeks ago.

But, sadly, the record has been greeted by a hail of bad reviews and has now dropped straight out of the top 50.

Things have not been helped by Dexy's change of image—from a joyous raggle-taggle band of tinkers into a group of pseudo-accountants.

Leader Kevin Rowland has also become pretty tedious company.

When I met him recently he gave me a long lecture on the evils of drink and drugs, flakiness of musicians and the silliness of fashion.

Come on Kev... time to remember what rock music is all about.

DEXY'S: Accountancy doesn't pay

and now...

Dexys Midnight Runners: the very antithesis of dumb-ass rock'n'roll

Knowledge of beauty

DEXYS MIDNIGHT RUNNERS
DON'T STAND ME DOWN
Creation
★★★★★

THIS is as good as it gets. I've checked. There's a perfectly feasible theory that suggests you'll find your pop greatness by soundtracking the *zeitgeist*. The plan that lets you make *With The Beatles* or *Dare* or *Morning Glory* or *Spice*.

Another option maintains you're best barrelling along two steps ahead of your peers (*Revolver*, *Smile*, *Sandinista*, *In Utero*). Heck, if it floats your boat, you can be vivaciously self-conscious (*The Who Sell Out*, *Lexicon Of Love*, *Songs For Sale*) or even enthusiastically pointless (everything by Baby Bird).

Or you could be Dexys Midnight Runners. Dexys defied the comfort of easy adoration. Every time you thought you were starting to understand what they were all about, they'd come along and completely reshuffle their intentions, offer up a whole new universe of possibilities. And they'd be right every single time.

Tracks: The Occasional Flicker • This Is What She's Like • My National Pride • One Of Those Things • Reminisce (Part Two) • I Love You (Listen To This) • The Waltz • Reminisce (Part One) • The Way You Look Tonight
Produced by **Kevin Rowland, Helen O'Hara, Alan Winstanley** and **Billy Adams**
Mixed by **Pete Schwier**, except Reminisce (Part One), mixed by **Colin Fairley** and The Way You Look Tonight by **Jimmy Miller**
Mastered by **Chris Blair**

So, you'd drench yourself in the Jesuit grace of their *Searching For The Young Soul Rebels*, then they'd slap you down and turn you around with *Too-Rye-Ay* and its hedonistic folky surge. You'd know that "Come On Eileen" was much, much more important than the loosened-tie office workers and gin-and-tonic giddy secretaries would ever understand. That when they were up and running, Dexys Midnight Runners possessed a fluid brilliance that few other bands on the planet could touch.

And on *Don't Stand Me Down*, Kevin Rowland's explosive genius bruised your soul. It's the greatest record ever made. And for those of us who've rather enjoyed clinging to an élitist appreciation of its life-affirming qualities, it's no end of a pisser that Alan McGee has seen fit to re-release it on Creation. With extra tracks and new sleeve notes, if you please.

Bastard. There goes the gang.

Consolation comes from the fact that at least people will think again about Kevin Rowland and maybe appreciate at last the wild tenderness that marks him as one of the finest poets on earth. Time to obliterate the injustice that decreed a man who dared to dream of everything got dismissed as a doltish chancer.

Not that Rowland himself was in a particularly confident state of mind when *Don't Stand Me Down* was originally released. The newly-penned sleeve notes reveal the turmoil and insecurity that accompanied his intent. "I was terrified at the release of the LP . . . I was consumed with self-loathing," he writes. "I sabotaged the record's chances of success by disallowing the record company from promoting it effectively. Just as well, I couldn't have dealt with its success at the time."

There's a weariness to this admission quite at odds with the breathtaking inventiveness of the record itself.

That something rather unusual was going on became evident right from the sleeve and the carefully crafted look that the band had adopted. Drawing on the American Ivy League sartorial style – Brooks Brothers shirts and expensive loafers – they came across as the very antithesis of dumb-ass rock'n'roll, imbued with a focused precision that deliberately set them apart from their peers. And, importantly, allowed them to reinvent both their own sound and the commercial baggage of their past.

The bad news about the re-release is that you don't get the original lyric sheet, a piece of text that stands up as a kind of vivacious cross between *The Wasteland*, Brendan Behan and a killer *Two Ronnies* sketch. The good news is that you get explanatory elaborations of all the songs, weighted with a confessional acknowledgement that the rest of the band perhaps contributed more than was admitted at the time.

There are nine tracks. Which is a bit like telling you how many vowels there are in *Hamlet*. You can't slice it up, though, a mistake made evident when, on its original release, the record company put out a grim, truncated version of "This Is What She's Like" as a single. This was an experience never meant for half-truths.

It starts with "The Occasional Flicker", and "*I don't want sympathy*" snarling its intent across your consciousness. The tone is set for a litany of savage, bitter contempt, constantly somersaulting into an unashamed celebration of unqualified emotion. It burns like hell with blue skies.

Never more so than on "This Is What She's Like" and "My National Pride" (formerly "Knowledge Of Beauty"). Getting on for 20 minutes of cathartic reappraisal of the things that matter, crass impress-your-mates radicalism drowned by the sweet soul torrents of a personal, bloodied manifesto.

The record constantly soars from introspection – "Reminisce (Part Two)" and "The Waltz" – to cascading reminders of Rowland's innate pop sensibility. If there's a record that can take the Earth out of orbit quite as consistently as "I Love You (Listen To This)", I've yet to hear it.

The new tracks are "Reminisce (Part One)" – a gorgeous, largely spoken-word affair – and an elegant cover of Jerome Kern's "The Way You Look Tonight". "*Here is a protest*," sings Kevin Rowland. And here, you think, is wild, irresistible genius.

The last of the true believers. Forever.
Paul Mathur

Albums

ROCK'N'ROWLAND

DEXYS MIDNIGHT RUNNERS. Poetry. Passion. Power. This is what they're like...

**DEXYS MIDNIGHT RUNNERS
DON'T STAND ME DOWN
Creation** (9 tks/55 mins)

I ONCE punched another journalist for telling me how much he loved Dexys. It was at Reading Festival, we were drunk, extolling the virtues of Kevin Rowland, bragging to each other about how much his singular soul vision meant to us, when suddenly I snapped. "Don't tell me how much you like f***ing Dexys," I roared. "You're not even worthy to speak their name." SMACK! Our editor had to pull us apart.

Crap, I know. But I use the incident as an example of the passion Dexys Midnight Runners still inflames. Not for nothing did Kevin Rowland refuse to allow alcohol at his live shows, not for nothing did he sack one band after making the finest debut album EVER ("Searching For The Young Soul Rebels") and then come back with a Number One hit, not for nothing did he disappear into self-imposed exile after making the greatest album EVER ("Don't Stand Me Down"). He'd mention Jackie Wilson and Van Morrison in his songs, but we always knew he was on a higher plateau. This man was IT. His impassioned rants/poems against love and the duplicity of those who made the rules littered B-sides like so many golden leaves sailing down the Rhine in Autumn. His much-vaunted new soul vision wasn't just a trend, it was *everything*.

"Don't Stand Me Down" was Dexys' third album, their most uncompromising and personal record, their finest moment. I'd never heard anything like it at the time. I still haven't. Tracks were mostly narrative, often falling back into spoken word conversations between Kevin and his main foil, guitarist Billy Adams. The brass sections blasted out harmony upon harmony of pure, clean contentment. Violinist Helen O'Hara's bow swept and dived across songs like it was possessed. Lyrics ranged from Kevin's rediscovered pride in his Irish nationality, trying to find some way of putting that indefinable, burning feeling into words, walking down Kilburn High Road on summer nights listening to Jimmy Ruffin, confusion, self-belief, self-hatred...

And it all hinged round one truly awesome song – the second track, a 20-minute epic entitled "This Is What She's Like". It started off with an argument between Kevin and mainman Billy about some girl or other, ran the gauntlet of emotion from hot to boiling to absolutely scalding, contained some great, great lines, slowed down, sped up, stopped when overwhelmed by emotion, touched upon class jealousy and pure desire, and contained the greatest violin part ever written...

Elsewhere, Kevin sounded simply sublime: the opening song "The Occasional Flicker" boasted the to-die-for line *"Compromise is the devil talking"*; "One Of These Things" harked back to the beginning of "Searching For..." with its sly digs at DJs, how they *"all sounded the same"*; "The Waltz" was as sweet and soulful and sad as its title implies. "I Love You (Listen To This)", meanwhile, was the most direct, moving love song to ever have been written by a white man – *"I was thinking of a compromise/When I saw the beauty in your eyes"*. The music owed plenty to the studios of Stax and Muscle Shoals, to the inspired lengthy jamming of early soul artists like Jimmy James & The Bandwagon, to any number of old skool Irish crooners. Some of these songs I still can't listen to without a tear coming into my eye...

This Creation reissue also contains two additional Dexys tracks: the spoken word, self-deprecating and wonderfully moving "Reminisce (Part Two)", wherein Kevin goes searching for the spirit of Brendan Behan in Dublin; and an impassioned cover of Jerome Kern's "The Way You Look Tonight".

What else can I say? This is as beautiful as music comes.
EVERETT TRUE

OTHER RELEASES
Searching For The Young Soul Rebels (EMI LP, 1980)
Too Rye Aye (EMI LP, 1982)

Brave review
Peter Paphides on 'Don't Stand Me Down'

Christmas Day, 1982. That was the day Dexys Midnight Runners changed my life. Sitting by my parents' stereo at 8am as Kevin Rowland fired these beautiful words into the middle of 'I'll Show You': 'It's hard to picture dirty tramps as young boys. But if you see a man crying, hold his hand, he's my friend. If these words sound corny, switch this off. I don't care. Nearby he's still crying, I won't smile while he's there.' From that point, I was his. It wasn't just the words. It was the anger. And the almighty upswell of a band united in pursuit of his vision. So when Dexys disappeared for three years after 'Too-

'If you ever understood anything of what Dexys were about, cowardice is the one thing you'd never accuse Kevin Rowland of.'

Rye-Ay', I never questioned it. I waited, patiently remembering how I'd felt that Christmas morning.

The first thing everyone noticed when Dexys preceded the release of 'Don't Stand Me Down' with an appearance on 'Wogan', was the attire. Gone were the dungarees of 'Come On Eileen'. Instead, Kevin Rowland and guitarist Billy Adams sported the Ivy League look that Kevin had long admired from his northern soul days. As such, the song they performed matched it perfectly. A horn-charged tirade of regret and devotion, 'I Love You (Listen To This)' threatened to combust by the time Kevin's last 'I love you's hammered into your heart. A week after that 'Wogan' appearance, on 'Switch', a despicably dense Muriel Grey asked them, 'What's with the double-glazing salesmen look?' Kevin, clearly incensed, spat, '*What* double-glazing salesmen look?' Things deteriorated from there.

By this time, with 'Don't Stand Me Down' now out, the second thing that people homed in on was the use of spoken dialogue. 'The Occasional Flicker', a smouldering Memphis soul meditation, sets the tone for the album: 'Compromise is the devil talking,' announces Kevin, before Billy tries to ascertain the nature of Kevin's 'burning feeling'. 'One Of

Those Things', ostensibly a song about the lack of decent music on the radio, is guided by a conversation between Kevin and Billy in which the music on Radio One and every right-on platitude of the day regarding Irish, Palestinian and Nicaraguan problems all begin to sound like the same old clichés. *Melody Maker* journalist Barry McIlheny later accused Kevin Rowland of cowardice because of what McIlheny perceived as ambiguity over the civil war in Ireland. He later seemed surprised when Kevin saw him in the street and punched him. But really, if you ever understood anything of what Dexys were about, cowardice is the one thing you'd never accuse Kevin Rowland of.

If only for its second track, 'Don't Stand Me Down' is the bravest album I've ever heard. 'This Is What She's Like' sees Kevin trying to pinpoint his muse's beauty by listing the types of people who disgust him most: 'You've seen the scum from Notting Hill and Moseley, the CND?/They describe nice things as wonderful/She never would say that.' As the song, a blistering northern soul tornado, reaches its climax, we find Kevin literally speechless, lost in tongues of adoration. In turn, the band, fired on by the electricity of his longing, simply transcend. At that point, I'd never even fallen in love. But 'This Is What She's Like' gave me a clue that something greater than I could comprehend was just around the corner. I carried on maturing with that song. Like 'I'll Show You' in '82, and 'My National Pride' and 'The Waltz' in '85, it taught me that righteous anger can show you who you are; and that humanity is a personal duty, not something to brag about.

Stories abound of the making of 'Don't Stand Me Down', that Kevin Rowland was so intent on finding the best musicians for the job that he carried on searching, even after the money ran out. After each audition, he'd pay them from his own pocket. Understandably, when the record didn't sell, Kevin took it uneasily. In the sleevenotes to the new re-release of 'Don't Stand Me Down', he admits, 'the criticism hurt, as did the feeling of being misunderstood'. Solace, however, was gleaned from comments of 'ordinary' folk who grasped all the sentiments missed by people who are *paid* to grasp these things.

They don't make records like 'Don't Stand Me Down' anymore. But then, they never did. Perhaps that's why, 12 years on, when 'This Is What She's Like' concludes, 'That's my story/The strongest thing I've ever seen', I'm compelled to to the same.

'Don't Stand Me Down', replete with two brilliant extra tracks, is released by Creation on Mon.

REISSUE
DEXY'S MIDNIGHT RUNNERS
Don't Stand Me Down
(Creation/CD only)

WAS 'DON'T Stand Me Down' the most cruelly ignored record of the last decade – one that at the time lost Dexys known mostly as the top 10 ton-full of people originally working this brilliant record fail to realise that they had not only a Dexys album at least as good as the previous two, but also one of the finest albums of music, passionate and beautiful albums of the mid-'80s? Few were they really that blinded by Kevin Rowland's choice of ivy League preppy wear for his group's new uniform (was the raggle-taggle look that much better?) that they couldn't even listen to a record made by a group who'd previously only delivered delicious fare?

These are all questions that must have terrorised Rowland in the wilderness years that followed the release of 'Don't Stand Me Down' in 1985 – and have hopefully ended with his new deal with Creation. In his sleevenotes to the reissue, however, Rowland (or 'Lucky' Rowland, as he signs it) says that he originally sabotaged the record's chances by disallowing his record company from promoting it properly, and that he's glad that he did because he couldn't have coped with success at the time. Still, a record as deep at this deserves a wider appreciation than it originally got, no matter how much its author needed a break.

Perhaps the record's key can be located in the first song, the thumping and groovy 'The Occasional Flicker'. 'Compromise is the Devil talking,' roars Rowland with sparkling venom, 'and I've spoke to 'im,' mentioned

Dexys: beige dungarees, suppose

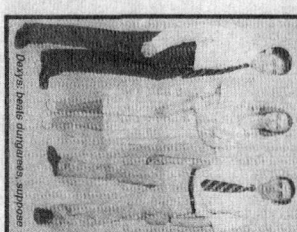

something of moving in..." This, therefore, is not an album tailored for radio, there are no avenues for single-length edit. Instead, it takes musical themes developed on Dexys previous two phases – horn-led soul power and fiddlesome Celtic pride – and weaves these around Rowland's most considered conversational shape, but this doesn't dampen Rowland's fire, but merely lends warmth and humour instead.

This is What She's Like starts with a sweet exchange – all reverence and guitar – between Rowland and guitarist Billy Adams, before Rowland runs through everything that his love isn't ("choice scumbags from Notting Hill and Moseley, the CND") through a soul/Beach Boys romp, 'Reminisce (Part One)' is a gentle narrative about a teenage love set to a van Morrison-ish shimmy, while the lolloping, hilarious Memphis stew of 'One Of Those Things' finds Rowland ripping into phonies and dilletants everywhere.

But this album is more than just a disparate collection of songs. It's a trio of back-to-back vocal tour de forces (a third backed by some genius session players) creating by some genius one of the term visionary songwriter. People use the term 'soul' lightly, but there was only one soul record made in 1985. This is it, and it's timeless. (9)

Ted Kessler

DEXY'S MIDNIGHT RUNNERS
Don't Stand Me Down
(Creation)

Some albums are just *too* good. When 'Don't Stand Me Down' first appeared 12 years ago, the general reaction was one of stunned bewilderment: a classic pop maverick what-the-fuck-is-going-on moment.

Gone were the proto-crusty dungarees, swapped for Wall Street suits and Martha's Vineyard preppie leisurewear. Gone, too, were the simple and assimilable soul-pop anthems, expanded into great glowering, mood-swinging epics punctuated by rants, reveries and conversations between Kevin Rowland and his faithful right-hand man, Billy Adams.

A commercial flop, it was fantastic. What's more, it still sounds that way in this revised version. With some new pics, strangely humble sleevenotes by Rowland, and two added tracks: an old B-side, 'Reminisce (Part One)', and a lovely unreleased croon through Jerome Kern's 'The Way You Look Tonight'. And hindsight shows us that we, the strong devoted, were right back in 1985: one of the very best albums of the decade. Believe it. **10**

John Mulvey

DEXYS MIDNIGHT RUNNERS

Don't Stand Me Down

Includes two extra tracks not on the original album. Out June 2nd. CRECD 154. A Creation Records Product.

DEXYS MIDNIGHT RUNNERS/ THE CELTIC SOUL BROTHERS
PAPA KEVIN'S GOT A BRAND NEW BAG
(containing: violins, records by Van the Man and some official announcements)
By Jan Libbenga, published in the Dutch 'Oor-Magazine' – No.11 2/6/82
(Translated for 'KOR' by Wim Bakker)

> 'There's a lot of confusion over us. Naturally, our adverts in music magazines can express what we want, but can also be misused by journalists who want to give us an image. That's why we use everything to communicate. Our records are not sufficient. There is a good reason why we don't talk to journalists: We are very committed to what we do and think that journalists know too little about our music to judge it. We also like to detach ourselves from music the magazines usually write about. We see no reason to give our work in the hands of the so called rock writers'
> **(from an official announcement by Dexys)**

Kevin Rowland, singer of Dexys Midnight Runners, has changed, as has his group. Gone are the wool hats; overalls will mark a new beginning of these future folk singers. The Midnight Runners have welcomed three new fiddlers. 'The Emerald Express' in their group. The band now has a total of eleven members. Soul Rebels with fiddles, the Celtic Soul Brothers!
Rowland hates this kind of journalistic peptalk, as he hates all articles of journalists, British in particular. Rowland buys a copy of the New Musical Express every week, just to irritate himself about the articles of journalists who think they know it all. But Rowland isn't a pop star who curses the media only after he gets bad reviews himself. Some people call him arrogant, but that's not a description that fits him. He's over-sensitive, which makes him suspicious and inconsistent. Before Anton Corbijn (the photographer) and I are travelling to the Genetic Studio's in the North of Reading, the London Record Company of Dexys told us that Rowland has become very easy to talk with. Well, they must have been mis-informed. The first thing Rowland asks us, is to sign a contract, which will forbid me to sell the interview to British magazines.

Punk is the thing that gets him in motion, just for a short while. In 1978 Rowland finds that Punk and New Wave are just empty balloons. A new world opens before him when his elder brother takes him to a concert of the legendary Geno Washington. That's how music has to sound. Rowland starts to form the Midnight Runners and is very careful in selecting the members. Before the Runners present themselves to the public they rehearse a lot in abandoned buildings. The police are chasing them a lot, so they're always changing the name of the band.

Dexys supported The Specials on there first tour. Today, Rowland claims that it was his group that inspired The Specials to use horns. He's very proud that he refused to sign a contract for the 2-Tone record label. He would of sold his soul to the devil.

Rowland gives himself totally before a crowd, a crowd that he also selects very carefully. He starts by performing for 15-year old teenagers in the suburbs of Birmingham. Out of this young audience he selects Billy Adams as a guitarist.

In the early 80s Dexys were touring 'Straight To The Heart', which is also the message of the first records Geno and Dance Stance. With the release of the album 'Searching For The Young Soul Rebels', the shows are called 'The Midnight Runners Intense Emotion Revue'.

In July 1980, when Dexys are getting a negative rock press, the band decides to stop talking to journalists. They only communicate with the public through adverts. In the same year many members quit Dexys to form The Bureau. They claimed that Dexys just isn't developing any more. Rowland claims they wanted him out of the band.

But what really happened Kevin?
I wanted them to play violin.
And?
They refused.

> 'Our music has soul. Soul is no form, as it isn't a particular sound. Soul is always pure and honest. We are not talking about black American soul of the 60s, 70s and 80s, we are talking about soul as an emotion. Who listens to real soul records, will believe that the musicians believe in what they play. Soul can not only be found in music, we also believe in soul books (drummer Seb Shelton mentions John Steinbeck's *Of Mice and Men*), soul movies (Kevin mentions *Mean Streets* and *Midnight Cowboy*) and soul life. We find our strength in soul. We have chosen the word soul, because we could not think of another name. It's not a good choice, people like Donna Summer have already claimed the word. If soul means 'revival' we are definitely not a soul group.'
> (From an official announcement by Dexys)

Are you planning to tour with the Irish group?
What Irish group? The Emerald Express isn't a group. I selected those people and gave them a name. But indeed, they're a part of the Midnight Runners.
Will the album be like the single 'The Celtic Soul Brothers'?
In the way that the role of the horns has been substained. In the future I would like to play acoustic folk.
Folk?
It's not that I love folk, I could not name a folk-artist I like, but I think it would be a good idea for the pop scene to play acoustic music. Celtic music.
You have succeeded in that field with the single
It's the best we have ever done. The album is even more extreme. I've never liked guitars, but now the horns are beginning to annoy me. Two years ago we we were the first group to use horns. Now there are as many horns as synths. That's why I want to do something different, the opposite of the pop scene, just to annoy them. Anyway, I never liked pop music.
It's superficial?
Not superficial, it's just shit! The record industry is complaining about a drop of record sales. They say people are not interested anymore. But why should they be? Most music

is garbage. The only music that's really worth something is music that is played from the heart. Soul, good and strong music. But, I'll stop cursing at other artists. Some of them don't mind they make trash. They even enjoy it. That's fine, that's their opinion.

When did you start to lose interest in pop music?
That's impossible to say. To be honest, I don't have an opinion of the pop scene as a whole, I can only place it in the framework of the Midnight Runners. I loved music, a lot even, but now I've had enough. Maybe it's my age. When I listen to music I listen professionally, not for fun.

Is there no music that interests you?
What do you mean? The British Funk maybe? That's something we've already had in 1978 and 1979. Those were the best years of the funk. The present funk is nothing more but an invention of the media. I have no contact with other musicians. I've got nothing against them, but we have nothing in common.

You still don't talk with British journalists?
I don't want to interfere with their work, let them. I just don't want them to interfere with my work either. It may sound arrogant, but I know they don't understand it.

And Dutch journalists do?
You're right, that's inconsistent, but I don't read foreign magazines, so I can't judge them. It may be even worse over there with you. Point is, people don't have a chance to read our opinions because they're never published or are totally placed out of context. Other groups can steal my ideas. But... you must not take it too seriously. It's all part of the Dexys legend. I just want to see the reactions of the journalists. There's no big deal. I read English magazines regularly.

But you have stopped with your adverts
That will start again. That even must start again, because rock journalists don't understand music. They say of this country that the fashion changes very fast. Bullshit, this country is very slow. We're still stuck with synth music. Good music is rare. There have been made brilliant records that have inspired millions of people. Two years ago we said our music had soul, eighteen months later every idiot said the same of their music. I want to hear music that's pure and emotional. The only musician who has kept his integrity is Van Morrison. The rest is shit. Well... Aretha Franklin, Burt Bacharach and Dionne Warwick are exceptions. It doesn't matter if a particular record represents a trend or an era, if that is captured in a good way. But aren't you the one that gave 'Searching For The Young Soul Rebels' a bad review?

As the interview continues Rowland has less to say, his answers are getting shorter, his paranoia returns. Rowland has only one ideal: Justice, not particularly for others, but for himself.

'Our live-performance are different from the usual rock concerts. We are entertainers, but that doesn't mean we are messing about to get some applause. We are obsessed with 'projection', we want to reach everyone in the audience. We want to lift, lower, lift them. We'd love to move you to tears. If it sounds cheap, sorry, we don't care. Alcohol before a show is forbidden, the performances have to be pure. We believe in self-discipline, that's why we rehearse a lot. To improve, keep yourself up, that's what it is all about (ask Candi Staton).'
(from an official announcement by Dexys)

The last single 'Show Me' was produced by Tony Visconti, the new album is produced by Clive Langer and Alan Winstanley, who are also responsible for the success of Madness. According to insiders, Langer had many difficulties with Rowland, who's grunging voice was interpreted by the producer as an annoying fit of coughing. However, both men have done a fantastic job. Rowland: 'We first made demos of of our songs and let Clive and Alan hear them. They gave a few good suggestions. We worked too much in one direction. We were reluctant to combine violins with horns. Now they connect.' The tape of the album is played and immediately with the first song I'm full of enjoyment. Against a pure and dry musical background Rowland is singing in the best tradition of soul and gospel. It seems the album is modelled after Van Morrison's 'St.Dominic's Preview', after I heard a version of Van Morrison's 'Jackie Wilson Said' I'm sure: Rowland sounds like a young and enthusiastic Van Morrison.

In the evening during dinner, Rowland confesses: He discovered Morrison only two years ago and he already knows all his albums. He even sent a demo of 'Jackie Wilson Said' to Morrison, who gave a positive reply and even sang the song with Rowland. 'I couldn't believe it', says Rowland, 'he just came to us, it was unbelievable'.

It's midnight when we return to London. The contract Rowland mentioned, hasn't been seen.

'We are no part of the music business. We go our own way. It's important for us to take risks. For us, everything is important: every record, cover, advert or photo can transfer emotion. Well, that's what we had to say. We apologise for raising the roof, that was not our intention.'
(From an official announcement by Dexys)

DEXY'S MIDNIGHT ROBBERS

'I stole our sound' admits Rowland

KEVIN ROWLAND has confessed that he "stole" the sound of his biggest commercial successes, the 1982 single "Come On Eileen" and album "Too Rye Ay", from his former Dexy's Midnight Runners colleague Kevin "Al" Archer, to whom he has apologised in a statement issued last week via Creation Records.

Archer was a member of the original Dexy's line-up, and he appeared on their debut album, "Searching For The Young Soul Rebels", before being sacked by Rowland. At the time, he was billed as Al Archer to avoid confusion with Rowland.

The statement issued by Rowland also explains the thinking behind "My Beauty", the album of covers he's now working on, and his plans to form a new line-up of Dexy's Midnight Runners with his long-time sidekick Big Jim Patterson. Rowland's statement reads as follows: "I'm really pleased to say that I've signed to Creation, and I'm excited about starting work soon. I will try to be worthy of the faith shown in me.

"The first thing I intend to do is start work on a solo record called 'My Beauty', made up of beautiful songs that I have heard throughout my life and that have touched me in the most powerful way. Often when I was sad, over the last few years, these songs resurfaced in my consciousness and helped me with where I'm going.

"Mostly I didn't buy these records when they were out, but they got into me and have lived in me, and when I needed them they were there, guiding me and expressing for me what I couldn't myself. They had always been there, I just didn't notice them. It's not about authenticity of original songs or arrangements or anything like that, because I own my experience of these songs – what they mean to me. That's what I want to express here, what I understand to be real beauty – my beauty.

"Following that, Big Jim Patterson and I intend to start work on recording the new Dexy's album. Before any of this, 'Don't Stand Me Down' will be coming out on Creation with a new sleeve and two extra tracks: 'Reminisce Part 1' and 'The Way You Look Tonight'. I'm really pleased about that.

"Most of all I need to say that 'Don't Stand Me Down' was/is important for me because it came after the 'Too Rye Ay' record. I experienced hollow success with 'Come On Eileen' and 'Too Rye Ay', the musical sound of which – folky fiddle and texture mixed with Tamla type soul – came from Kevin Archer and not me, as I claimed. The idea and sound was his. I stole it from him, hurting Kevin Archer deeply in the process. I conned people all over the world – the people close to me, the people I worked with, the fans, the radio and TV programmers – and I made a lot of money.

"To everybody I conned, I'm sorry. To my beautiful friend Kevin Archer, I love you. I'm sorry I hurt you. I was jealous of you and your talent. You deserved better. I hope you get what you deserve.

"Appropriately I felt like a total fraud, and unworthy and unable to deal with the acclaim that came my way.

"Best wishes, Kevin Rowland."

After one tabloid newspaper ran a story suggesting that Archer had written "Come On Eileen", Rowland retorted with a second statement clarifying the situation. It reads: "I am angry that what I wrote has been misinterpreted. I didn't steal the song 'Come On Eileen'. I wrote it together with Jim Patterson and Billy Adams, though the breakdown and build-up section of the song was heavily influenced by a section of one of Kevin Archer's songs.

"I stole *the style of music* (the blend of folk and soul, the combination of instruments) that was Kevin Archer's, for which I am deeply sorry and regretful. I did not steal the song."

"Don't Stand Me Down" will be reissued by Creation in April. Asked when the Rowland solo album could be expected, a spokesman for Creation replied: "They're at an early stage in the recording process, so it'll be a while yet. But I think it would be reasonable to expect it this year."

I stole song glory says Dexys star

POP singer Kevin Rowland last night apologised to a band member – for stealing his song.

The ex-Dexys Midnight Runners star had always taken the credit for the 80s mega-hit Come On Eileen.

But yesterday Rowland, 43, admitted the group's Kevin Archer had come up with the idea for the song's folk-soul mix, not him.

He said: "The idea and sound was his. I stole it from him. I conned people all over the world and I made a lot of money. To everybody I conned I'm sorry."

Rowland, who has just signed up with Creation Records, added: "To my beautiful friend Kevin Archer I love you, I'm sorry I hurt you. I was jealous of you and your talent."

BROKE AND BITTER, MAN BEHIND A MEGA-HIT TELLS OF MISSING OUT ON £500,000

Daily Mail, Wednesday, January 29, 1997

How Dexy did a runner with the song I inspired

From ANNE SHOOTER in Hamburg

FOR a former member of a hit pop group, Kevin Archer cut a rather pathetic figure.

Drawing on yet another cigarette in his sparsely-furnished flat, he wondered where next month's rent was coming from and admitted he is a bitter man.

Not surprising from a musician who believes he lost out on fame and a £500,000 fortune through the actions of someone he considered a friend.

His story centres on top 1980s band Dexy's Midnight Runners and the recent confession of the group's lead singer Kevin Rowland.

Rowland admitted that it was Archer who deserved the credit for the No 1 single Come On Eileen, one of the biggest-selling singles of the decade, and the album Too-Rye-Ay.

Rowland issued a statement which said: 'To my beautiful friend Kevin Archer, I love you, I'm sorry I hurt you — I was jealous of you and your talent. I conned people all over the world and I made a lot of money. I'm sorry.'

Archer, 38, surveyed his cold, damp flat in one of Hamburg's less luxurious quarters, and said: 'I've called him and said that it's all very well being a beautiful friend — but where's my share of the money?

'What he did to me was terrible and he knows it. Look at where I am now. I have nothing and it's all because of what happened with that song.

'I can't listen to Come On Eileen — I turn off the radio whenever I hear it, it makes me so angry.'

Archer said he has received nothing for Come On Eileen or Too-Rye-Ay, although he still receives approximately £12,000 a year in royalties for Gino — an earlier hit by Dexy's Midnight Runners.

Life is a struggle. He has to borrow money from friends. Last week he was arrested for stealing food from a supermarket. The seeds of his downfall were sown in 1981.

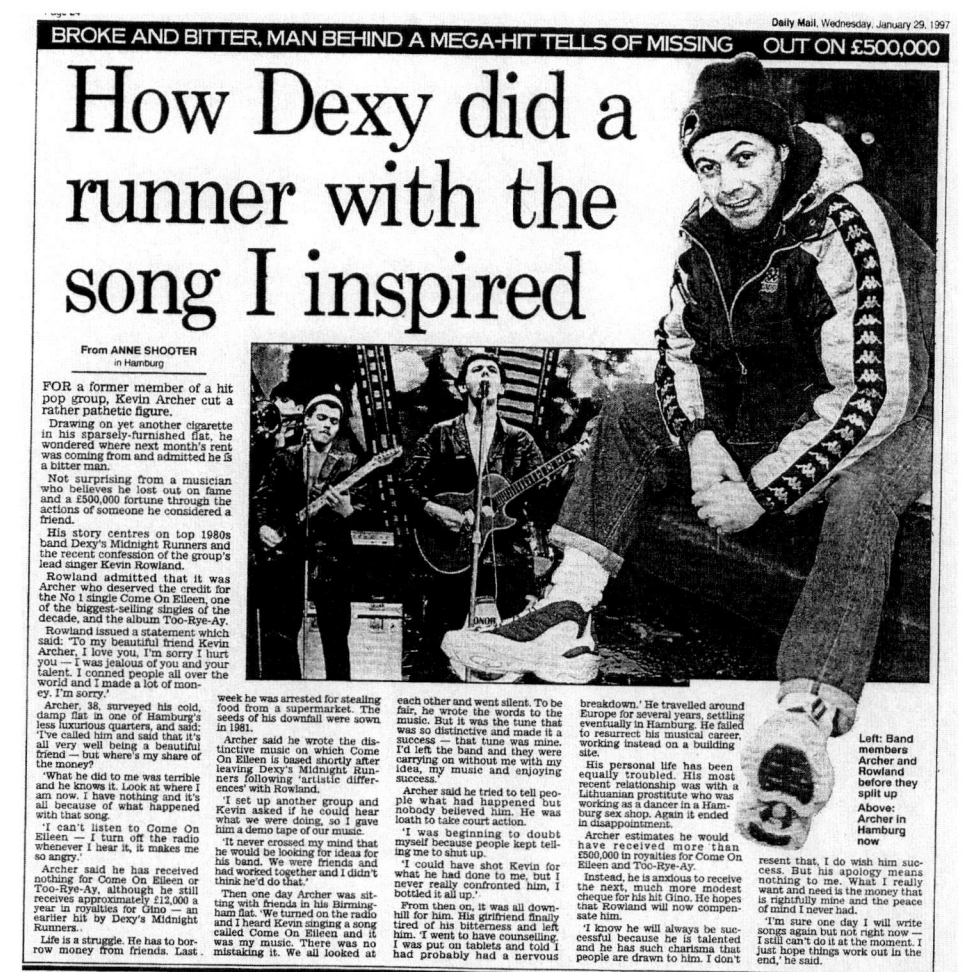

Archer said he wrote the distinctive music on which Come On Eileen is based shortly after leaving Dexy's Midnight Runners following 'artistic differences' with Rowland.

'I set up another group and Kevin asked if he could hear what we were doing, so I gave him a demo tape of our music.

'It never crossed my mind that he would be looking for ideas for his band. We were friends and had worked together and I didn't think he'd do that.'

Then one day Archer was sitting with friends in the Birmingham flat. 'We turned on the radio and I heard Kevin singing a song called Come On Eileen and it was my music. There was no mistaking it. We all looked at each other and went silent. To be fair, he wrote the words to the music. But it was the tune that was so distinctive and made it a success — that tune was mine. I'd left the band and they were carrying on without me with my idea, my music and enjoying success.'

Archer said he tried to tell people what had happened but nobody believed him. He was loath to take court action.

'I was beginning to doubt myself because people kept telling me to shut up.

'I could have shot Kevin for what he had done to me, but I never really confronted him, I bottled it all up.'

From then on, it was all downhill for him. His girlfriend finally tired of his bitterness and left him. 'I went to have counselling. I was put on tablets and told I had probably had a nervous breakdown.' He travelled around Europe for several years, settling eventually in Hamburg. He failed to resurrect his musical career, working instead on a building site.

His personal life has been equally troubled. His most recent relationship was with a Lithuanian prostitute who was working as a dancer in a Hamburg sex shop. Again it ended in disappointment.

Archer estimates he would have received more than £500,000 in royalties for Come On Eileen and Too-Rye-Ay.

Instead, he is anxious to receive the next, much more modest cheque for his hit Gino. He hopes that Rowland will now compensate him.

'I know he will always be successful because he is talented and he has such charisma that people are drawn to him. I don't resent that, I do wish him success. But his apology means nothing to me. What I really want and need is the money that is rightfully mine and the peace of mind I never had.

'I'm sure one day I will write songs again but not right now — I still can't do it at the moment. I just hope things work out in the end,' he said.

Left: Band members Archer and Rowland before they split up
Above: Archer in Hamburg now

KEEP ON RUNNING
ISSUE 9 OCTOBER 1997

"Poor old Johnny Ray
Sounded sad upon the radio
He moved a million hearts in mono
Our mothers cried and sang along
And who'd blame them.
Now you're grown, so grown..."

COME ON EILEEN (No. 1, July 1982)

Reminisce Part Six

Stephen Fry once made a joke about the assumption that President Kennedy's assassination was a key moment in everybody's life -
"Yes, I can remember exactly what I was doing when I first heard Kennedy had been shot... I was listening to the news on the radio."
I'm probably not the best person to reminisce on discovering Dexys. I bought the singles off 'Too Rye Ay' when they came out and often enjoyed playing them. Many years later I bought 'Don't Stand Me Down' in the sales for about fifty pence and was so impressed that I've been slightly obsessed with them ever since. It's not much of a story is it? However, I would like to say this...

I've seen quite a lot in my twenty-three years, and heard a fair bit too, but few things compete with the voice of Kevin Rowland. 'Keep It', 'One Way Love', 'Show Me', 'I Love You (Listen To This)', - so many of his songs – all of them in fact, mean so much to me. My introduction came via 'Eileen'. I can remember it being played at parties and seeing the video on Top Of The Pops, it was always on the radio, and people would often go 'round singing it – Happy Days.
'Old' was probably the next to blow me away, the lyrics still move me a great deal. Kevin is an unusually compassionate fellow. 'I'll Show You' and 'Young Man' are two other obvious examples of his ability to really express his concern for others and takes the heart of the listener.

His choice of cover versions also show him to be a man of great taste. The last few minutes of both 'The Way You Look Tonight' and 'The More I See You' really get the hair on the back of my neck sticking up. And as for 'RESPECT', I think it's true to say he did Otis and Aretha proud.

The fact that there's more to come and that I may finally get to see him play live is the best news I've heard in years. The songs he did on the Jonathan Ross show proved that he hasn't lost his touch as a songwriter or as a performer. Ironically in one of the songs he sang '*I was wrong*' – Everything he did seemed right to me.

Harry Pye, London

DEXYS MIDNIGHT RUNNERS

Intense Emotions Limited, 4 The Willows, Four Oaks, Sutton Coldfield, West Midlands

July 1st   Intense Emotions Circle.   Newsletter 2

Dexy's Midnight Runners Team is:

Seb Shelton	- Drums
Steve Wynne	- Bass Guitar
Big Jimmy Paterson	- Trombone
Micky Billingham	- Organ and Piano
Paul Speare	- Tenor Saxophone
Billy Adams	- Guitar
Brian Maurice	- Alto Saxophone
Kevin Rowland	- Singing
Paul Burton	- Manager
Pete Barrett	- Crafts and Design
Suzanne Kenna	- Secretary

Hello again, this time I'm writing, Billy Adams. I've been in the group since January after Al decided to leave. I knew Kevin 2 or 3 years ago when Dexys were playing at small clubs around Birmingham and told him then that I would like to join the group. He remembered and when Al decided to leave, contacted me and asked me to join. Of course, I accepted straight away and since then, well you know the rest.

Back to the present we're just back in England after spending 2 or 3 weeks playing in Holland, Norway and Sweden. All the shows over there went really well, apart from a couple of problems. You may have heard about the trouble we had at Hamar festival in Norway. A few petty minded groups tried to stop us from playing when they found out that they weren't going to be payed (as the promoter had gone bankrupt). We were determined to play though as we'd been travelling for most of the day to get there, not to mention for the sake of the audience. They'd been left waiting for 3 hours without even an explanation as to what was going on. Mind you it was worth it when we did go on as we got a great reception.

After that we played a couple of show in Stockholm, Sweden (both went well) and then off to Amsterdam in Holland. Most of the shows in Holland were open air festivals and at one or two it poured with rain. It really lifted me though to see how enthusiastic the audiences were when they had'nt all necessarilly come to see us anyway. The national radio stations showed a lot of interest too, as they recorded two of our shows and broadcast one live.

Anyway on the whole we got a great reaction and I hope we left a good impression. I particularly liked Stockholm, it just seemed cleaner there and the people more relaxed.

With the newsletter this time we've sent you a pre-directory address sheets. These are in advance of the actual directory for those of you anxious to contact each other. Oh and by the way when we first suggested the directory we said that ages and telephone number should be included. Some people have'nt included these details so if you wish them to be included in the directory then make sure you've sent them to us.

Since the last newsletter we've also recorded the Projected Passion Revue for Radio 1. It was broadcast on May 30th and it featured both us and the Outer Limits. Unfortunately we did'nt have chance to warn you about it in the last newsletter but for anyone who did catch it, it was a good opportunity to hear the new group and some of the new ideas. The BBC did'nt make a very good job of the sound but everyone was pleased with the performance and I think that came through.

We can give you warning though that we've just recorded a number of new songs for the Richard Skinner show on BBC Radio 1 to be broadcast within the next fortnight.

We've finally found a suitable record company: Phonogram records, which means that the new single "Show Me" has at last been released. It was released on July 3rd on their Mercury label and we feel confident it will do well. This time we've got the full backing of a record company that believes in us.

Also since the last newsletter we've got a new member to the team: Susanne Kenna. She's been a long standing friend of the group and will be taking over as secretary from Jenny who unfortunately proved to be unsuitable.

So it seems that most of our problems are resolved now and with our recent success in Europr and the recording of the new L.P. to look forward to the feeling within the group is stronger than ever.

Thats all for now and thanks for your support.

Billy Adars

P.S. Sorry about the membership card delay we havn't forgotten them!

**A SPIRITUAL PASSION AND A CRAFTSMAN'S CARE
A POSITIVE FORCE WITH A HINT OF DESPAIR**

DEXYS MIDNIGHT RUNNERS

Intense Emotions Limited, 4 The Willows, Four Oaks, Sutton Coldfield, West Midlands

Dear Clive,

Thanks for your letter. We'd love a copy of Mean Street on video and we'd be really grateful if you could get a copy. Our manager's the only one with a video player (it's a V.H.S type, I think that they aren't compatible or something are they?) so if you could get a copy write & tell us how much you want for it. Unfortunately we've only got one copy of the "Boom Boom out goes the lights" video but if you've got the facilities to copy it write & tell us and I'll send it to you. It wasn't all that good actually as it was recorded in January. (Although they didn't show it till around April.) I personally had only been in the group a fortnight. We recorded Show me (slightly different early version), plan B, soulfinger & keep it but they only used the first two (although they were going to use the others on a later programme). The main reason its not all that good is that visually there's not much movement (we hadn't time to work on stage act) but I suppose if you've got all the other video's you'll want it. If you collect videos you'll probably be pleased to know that on August 16th we're recording a show to be shown on television. Its for some new series and I'm afraid as yet I don't know the name of it or when it

"SPIRITUAL PASSION AND A CRAFTSMAN'S CARE A POSITIVE FORCE WITH A HINT OF DESPAIR" will be broadcast. They want us to do a 15 minute set so hopefully all of it will be broadcast.

Incidentally there is some other live recording about somewhere, I don't know whether it will ever be broadcast on T.V. though. When we played at the Venue in aid of Multiple Sclerosis with some other groups it was filmed.

The talking at the beginning of "Show me" was just a bit of chat recorded accidentally, but we just thought it sounded good & left it. Phonogram for some reason didn't put it on the first batch that were made (something about DJ's not liking it).

Anyway thanks & write again

Billy Adams.

P.S. I'm afraid we've got no posters yet & if you're in the circle you must have all the photo's that have been done so far — there should be more soon though but you'll be notified through the circle of what's available.

I don't believe you really like Frank Sinatra...

Chuck Woods – Seven Days Too Long

Whenever I played 'Soul Rebels' (3-4 times per evening, generally), this song used to haunt me. Where had I heard it before? Why was it so familiar, it not having been a UK hit? Then I dug out a pile of old Northern Soul compilations that had been neglected at the back of a cupboard, and there was Chuck Woods' floor-filler from 1968, sounding as fresh as it had when it was played at All-Nighters in 1974. Apart from the whoop at the start (credited to Pete Wingfield by Kevin in the sleevenotes to 'It Was Like This'), and a more insistent driving delivery, the band sticks closely to Chuck's arrangement. An obvious difference is the one *acapella* chorus that the band sing (no instruments backing them) two from the fade. Kevin also puts a bit more passion into it than the mysterious Mr Woods. One of Soul Rebels' highlights.

David Innes

EXCLUSIVE

BIG JIMMY
Q & A

Big Jimmy...
The most powerful trombonist in the business...
Kevin's most faithful and longest serving right-hand man...
The man responsible for the most explosive start to an LP ever -
"Big Jimmy, Al, ah for God's sake, burn it down..."

So how did you really get to join Dexys, or did you really hear of a 'big one going off in The Midlands'?
I saw an advert in Melody Maker. It read; "Trombone and trumpet wanted for new wave soul band." I was living back home in the north of Scotland, and I didn't get the paper till Friday. I didn't have the bottle to answer the ad, but I went to the pub at night and phoned up when I came home about 11.30pm. I spoke to Pete, Kevin's brother, who must have thought I was a total pillock. I think Pete or Kevin phoned me back on Saturday and arranged for an audition the following weekend. I went down to Birmingham, travelling all night, arriving at New Street at 6.30 in the morning. It was late October and they auditioned me at 10.00am in a garage and I was freezing and knackered. As soon as the band started playing, that was it, I've never felt anything like it. My heart was pumping and I was totally unaware of my tiredness and coldness. It was the best musical experience I had had in my life.

Is it true that you used to drink half a bottle of whisky before each show?
Yes, although that was probably an underestimation. I always tried not to have too much, but a half bottle was about right, depending how much I'd had during the day or the night before, and also how much I'd had to eat as well.

What was it like being in Dexys in the early days and how do you look back on it now?
It was a new experience for me. I'd only done classical, jazz and brass band stuff before. It wasn't so much the music as the different life style. It did feel like being on some sort of crusade, being part of something new and refreshing and exciting, being part of a gang of people that actually meant something. It made me realise that music is not just about sitting down reading notes on a page. It's about giving something of yourself.

You co-wrote most of the tracks for the 'Too Rye Ay' period, yet you left prior to it's success. What were your reasons and how did you later feel?
Jealousy mainly, I was jealous of the string section, I thought the brass section was the most important part of the band. I felt redundant, I thought I was being shoved out. I was drinking a lot and you have to understand that my mind was not well. Brian Maurice was leaving and I thought it was time for me to go as well. I did regret it but at the time it seemed like the best thing for me to do.

What song are you most proud of being involved with?
'Old', mainly because of the way the melody came about. We were rehearsing one day, we had most of it written, but we didn't have a melody for some of it. When it came to having a break, Kevin said, "Could you stay here and see if you can write a melody." I don't know where it came from but by the time the group came back I'd written the melody. I love that song anyway, Kevin's lyrics makes me cry.

You've been a major part of Dexys really from day one, what have been your highs and lows?
There have been too many highs to mention really, although being on Top Of The Pops for the first time was really special. I told my Mom and Dad when I was about twelve that one day they would see me on there. I think every time I was on stage was a high. The lows, probably the worst was when the first group split up. I felt like it was the end just as we were getting started, but I took things too personal and felt like packing in music altogether.

Did you find it annoying at times (ie. 'Don't Stand Me Down' era) that you were involved but had to like take a back seat view?
Not really, I'd made my decision to leave so I couldn't expect things to be like they had been. Helen and Billy were the new hub of the band with Kevin, and I didn't have any qualms with that. Playing the trombone is hard enough so I was quite happy.

Kevin and Jimmy back together in '93 and now stronger than ever

If you could change anything from your past with Dexys what would it be?
Mainly the times I did drink too much and made a complete prat of myself. Hopefully that wasn't too often, but once is once too often.

As well as being in The Blue Ox Babes you were also in a group called The Neighbourhood in the late 80s, could you tell us about these?
I can't remember how I joined The Neighbourhood. Geoff Blythe and myself were both in the group. The music was quite funky. The lead singer/songwriter Tim Hutton was a big George Clinton, Prince fan, so you can imagine what we sounded like. We were signed to EMI, but we fell apart because of bad management. I was never really in The Blue Ox Babes. Again Geoff Blythe and myself were involved. We only did a couple of sessions for them. We recorded some songs at Chipping Norton where we recorded 'Searching For The Young Soul Rebels' and the producer was Pete Wingfield which was quite a strange experience.

Have you been involved with any other bands?
I've done loads of sessions but the only other band I actually joined was a band called Pure Junk, which was a Jamiroquai sound alike. We didn't become successful as you can probably guess.

So how does it feel to be involved with Kevin and Dexys again?
It's great and it feels completely natural. Kevin and I have known each other for eighteen years or so, we know our good and bad points pretty well. Dexys is the only group that I can say I really felt part of. Although I don't drink now, I'm still a bit of a nutter and if Kevin can put up with me, then that is the best compliment anybody can pay me. I think we work well together and I think musically we are quite a good partnership.

Can we expect any more vocals from you again in the future – or are we safe? (Manhood '93)
How dare you! I admit I'm not a singer but I didn't think I was that bad. I probably will be singing again, but I'm sure if you got a petition together and got a few signatures, sent it to Kevin, by public demand I'm sure I could be stopped.
(Please send your replies to 'KOR' for passing onto Kevin!!)

What artists do you now listen to and who do you really admire?
I don't listen to anybody in particular, but if I hear something on the radio that catches my ear, then I stop what I'm doing and give it my full attention. I still prefer melodic stuff, but some rapping and rythmic things are very effective. I admire anybody who is successful, but that doesn't mean to say I like successful music. I like people who make music for the right reasons, not people who are just in it for the money. For me, a beautiful voice or a wonderful song is something to cherish. A gift shouldn't be abused or wasted.

If you could change anything in the world what would it be?
Where do you start to change all the bad things in the world? Greed is probably the cause of most wars, money seems to be more important to some people than life, I suppose I would make greed an offence. I don't know how you can change the way people think.

Your desert island disc would be?
'Schools Out' by Alice Cooper. When I saw them on Top Of The Pops, I was sixteen, at that age where you are discovering a lot of things that are probably going to change your life forever. I loved the theatrics of it and the rebellious side of it. It was the right song at the right time of my life.

BIG JIMMY *credits...*

1980	I Couldn't Help If I Tried	Rowland/Paterson
1981	Plan B	Rowland/Paterson
	Show Me	Rowland/Paterson
	Soon	Rowland/Paterson
	Liars A To E	Rowland/Paterson/Torch
	And Yes, We Must Remain The Wildhearted Outsiders	Shelton/Paterson/Billingham
1982	The Celtic Soul Brothers	Rowland/Paterson/Billingham
	Let's Make This Precious	Rowland/Paterson
	All In All (This one last wild waltz)	Rowland/Paterson
	Old	Rowland/Paterson
	I'll Show You	Rowland/Paterson
	Until I Believe In My Soul	Rowland/Paterson
	Come On Eileen	Rowland/Paterson/Adams
	Dubious	Rowland/Paterson

It was August 1997...

I was searching for the spirit of Kevin Rowland in the town of Brighton, I went to Penny Lanes, I went to Donovans, like in the song, y'know the one where he's reminiscing. About fifteen years ago I began my quest, in fact I think it might be a bit longer than that, and from then 'til now I've searched...

And on Friday 15th August my searching had come to an end and I had finally found, yes I finally met up with the great man. I wasn't even in my teens when I first met Kevin back in 1980 as a starry eyed autograph hunter! ("Can I have your autograph please? I seen you on Tiswas this morning!"). This time it was to be different...

We'd arranged to meet up at 12.30pm until about 6.00pm and then meet up again on the evening as Kevin had been invited to a party celebrating the opening of a new recording studio and invited me along with him, then we were going to this club afterwards. Kevin said he would meet me where I was staying, a little Bed & Breakfast on Charlotte Street. It was OK, it was alright – I would have slept anywhere.

I arrived in Brighton about 7.00 on the Thursday morning, the journey didn't take as long as I had anticipated, and I never went over seventy mile-per-hour honestly! I tried to keep a pretty low profile throughout the day as I didn't really want to bump into Kevin accidentally, I wanted it to be as it was planned.
On the Friday I woke up about 8.00am, went down for breakfast about 9.00 and returned to my room to get ready for a very special day. The time was getting nearer, I don't think that I was really nervous, apart from the fact that I nearly used hair gel instead of shaving cream!

12.30pm there was a knock at the door, a shiver went down my spine, "There's a gentleman waiting to see you downstairs," I was told. 'Well, this is it' I thought. My legs did feel a bit jelly like walking down the stairs as I took a few deep breaths, I went into the reception area. "Hi ya Neil," "Alright Kev, it's been a long time," "About fifteen years, you were only about nine wasn't you? I recognise you now" replies Kevin. Anyway, we leave the B&B, I tell Kevin about my feet being covered in plasters after all the walking I did the previous day. "So you wont want to do much walking then, how about we go for something to eat and then go back to my place, my car's just around the corner," was I pleased, I don't think my blister covered feet could have taken much more walking. We arrive at the cafe, have something to eat along with a cup of tea (of course!), Kevin is taken by a tune playing in the background so he asks the waitress who it is, it's a CD playing by Roy Ayres, he wasn't too keen on the other tracks though. Conversation was not easy at this point, I think we were both feeling a bit nervous so we talked about Dexys for a while and how he's feeling, to *kick off the proceeding*s as it were, y'know?

We return to Kev's place. Kevin makes the tea, a nice strong cuppa! "I'll play you some demos for the Dexys stuff if you want?" I was hoping he'd say that! I wasn't going to ask him as I knew that if Kevin didn't feel comfortable about me hearing them then he wouldn't have asked me, and I was touched by the fact that he had. He plays me 'Manhood' and 'If I Ever' – the songs he did on the Jonathan Ross show a few years back. Kevin sits on the floor listening closely, I'm on the edge of my seat miming silently. The music finishes, Kevin turns around to me, "Fuckin' brilliant Kev" I say, and I truly mean that. I know you're probably thinking 'Well, he'd say that anyway,' but I'll tell you that it really was quite unbelievable.

Kevin asks if I'd like to have a walk over to his local park, so that's what we do. We sit down on the bench, it's a nice view and you can just about see the sea-line in the distance. It seemed like an ideal place for thinking. I think we were getting a bit more relaxed now and the conversation turns to more personal things. I tell Kevin about my problems in the past, although he already knew about most of them. I told Kevin about the time I was forced to get help for being obsessed with Dexys Midnight Runners, and the Doctor was told "He's obsessed with Dexys Midnight Runners," Kevin asks "and what did he say?", "Who's Dexys Midnight Runners?" I reply! And that started us laughing. But thanks to a telephone conversation that I had with Kevin previously and also a letter that I received from him I do now have things in more of a perspective. But do not get me wrong, Dexys are a big part of my life whereas before it was like they was my life, it was like Kevin was my only real friend although I know that he didn't really know me. Anyway, that's enough about me. We talk for a little while longer and Kevin asks if I would like to join him tomorrow afternoon with another friend for a cup of tea and something to eat in his local cafe, obviously I say "Yes," as long as he doesn't mind, well he wouldn't have asked me otherwise would he? Kevin says that he's now feeling a bit tired, I ask if he would like me to go and I'll see him later, he says "No, you can watch the television or something while I have a lie down for half an hour," "Or I could listen to the demo tapes again" I reply cheekily, "Yeah, OK" says Kevin.

We return to Kev's place, he shows me into the kitchen - "There's the kettle, sugar, better get some tea bags (there's only one left!), I'll go over the road," "I'll go" I tell Kevin, "then you can get your head down for a bit," "OK" says Kevin and he gives me the keys and sorts out the demo tapes that I can listen to. I return and make a cuppa, ready to settle down to the demo tapes. I rewind them both to the start, making sure that it wasn't on to loud as I did not wish to disturb Kev's rest. Thinking about it now, I guess I could have done anything while Kevin was away, I could have played some other tapes whatever, but I didn't, the thought never crossed my mind, Kevin had put his trust in me and I had no intention of dishonouring that trust and I was just so took back by the demos that he did let me play. As well as 'If I Ever' and 'Manhood', I'm also welcomed by some other new Dexy tracks – 'You Are The Rose' (to be changed to 'I Don't Know You' Kevin later tells me), 'She's Got A Giggle That Makes My Heart Melt' and another two stunning tracks - 'My Life In England' and 'I'm Coming Home' which are absolutely breathtaking. I was just sitting there on the floor completely dumbstruck, I knew the demos would be good but these were just totally unbelievable. Kevin has been taking singing lessons over the past year or so and on the evidence of his vocals on these demos I don't know why, he sounded absolutely great, similar to his vocals on 'Don't Stand Me Down'. Kevin returns to the room, I could turn it up now, "There was no need to have it on that low" says Kev, so I turn it up a bit and Kevin goes over and turns it up some more. Kevin is going over some of the demos "This is going to be changed to this" etc. This was brilliant. I tell Kevin "You're going to do it," "I hope so" he replies. Anyway, we have a few more cups of tea and Kevin drops me back to my Bed and Breakfast at about 6.00pm. "I'll pick you up about 9.30" says Kevin, we shake hands and depart company until later...

Kevin picks me up at 9.30pm, I had brought with me a tape that I had just got hold of by Geno Washington which included 'Michael', Kevin puts it in the tape player in the car and fast-forwards it to 'Michael', "I haven't heard this for about ten years" he says. 'Michael' comes on and Kevin's singing along, waving his arms, clapping his hands and swerving the car all over the road in the process! This was another brilliant moment, it was really good seeing Kevin giving it some and really enjoying himself. Kevin later says that Geno should have changed the lyric 'Michael the lover lord' to 'Michael the lover boy', has Kevin got a plan in mind?

We eventually find where we are going, we were *right the first time*, but given false information. It was not really what we expected, a kind of heavy rock gig, and Kevin was not too impressed although he was quite impressed by the bass player with the second band that came on. Kevin met up with the person who used to write all the hit records for Leo Sayer and Adam Faith was also there. During the time we were there this person came up to Kevin, who he does not know, but he's quite used to that! This person asked Kevin "What is the most recent best record that you've heard?" Kevin replies "That would be in the car coming here!" - another great moment. Kevin is quite pleased with the number of people who are now coming up to him and saying that they've got the new release of 'Don't Stand Me Down', I say to Kevin "Ah, but do they have the original?" Kevin laughs. Anyway, it's a very pleasant change from people mentioning 'Come On Eileen' to him! It's about 11.30pm when we leave to go to another club, and Kevin felt like going back to his place first for a cup of tea and toast, good idea I thought, so that's what we did. Kevin checks the answering machine, a friend phones from London to say that he's coming down to Brighton tomorrow and Anne Nightingale phones to say that she will be at the club where we were going on that night and that she would love to see him there. Kevin and I were finding it quite amazing all these coincidences that were happening the time that I was there, "I'm never usually invited anywhere, it's just because you're here" Kevin says with a smile.

So we set off for this club. The music is Big Beat, not really my style (give me Dexys any day!), although Kevin is actually quite in to it and having the occasional groove. We fight our way through the crowds and see Anne Nightingale, she is quite delighted at seeing Kevin and they chat for a while, and Anne gets up from her chair and has the occasional dance, "You wouldn't believe she only had an operation two weeks ago would you" says Kevin, and you certainly wouldn't and she was really enjoying herself. I was trying to get in to the music a bit and practisin' the occasional step. Kevin said "Just close your eyes, listen to that bass," I did and I must admit it did sound better, still it was not really my scene, I'd rather go to a club where they're playing the old classics from the 50s and 60s, but it was great to see Kevin out there and really enjoying himself. The DJ's that night were Mick Jones (The Clash) and Norman Cook (Housemartins), also there, I was told was Wendy James (Transvision Vamp) who I used to think was sex on legs! But I didn't bother searching for her as tonight I was with Kevin, although his attention was focused elsewhere at times (eh Kev!?), and who'd blame him!? Actually, thinking about it, maybe I could have got off with Wendy... nah! There were also people there from the local press and the manager of Skint Records Damian Harris who told me - "I can't believe it, in one night I've met Kevin Rowland and Mick Jones," how did he think I felt!? Kevin introduced me to them all and I usually got the "Are you in the band?" question, unfortunately I had to say "no," maybe I should have said "yes" and then I might have pulled! We leave the club at about 2.00am and Kevin says that we'll go to his place for a cup of tea and then he'll drop me back. Brilliant I thought.

So we have a cup of tea and chat. I didn't drink any alcohol in the club that night, and I do usually like a few drinks. Kevin asks me why I hadn't had a drink, I reply "Because I wanted it to be pure" - it had to be and it was. Kevin asks if there was anything that I wanted to know, apart from any details of the 'My Beauty' album, "Although you've asked quite a few questions already" Kevin said, I didn't think I'd asked that many! I asked him about the donkey (like in the song, y'know the one about the donkey), Kevin informs me that it was taken from the Val Doonican song 'Delaney's Donkey', although he doesn't like the song y' understand. Then Kevin talked of the very big part that Big Jim Paterson is playing on the 'My Beauty' album, so much so that Kevin was actually thinking of doing it under the Dexys name, but Jim refused, "It's your album" he told Kevin.

I can inform you that the Dexys album will definitely happen with an option on a third album. Kevin told Alan McGee that he really wants it to be a success, Alan McGee replied "Don't worry about it, if it's not we'll just go onto the next one and then the next one after that until it is a success, I'm just really glad that you're on the label." Kevin is very pleased with all the support that he is getting from Creation, they have just left him to his own devices, and as we know, that is the way he likes it. Kevin told me that he could have had the album finished by now, but he's not doing it for the money (we know that anyway) and he just really wants it to be really good. Kevin admits to being a perfectionist and says that he does need to try and relax a bit more as it does just put more pressure on. The set-up is going to be very similar to 'Don't Stand Me Down' with all the group being in the studio at the same time. This has turned out a bit like an interview and I wander if Kevin subconsciously liked it this way, I don't really know. Anyway, it's about 3.00am and Kevin drops me back to my Bed and Breakfast, I offered to walk back as it wasn't too far, but Kevin wouldn't have it. Kevin thanked me for a really good night,

"Best night I've had out for a long time" he says, "Nothing to do with me" I replied, "Oh it was, you were the second half" he said. My stomach tingled. I returned to my room, switched the light off, lay on the bed, my window was only slightly open and there was a single lonesome star shining brightly down positioned right in the middle.

We met up at three o'clock on the next afternoon along with one of Kevin's friends from Brighton and the one who had come down from London. We drink tea and chat, Elvis is playing in the background, twenty years ago to the day that he died on 16th August 1977, Kevin remembers hearing the news when he was in a punk club in Birmingham - "When I probably had blue hair!" Kevin says with a smile, he remembers the dis-taste of the DJ as Kevin quotes in a brummie accent - "If any of you are interested, we've just had news that Elvis has died" and then the DJ went on to play the song '1977' by The Clash and Kevin thought that this was very distasteful. The friend from London departs to hit the beach, and the three of us walk around town. I ask Kevin if he doesn't mind me hangin' around, he replied "You're not hangin' around, you're with us," and that was nice. The other friend later departs and Kevin and I walk for a while, we get an ice-cream and head for the park in The Pavilion. There's quite a few people there and deckchairs are spread across the lawns, all of them in use apart from two lonesome deckchairs ideally situated right in the middle, just there, as if they were waiting for us, "Just look at that" said Kevin, seemingly bewildered by all these coincidences. We finish off our ice-cream and have another little chat. I asked Kevin where the title 'Don't Stand Me Down' actually came from, he said that he was just in the studio one day with Billy and it just came out, he just said to Billy "Don't Stand Me Down." Kevin thought about what it actually meant, he said that he thinks it was like that he was saying to Ireland not to reject him, and also to everybody else out there. Kevin also remembered a Bill Wither's song he heard after Don't Stand Me Down was released titled 'Use Me Up' which included the lyric – 'someone tried to stand me down', so Kevin said that he may have subconsciously heard the lyric before Don't Stand Me Down was recorded. I said to Kevin that it is a very powerful title, "Powerful" said Kevin, "Yeah, I suppose it is." Anyway, it was now about 6.00pm and I gave Kevin a lift back to his place, the end was near.

We talked for a while in the car before Kevin departed. Kevin asked me how I felt, I said that I don't think I've been as nervous as I thought I would have been. I told him that I know that he is only a normal person, and when I say 'normal person' I mean that everybody is just a normal person, no matter who you are or what you do. I don't think that Kevin really enjoys being referred to as the 'great man' or 'legendary' whatever, because Kevin knows that he is only a normal person, although he obviously has a very unique and special talent.

Kevin said that he too felt nervous, and I think I expected that too. I think that Kevin might have felt like he was on show to a certain extent, but I did not want him to feel that way, he certainly was not on show to me. He is my friend. A girl asked me when we were in the club on Friday night if I loved him, and I said "yes" because I do, and if that sounds corny then too bad. Anyway, it was time for Kevin to go, we shook hands like we hadn't before, I said "Just get out there and do it," he said "I'll try mate, I'll try," and that was the end.

It had worked out the way I thought it would, and the strange thing was all the coincidences that happened over those few days. First of all it was August (*It was August 1980* – Reminisce Part 1); Kevin had that invite to the party and the friend phoning on the Friday to say he was coming down on the Saturday; Anne Nightingale phoned; 'Come On Eileen' was at Number 1, fifteen years ago to that week; Elvis died on the Saturday twenty years ago; those two deckchairs nicely positioned right in the middle, just like the star; the Sunday was Kevin's birthday. I returned home and found that I had the original CD release of 'Don't Stand Me Down' waiting for me – I'd been searching for years.

People say that meeting your idols usually leaves you with false hopes, and that it destroys all myths and legends, whatever, and that you usually end up disappointed. In my case this was just simply not true, maybe this was due to me respecting Kevin Rowland as being just a normal person, just like you and I, and I think it turned out to be just like what I was expecting. I returned home and felt exactly the same now as I had before and I think that says it all.

That's my story, the strongest thing I've ever seen.

Neil Warburton

I don't believe you really like Frank Sinatra...

Otis Redding – RESPECT
This song was a live favourite throughout Dexys' career. It first surfaced on Otis Redding's 1965 masterpiece 'Otis Blue', but the Dexys' version owes much more to the hit version recorded by Aretha Franklin which reached 10 in the UK singles chart in 1967. In 'Mojo' May 1997, the story of the differences Aretha introduced to the track are explained, including the bridge section to which the Runners adhered faithfully, and the spelling out of the R-E-S-P-E-C-T motif. Otis' version has been viewed as a cry from the heart of young black America for equal treatment in the context of the rise of black awareness through Martin Luther King and others. Aretha's version, poppier and more uptempo, has been seen by some as a call to arms to black women to demand respect. Kevin's spoken passage in the various versions that are available either officially or otherwise make demands for respect for the power of soul – but you knew that.

M.F.S.B. – T.S.O.P.
From the 12" of Jackie Wilson Said. T.S.O.P. (The Sound Of Philadelphia) is an instrumental recorded originally by M.F.S.B. for Gamble and Huff's Philadelphia International label in the mid 1970s. M.F.S.B. was claimed to stand for 'Mother, Father, Sister, Brother', but those in the know at Philly claimed that it was an abbreviation of 'Mother Fucking Sons of Bitches'. Charming. Dexys' version follows the original very closely. An ideal opener for the '82 show, showcasing the strings, but leaving an opening for some great hornwork.

David Innes

KEEP ON RUNNING
ISSUE 10 JANUARY 1998

"Jackie Wilson said it was reet petite
I kind of love you
Yes it knocks me off my feet
Let it all come down
Oh let it all come down..."

JACKIE WILSON SAID (No. 5, October 1982)

I don't believe you really like Frank Sinatra...
MENTIONED IN PASSING...

Not only have Dexys and Kevin recorded and performed live several cover versions, our favourite minstrel has also mentioned songs in passing, giving vital reference points to the influences that helped create the sound, the attitude and the soul.

First up, on **Geno**: *"you were Michael the lover"*, **Michael** having been a minor hit (number 39) for **Geno Washington and the Ram Jam Band** in February 1967. The position reached by Michael (or 'Mike' to his friends) was Geno's greatest singles chart achievement, equalling the position reached by **Water** nine months earlier. It appeared on his 'live in the studio' album *"Sifters, Shifters and Finger Clicking Mamas"*. I know the editor has a copy of this on tape. It was me who bootlegged it for him.

Chronologically speaking, **Plan B** was next to reveal a marker in the quest for Dexys' sound. *"Bill Withers was good for me – pretend I'm Bill and lean on me..."* Kevin informs us. **Bill Withers'** superb output included **Lean On Me**, a massive hit in the USA in Summer 1972. Here, it only reached number 18, because the singles-buying public was besotted with Blackfoot Sue, Gary Glitter and Alice Cooper (eh, Big Jimmy?) at the time. Lean On Me is an excellent example of Bill Withers' talent, and there's a fine compilation available which contains **Lovely Day**, **Ain't No Sunshine** and **Oh Yeah** among others. Seek it out. In Plan B, of course, the band are quoting from **The Hollies'** number 2 hit of 1966, **Stop Stop Stop**, but we're not counting this, OK?

Next up, in **Respect** from the Radio One In Concert (*the in-a-tent emotion revue, as Kevin dubbed it*) from Newcastle, The Artist Formerly Known As Carlo lets us into a confidence. He, like many of us with tennis rackets pretending to be the late Rory Gallagher, sometimes stands in front of the mirror and pretends to be **Al Green** when he's singing **Tired Of Being Alone**. Al Green's influence on a generation of singers cannot be overstated, and Tired Of Being Alone is a nice (I would have said 'wonderful', but she never would say that) example of the man's talent. It reached number 4 in the UK charts in 1971. One of the Rev Al's other great hits – **Let's Stay Together** – was notoriously ruined by Tina Turner some time ago. Any of Al's albums are worth a look. Demon

Records have a Greatest Hits on the market mid-price which contains most of the best stuff. For real Memphis soul junkies, the Hi box set is essential. Listen and wonder. And talking of wonder...

Reminisce Part One, originally found on the B-side of the re-released *Celtic Soul Brothers* in '83 and tacked on to the end of the new CD release of *Don't Stand Me Down*, mentions in passing *Higher Ground*, a hit for *Stevie Wonder* in 1973, reaching number 29. Kevin 'didn't like the song you understand'. I did. Still, we can't always agree, can we? Like most of Wonder's songs at the time, it *funks*, driven by a clavinet and a real drummer. Wouldn't be allowed now. Also on Reminisce, the song, 'y'know the one about the donkey' gets a plug. Neil and I agree that this has to be *Delaney's Donkey*, made famous by the Singing Pullover *Val Doonican*. Surprisingly, this was not a hit, but was played every Saturday and Sunday morning on the kids' request show on the radio. Perhaps it was a rare B-side, an alternative mix of *McGinty's Goat* (also, shockingly not a hit) that was for hardcore Val club consumption only. The Forest and Heller mixes, Midnight and 3AM? Bollocks.

And finally, mentioned in passing are four songs from 1970. Funnily, Kevin dates them as 1969. Even the most talented artists get it wrong sometimes or was he welcoming the New Soul Vision by looking into the future even then? In *Reminisce Part Two*, from *Don't Stand Me Down*, Kevin's tale of teenage romance, the summer of 1970 is brought alive by the four songs mentioned: *Lola* by *The Kinks* (number 2), still available on any number of compilations, the story of a young man's misplaced love for a transvestite who 'drinks cherry cola'; *Wedding Bell Blues* by *5th Dimension* (number 16) which I cannot remember but do know that it was written by *Laura Nyro* who sadly died in April 1997; *Leaving On A Jet Plane*, originally written for *Peter, Paul and Mary* by *John Denver* (who later recorded the song himself) who was tragically killed in a plane crash in October 1997 was a number 2 hit in January 1970 for *Peter, Paul and Mary*, who are not to be confused with *Emerson, Lake and Palmer*. Finally, *I'll Say Forever My Love*, the refrain of which provides eye-moistening backing for Kevin's monologue, was a beautiful song taken by *Jimmy Ruffin* to number 7 in July 1970. Do us a favour and record it Kevin... and how about putting the same artist's *What Becomes Of The Broken Hearted* on the B-side? More please. Thank you.

David Innes

BBC ban for Dexy's video

Oldbury pop group Dexy's Midnight Runners, above, have run into a censorship row at the BBC over a video to promote their chart topping disc Come On Eileen — and TV chiefs have refused to show the film.

Although the single is No. 1 for the third week running, the video will not appear on Top of the Pops tomorrow because the Beeb is sensative about a scene in the film.

The BBC has tken exception to a scene including Birmangham girl Helen O'Hara — formerly Helen Bevington, violinist at the Birmingham School of Music.

She is seen pushing a baby in a pram when she and actress Moira Faley are grabbed and shaken by the other members of the group loitering on a street corner.

The baby starts to cry and the BBC decided that was enough to stop the use of the video film on this week's "Top of the Pops."

Instead the No. 1 spot on Top of the Pops will be a recording of the band, seen by viewers last week.

The video was the brainchild of group leader Kevin Rowland, who started the band from his former Apollo Road, Oldbury home.

I don't believe you really like Frank Sinatra...
Geno Washington and The Ram Jam Band -
(I Gotta) Hold On To My Love

WHAT? You say. Well you all know the instrumental prelude to 'Geno' that Dexys very often used in their live shows and you all wandered where it came from, well it originated from this classic Geno track which Kevin and brother Pete must have been practisin' steps to back in '68 in a sweaty club, although the idea to use this actually came from Kevin Archer. Taken from Geno's studio album 'Sifters, Shifters, Finger Clickin Mamas' which also includes a version of 'Que Sera Sera' and yes, this is the only version that gets me rockin! Also included on the LP is 'Michael', y'know Michael, the lover, he was the fighter that won.

Neil Warburton

DEXYS MIDNIGHT RUNNERS

Intense Emotions Limited, 4 The Willows, Four Oaks, Sutton Coldfield, West Midlands

September 1st   Intense Emotions Circle.

Newsletter 3

Hello there,
          It's a few words from me this time,
Mick Billingham. I joined the group in November 1980,
just after Seb. I had a phone call at work from Kevin
one afternoon and almost a year later here I am writing
this newsletter. I'd only been messing around with
small time affairs, none of which had been
satisfying at all, so Dexy's was like a chance
of a lifetime when it happened. Serious,
sincere music at last. I found that joining
a group who constantly strive for perfection
offered me a challenge which was well worth
waiting for, and I still feel that. Also,
the group's deep spiritual feel suits my
way of living. I belong to the Mormon church
and I wouldn't feel easy playing
uninspired music anymore. Anyway, enough of
me, more about the group.

Our next single, entitled "Your Own" will be
released very shortly. Some of you may have
heard it already, either on the Richard Skinner
session or at our shows. We're very proud of it.

Recently we played a show at the Theatre Royal,
Nottingham which was recorded for television. It should be screened in the
late autumn, so keep your eyes peeled for that one. The only other performances
really, were two in Portugal which I found exhilarating. Personally I've never
played in front of so many people before (5000) and I'd be telling lies if I
said I wasn't nervous. I find that with this group, it requires so much physical
and spiritual strengh on a performance that the thought of being stimulated by
any other means than sheer personal drive, would ruin the sincerity that I
hold so dear. As far as I'm concerned, nerves is the only high that I need.
We're planning another one-off performance in Portugal in September. Other
than this there are no other shows planned yet.

The pre-directory sheets sent out with Billy's newsletter are already being
taken advantage of by some of you. It was an idea that we all felt would be
different and exciting, so we hope that a lot more of you will use them.

Now then, we have in our midst a shady set-up who call themselves "Wind-ups
Anonymous", masterminded by two admirers called Stennet and Noz. While being
quite loopy, take it from me they're quite harmless, so if their wind-ups
stretch to you, just take it with a pinch of salt. They might go away, but
then again .... etc.

"SPIRITUAL PASSION AND A CRAFTSMAN'S CARE A POSITIVE FORCE WITH A HINT OF DESPAIR"

We'd like to give a special thanks to Clive Gray who sent us a video copy of "Mean Streets", which he informs us he can supply Circle members with, plus other videos, so any of you who are interested, contact Clive.

Finally, we would also like to say that any rumours you may have heard about Brian leaving the group are utter nonsense. He's still with us, so ignore anything you might hear.

Well, many thanks for bearing with me, and I'd like to leave you with these few words to ponder on:
"If any of you lack wisdom, let him ask of God that giveth to all men liberally and upbraideth not, and it shall be given him".
James Chapter 1 Verse 5.

Regards,

Mick Billingham

P.S. As we try to keep the organisation of the Circle fairly simple, when you receive your membership card we would be grateful if you would include your membership no. on any letters you send, together with a stamped addressed envelope. It will help Suzanne a lot.

I don't believe you really like Frank Sinatra...

Zoot Money's Big Roll Band – Big Time Operator

When first I heard Dexys, I was mightily impressed, but wandered at the substance behind the brass and the obvious passion. Dubious? I need not have worried. In an interview with one of the dishonest hippy press, Kevin talked about his musical influences. Included was Zoot Money's 'Big Time Operator', a soul landmark, but unusual in that it emanated from the UK, one of very few great soul songs to have it origins in this country. Others that spring to mind pre-Dance Stance are 'Handbags and Gladrags' and 'The First Cut Is The Deepest'. Zoot, more famous as 'the Flamingo Club Flasher' (work it out yourselves) recorded some fine songs in his time, including the dance classic 'The Uncle Willie', but never got the recognition his talent deserved. Destined always to be a side-man to others' success. 'Big Time Operator' was a regular in Dexys' live set in 1979 and 1980, and the arrangement sticks close to the original, with as usual, Kevin injecting more angst into the singing and the brass more prominent than on the 1966 EP release from one of the first wave of Young Soul Rebels. Other tracks on the original (Columbia SEG 8519) are 'Should Have Been Me' (also the title of Zoot's first album), 'Florence of Arabia' and 'Chauffeur'.
Searching for a copy still. Very rare. Very expensive.

David Innes

Dexys Midnight Runners

Dear Clive,
Thanks alot for the video. We've been really busy lately and as yet I havent had chance to get over to Four Oaks to see it but intend to as soon as possible. You asked if we could mention in the next newsletter to any interested circle members so I'll tell Mick who's doing the next one.

No news as yet about the L.P. though "Until I believe in my soul", "Spiritual passion", and "Your own" will be on it amongst others.

I'm afraid & as far as I know we havent got a copy of the video of "Dance Stance" though I'll ask around. Here's the "Boom Boom out goes the lights" video anyway.

We'd love a list of the videos you can get but I hope we're not imposing on you too much.

Have you got Midnight cowboy Kevin asked and Seb said he'd like

Taxi driver if you've got it. They said they're both really good films.

I don't think there's a song book out or likely to be. Do you play an instrument or something?

Anyway thanks again for the video

Billy Adams.

DEXYS
MIDNIGHT RUNNERS

ISSUE 11   APRIL '98

KEEP ON RUNNING
ISSUE 11 APRIL 1998

"What's that? What's that on the start?
Let's get this straight from the start
Who's that? Who's that? What's his part?
Tell him to come back tomorrow to start
You keep saying, so what did I say...?"

LET'S GET THIS STRAIGHT (No. 17, December 1982)

I don't believe you really like Frank Sinatra...

Johnny Johnson and The Bandwagon – Breaking Down The Walls Of Heartache

One of the high spots of the summer of 1968 was Johnny Johnson and The Bandwagon's only UK hit. It reached number 4 in the chart, but little more was ever heard of JJ and the B. As with the Dexys' version to be found originally on the B-side of 'Geno', the song is brass-driven, in top gear from intro to outro and made for dancing to. Dexys take the song, replicate the arrangement, but make it their own in a barnstorming performance that quite rightly, saw it voted as best Dexys' B-side in the 1995 KOR poll. I read somewhere once that Kevin would order the brass section's microphones to be turned down to make them play harder. Did Big Jimmy, JB and Steve Spooner ever blow more fiercely? Hats and wigs were held on to in the front row as this hurricane was released on audiences. A great original, surpassed by an even better cover.

Status Quo – Marguerita Time

Having recorded 'Respect', a Van Morrison cover and a classic Northern Soul song by Chuck Woods, who would ever have believed that Dexys would opt for a then recent Status Quo hit as a B-side for versions of 'This Is What She's Like'? Whilst Rossi, Parfitt and Co toned down their normal cacophonic three-chord Telecaster-driven racket for this December 1983 flirtation with mellower, verging-on-country sounds, it took a Jonathan Edwards size leap of imagination to even guess at what Kevin and his trustees might do with this. However, some word changes, the replacement of electric guitars (too noisy and crude by far, apparently) with acoustic strumming and Helen's masterly fiddle fills silenced those who questioned the band's sanity in taking on this minor classic. Would not be out of place on 'Don't Stand Me Down' or 'The Wanderer'.
Right again. Good old Kevin.

David Innes

DEXYS MIDNIGHT RUNNERS

Intense Emotions Limited, 4 The Willows, Four Oaks, Sutton Coldfield, West Midlands

INTENSE EMOTIONS CIRCLE

November 1st, 1981   Newsletter 4

Dexy's Midnight Runners Team is:

Seb Shelton - Drums
Giorgio Kilkenny - Bass
Billy Adams - Guitar
Mick Billingham - Organ and Piano
Paul Speare - Tenor Saxophone
Brian Maurice - Alto Saxophone
Big Jimmy Paterson - Trombone
Kevin Rowland - Singing

Paul Burton - Manager
Pete Barrett - Crafts and Design

    When I was first asked to write this newsletter, I wondered whether I'd be able to think of anything to say apart from recounting what we've done over the past two months, but when I got working on it, a few other things came to mind. I thought I'd start by telling you a few things about myself.

"SPIRITUAL PASSION AND A CRAFTSMAN'S CARE A POSITIVE FORCE WITH A HINT OF DESPAIR"

Kevin knew me through a mutual friend and asked me to join the group last December. I knew very little about them before that as I hadn't been listening to the radio or following the charts for two years or so. I was more interested in jazz and funk which at the time weren't making it commercially. In fact, around that time I was playing in a jazz-funk group called Pyramid, who were based in Birmingham, but I was beginning to feel the need to become involved in music with more meaning to it.

After I'd met Kevin and Jimmy for a talk about the group, they asked me to go along to a rehearsal, which I did. It was then that I wondered whether I'd be doing the right thing to join. The "rehearsal room" was part of an almost derelict warehouse in a dubious back-street of Birmingham, and it was warmer outside in the snow and dark than it was in the building. (We now look back and call it affectionately "The Fridge"). From the middle of the ceiling hung a wire, on the end of which was a solitary light-bulb - the only source of light and heat in the whole place.

No one said very much and I felt quite uneasy, not helped by the fact that I was shaking with cold and also had flu. Anyway, as soon as they started to play I realised that this was no ordinary "band". They were tight, dedicated and disciplined, and I knew this was right for me. The only doubt left in my mind was about giving up my comfortable day-job.....

When I joined the group, it was the first time I had ever truly rebelled against anything in my life. Most people go through a phase of rebelling, and it remains with some, but I hadn't. I had done everything that was expected of me at home, at school, at college, at work, in every way - and I _was_ happy like that. However, when the opportunity to join presented itself, it made me question my whole life-style. It would have been an easy decision to join a really big group who had no financial worries, but Dexy's? There was just something about the insular feel they had that I couldn't resist.

Some of my friends and relatives thought I'd gone mad. Others said it was the best thing I could ever have done, but they were the ones who expected me suddenly to earn lots of money and move out of my beloved council flat in Smethwick as if it wasn't good enough for me anymore.

Well, I don't earn lots of money, and I still live in the same flat, but I've never looked back as I now have a real direction in life, although I can't explain it or know where it will lead.

Anyway, I'll leave the subject of me now, and tell you what's been happening in the Midnight Runners camp over the past couple of months.

Firstly, Steve Wynne is no longer with us. He didn't have the commitment to the group that is so essential for what we are doing. The new bass player is called Giorgio Kilkenny, and he's been working hard over the past few weeks learning all our songs.

This brings me to the subject of our new single which we recorded just after Giorgio joined us. It's a song which you've probably heard us play under the title "Your Own". It's now called "Liars A to E" and was released at the end of October. The brass isn't used on the recording, being replaced by strings played by Jimmy, Brian and myself, and this heralds the beginning of a new direction for the group.

However, the B side of the single still features the brass. It's an instrumental written by Seb, with help from Jimmy and Mick called "And Yes We Must Remain the Wild-hearted Outsiders".

We are constantly being questioned as to when the new L.P. will be available. Well, we hope to be recording it over the next few weeks, and it should be released at the end of the year. No excuses. 'Good' is not good enough - it's got to be great. You can mass-produce baked beans but not great music.

After the release of the L.P. we intend to start work on a new show which we'll be staging next year. In the meantime we'll be presenting the Projected Passion Revue at the Old Vic Theatre, London, for the last time. The dates are the 13th. 14th. and 15th. November.

I thought I'd clear up a few points about the group in this newsletter which people are sometimes confused by.

Firstly, despite the fact that we feel it's important to get through to people, success isn't uppermost in our minds. We were pleased at the success of "Show Me" and had thought of following it with "Let's Make This Precious", but the time had come to change so we decided to go out on a limb and record "Liars A to E". Besides, everyone seems to be using brass at the moment - we want to be different. For me, this has meant brushing the cobwebs off my viola and learning to play again from scratch which has been quite a challenge.

We are well-known for being very close and insular; interpreted by many as being hostile and unsociable. They miss the point. We described ourselves in the essay with "Show Me" as a group, not a band. I feel we are more of a gang - a very positive gang, and from this I believe comes our strength.

Many people ask us if we're ever annoyed by music press reviews about us. We have no respect for the music press, but in a strange way we find them encouraging - if they are running us down, it gives us even more conviction that we're on the right track.

Another thing we are always being asked about is our opinion on other groups. Really it's quite simple. We haven't got anything against other musicians, it's just that they're so boring with their typecast habits, dress, opinions and sound, and we'd rather not associate with them.

Just to round off this newsletter, a couple of points concerning the Circle itself.

We are grateful to Paul Burns for helping out running the Circle and answering letters - it's really taken a lot of pressure off us.

We've enclosed about ten stickers with this letter which we trust you'll put in prominent positions where they'll be seen.

Well, I think that just about wraps everything up for now. Thanks for your continued support.

Sincerely,

Paul

DEXY'S MIDNIGHT RUNNERS

MEMBERSHIP NO: 460

Name..........................
....
Address..........................
....
....

Expiry Date: Nov 83

HELEN O'HARA SPECIAL
FEATURING PREVIOUSLY UNPUBLISHED INTERVIEW

Dexys' fiddler from March 1982 to 1986, and musical director in the band's last months. Now married with two children. "When I joined the band they were worried it would collapse if we didn't succeed commercially. But I just felt sure it would work. It was brilliant. One of the happiest times of my life was my first Dexys tour. It was the soul that got me. Or maybe passion is a better word. Those songs really pulled the heartstrings and made me play with a lot more expression than I ever thought I could. It drew something out of me, I felt that very strongly. I was starting to let go within myself. Kevin's got a brilliant mind and he's such a perfectionist with amazing ears. He could hear detail better than any of the classical tutors who taught me at college, although he had no training at all. Naturally, it can be hard working with a man like that. There were times when I thought, 'I just can't play that any better', but he'd make me do it again and usually it turned out that I could go one step further. I learnt a lot from him then and I still do when I have a chat with him. He's never boring, that's for sure. An awful lot of work went into Don't Stand Me Down and it was very disappointing when it failed, but ultimately Kevin felt it more than any of us. He wouldn't show it though. He wouldn't be self-pitying. He was always ready to move on."

(From 'Q Magazine' August 1993)

Helen took to playing the fiddle when she first picked it up at the age of 9. Right from the start she preferred to play by ear rather than from written music.

As well as the school band, Helen played in the Bristol Junior Orchestra until she was 11 and then went on to play for the Senior Orchestra. This meant that most of her school holidays were taken up by travelling abroad, but she loved it. They went to the U.S.A. ("a bit overpowering at my age"), Canada, Norway, Germany and all around Britain. However, the travelling proved too much for Helen at the age of 13. The rest of the orchestra were aged between 18 and 21.

At 16, Helen was due to lead the orchestra the following year, but finally decided she'd had enough and to the dismay of her family, she left the orchestra. She was slowly losing interest in classical music and, after a term at technical college, packed it all in to leave home and join a local jazz-rock group – a "horrible arty-farty hippie group" in Helen's own words – who toured around Britain and Holland. Members of Helen's family went along to give support, but ended up falling asleep. The group then started slowly turning into a P.A. Company and Helen got sick of humping speakers around. They eventually noticed that their P.A. system was more in demand than their musical services. She'd joined to play violin not become a roadie!

Anyway, sick of all that, Helen joined another local hippie group called "Uncle Po". She had to join as a pianist (intending to sneak the violin in somewhere) and they played 2 or 3 nights a week in Bristol, London or anywhere that would have them. They won a competition on Radio 1 to record a single, but only the group ever got copies so it was a bit of a pointless exercise really. Another competition they went in for was sponsored by a deodorant company. They got through to the finals and ended up with loads of free deodorant, but little else. Finally, the group ran out of competitions and after a short spell backing Al Mathews, Helen decided she'd had enough.

She wanted to concentrate on something worthwhile and improve her violin playing. So with that aim in mind, she went back to Bristol, locked herself away and spent six months practising 8 hours a day. At the end of it all Helen applied to go to the Birmingham School of Music and managed to convince them at the audition that she'd finished with groups and would work hard.

And for the best part of her four year course that's what she did. In her final year Helen led the school's Symphony Orchestra and the Opera Orchestra, the Chamber Orchestra and the String Orchestra. During that final year Al Archer (the original Dexys guitarist) was looking for a violinist and was put in touch with Helen. She played on some rough recordings that he made and Al told Kevin about her. Big Jimmy Paterson was then dispatched off to the school and frightened the life out of her when he walked into a small practice room she was using. She was playing a sombre Mozart piece when Big Jimmy barged in and asked her if she'd come and play on some demo's we were planning to do.

At first Helen refused, but Jimmy insisted and in the end she decided that she had no choice but to accept the offer. Although she was very reluctant at first, when she heard a tape of the finished songs Helen really loved them and knew she could never see classical music in the same light again. It was precisely what she'd been trying to avoid while at college!

The first time around, Helen brought a cello and viola player but it was obvious that what really made it work was the fiddle. So the next time around she brought two other violin players. They played on 'The Celtic Soul Brothers' and became known as the "Emerald Express".

Slowly, the group started to take priority over college for Helen and Steve Brennan (one of the other fiddle players). Rehearsing with us to record our next LP. 'Too Rye Ay' started to eat more and more into time they should have been spending at college. Helen was getting a lot of stick from all sides – teachers, pupils and family especially. The time that they spent recording the LP with us at Genetic Studios in Streatly, Helen should have been leading the Opera Orchestra for a performance at the School of Music. When she returned, there was an official letter waiting from an outraged Principal. Helen said that she'd been very ill while recording and couldn't get back. She also said that she'd had enough of playing with "Pop groups" which pleased them no end. Unfortunately for Steve Brennan, when he tried the same excuse he wasn't believed for one minute. It didn't help that they'd both rushed back to college for concert rehearsals plastered in make-up after doing TV shows.

Helen had passed all her exams in the third year and spent the last term auditioning for classical orchestras. She was accepted for a job in Spain with a professional symphony orchestra and everyone was relieved. At last, she'd seen the error of her ways and settled down to a proper job – it was even announced on graduation day at the School of Music.

The following day Helen went to do a TV show with us and joined the group.

Billy Adams

Previously Unpublished Interview
"Helen's doing solo instrumental music, violins mostly; it's really beautiful" - Kevin Rowland, Summer 1988

She wears neither dungarees nor a Brooks Brothers suit. "These days I'm wearing what I'm wearing – it's as simple as that."

Helen O'Hara has put her Dexys era behind her. Recently she's been demo-ing tracks for a solo album that links country music, Celtic sounds and a modicum of rock in a manner that refuses to be categorised. "My music is purely instrumental. What I'm trying to do is combine my love of classical music with the sensibilities, structure and directness of pop, adding some of the beauty and melody that stems from Irish and country music but shaping everything in a style of my own. What I'm doing is providing music for older people, music fans, rather than pop kids. I'm concerned that my music is melodic, rhythmic and interesting."

The musicians with whom she's been working with recently include: Robin Williamson (of Incredible String Band fame), ubiquitous Steelie B. J. Cole, and pianist Nicky Hopkins, who's graced sessions with everyone from the Stones, Beatles, Who and Kinks through to Quicksilver Messenger Service. "Nicky Hopkins is a brilliant player and great to work with. It's so exciting when you're working with someone you consider to be the best. All you have to do is just sit down and play. You don't have to say an awful lot."

Helen O'Hara is hardly your starter for one when it comes to musicianship. Bristol born, she began playing the violin at 10, latching on to the sounds of pop radio rather than those of classical music. After some classical training she left home and worked with some local groups and solo acts, including Al Mathews, but found she was unable to play some of the things that came her way. "I thought, I've got to sort this out. So I locked myself away for a year and just practised and practised. Then I applied for a place at Birmingham School of Music – I spent four years there on a performing course, eventually leading the school's Symphony, Chamber, String and Opera Orchestras and graduating with distinction in Performing Studies. It was during my last year that I met up with the Dexys."

"In early '82 I was asked by Kevin Rowland to play on the 'Too Rye Ay' sessions. I found two other fiddle-players and formed the band's 'Emerald Express' section, arranging the string parts. I was then offered a full-time position with the band the very month I was leaving college – so it all tied up. The funny thing was, that at the very same time, I was offered a job with a Spanish symphony orchestra. To be honest, I never had any intention of working with an orchestra, but the very fact that it was in Spain and I'd be playing Spanish music did appeal to me at the time.

Instead, she opted for life with the Dexys, immediately stamping her own mark on the band's musical output. "Jim Paterson was very close to Kevin at that point. He was kind of the band's MD. But by the time of the 'Don't Stand Me Down' album, I'd become more involved with the group and had taken over from him. Being the Dexys' musical director was my job for the last couple of years and it was great." She became, as one Dexy claimed, 'the engine room of the band', recruiting the whole line-up that played on 'Don't Stand Me Down', arranging, rehearsing and providing the band's routines, also co-writing such songs as the controversial 'This Is What She's Like' and 'Knowledge Of Beauty'. In an interview given at that time, Rowland himself said, "She's really in charge now, she's the boss."

Come 1987, after contributing musical backdrops to BBC TV's 'Brush Strokes', a series for which she also co-wrote the hit 'Because Of You' theme, O'Hara had decided that it was time to move on and shape her own musical destiny. Soon after, Rowland headed for the States to fashion 'The Wanderer' an album produced by Deodato (which includes 'Remember Me', yet another song that he and Helen co-wrote).

After spending a year concentrating solely on writing her own music, O'Hara began to miss playing live. In the summer of '88, Tanita Tikaram asked if she would play on the hit 'Good Tradition', and subsequently invited her as guest violinist on tour with her around the world.

O'Hara is now keen to see her own album released which she plans to follow with a series of live dates. "I've got some really strong ideas for concerts, integrating some of the musicians and instruments I will be using on the album."

Fred Dellar
Helen O'Hara

Artists Questionnaire

In 1987 I began to concentrate solely on writing instrumental music. I was certain that there was a huge audience who would appreciate accessible instrumental music. Although a lover of 'Classical' music, I always felt there was often a snobbery attached to this music and its followers, and that it had social class barriers. My aims when writing my music were to be soulful, melodic and concise.

Mentioning my project to others I learnt that there was instrumental music written by contemporary composers going out under the name "New Age". I discovered a wealth of instrumental music of all types. Some record shops were even including composers such as Erik Satie and Albinoni under the New Age label. I found that this music was very popular and that came as no surprise.

Most New Age music to me conjures up relaxing, tranquil and meditative moods, however, I feel the movement is now changing to include other moods and emotions e.g. energetic, uplifting, romantic and so on.

New Age music although discovered and listened to by an audience with perhaps 'alternative' lifestyles and some kind of ecological attitude is now, I believe, crossing over to reach others who are purely interested in the music and its composer/s. The music lovers of the 60s have grown up wanting an alternative to most current pop music and often elitist classical and jazz music. I am sure that the different types of instrumental music going out under the title New Age will attract such an audience. Perhaps New Age music will become the current 'classical' music without the barriers.

Where were you born and raised?
I was born in Bristol, England on the 5th November 1956. My mother's grandparents were from Eire. Perhaps this is where my love of Irish music comes from. My father's family were organ builders. There are still many Bevington organs around the UK. Unfortunately the inclination to build organs dwindled through the generations and the company BEVINGTON & SONS no longer exists.

Musical influences
I listen to and enjoy a wide range of music including the following –
Country – the 'old' school e.g. Hank Williams, Patsy Cline through to the 'new country' artists e.g. Randy Travis, Nanci Griffith, Dwight Yoakam.
Classical – Bach, Beethoven, Mozart.
Irish Music – Traditional songs such as Carrickfergus, Raglan Road, The Curagh of Kildaire.
Dances – jigs/reels etc. and slow airs.
Ennio Morricone, Van Morrison, Al Green, Otis Redding.

Lifestyle
I am for the discovery and use of new and original sounds. To try and replace the sound, feel and emotion of e.g. a violin or cello is, I think, a long way away. Some instruments cannot easily be imitated. The fact that electronic instruments are now so widely available is a good thing as it encourages more and more people to make music. If the music has soul, then the instrumentation, whether it is human or electronic is irrelevant.

My main objective with composing is purely personal. It is a way to express myself. The satisfaction comes when people enjoy my music. I would like to reach an audience as possible all over the world. I plan to constantly develop, improve and move forward. At some point I would like to write music for films and television.

Helen O'Hara Discography

DEXYS MIDNIGHT RUNNERS
Albums

1982 TOO-RYE-AY
1985 DON'T STAND ME DOWN

Singles

1982 COME ON EILEEN
1982 JACKIE WILSON SAID
1982 LET'S GET THIS STRAIGHT FROM THE START/OLD
1983 THE CELTIC SOUL BROTHERS
1985 THIS IS WHAT SHE'S LIKE/MARGUERITA TIME
1986 BECAUSE OF YOU/KATHLEEN MAVOURNEEN/SOMETIME THEME
1988 THE WAY YOU LOOK TONIGHT (B-side, recorded 1984)
1988 KEVIN ROWLAND'S BAND (B-side, recorded 1984)

GENERAL

1988 GOOD TRADITION – Tanita Tikaram
1988 RED RIBBON – Mary Coughlan
1989 5 Tracks – The Adventures (Album)
1989 1 Track – Vera Vitale
1989 4 Tracks – Tanita Tikaram's 2nd Album

COMPOSITIONS

1982 LET'S GET THIS STRAIGHT FROM THE START Rowland/Adams/O'Hara
1984 KEVIN ROWLAND'S BAND Rowland/Adams/O'Hara
1985 THIS IS WHAT SHE'S LIKE Rowland/Adams/O'Hara
1985 KNOWLEDGE OF BEAUTY Rowland /O'Hara
1986 BECAUSE OF YOU Rowland/O'Hara/Adams
1986 SOMETIME THEME Rowland/O'Hara/Adams
1987 THEME MUSIC – BBC TV 'BRUSH STROKES' Rowland/O'Hara/Adams
1987 INCIDENTAL MUSIC – 'BRUSH STROKES' O'Hara
1988 REMEMBER ME Rowland/O'Hara

(Special Thanks to New World Music)

This Is My Confession

Return of the Genius!

Rowland 'ready to return' as Dexys star

I stole song glory says Dexys star

Scruff Wonder

Come off it, Eileen

Geno-genies

DEXY'S MIDNIGHT ROBBERS

"Stop arguing and get on with making music"

KILLJOYS!

Pop star meets 'lost' daughter

Rowland: Come on, come clean!

> **KEEP ON RUNNING**
> *ISSUE 12 JULY 1998*
>
> *"Because we've sat back looking and nearly been took*
> *even been scared but now I don't care*
> *and I'm telling anyone who'll listen*
> *I've seen what's on show*
> *and now there's no more to know..."*
>
> THE CELTIC SOUL BROTHERS (Re-Release, No. 20, April 1983)

INTENSE EMOTIONS
a letter straight from the heart

Dear Neil,

First of all, thanks for the back issues. I feel that you deserve great praise for your work with *Keep On Running*. Long may it continue.

Reading the interviews, reviews and personal accounts regarding Dexys has been emotionally draining. By your efforts, I have been deeply touched, reinvigorated and indeed vindicated in my admiration of Kevin Rowland. My only regret is that I did not have faith enough to subscribe earlier. For that I apologise.

However, the main purpose of this letter is to air my ideas and views to someone who might be remotely interested. Although deriving from very different circumstances, it seems that aspects of our obsession are similar, and I feel compelled to share my thoughts with you. I have never before corresponded or met anyone who perceives Dexys in the way that I do, but, then again, I've never classed myself as a fan in the conventional sense.

I always considered myself an equal to the group and the man. Somehow, I sensed that this was what he wanted. True Dexys appreciation is not about idol worship, it's about sharing and communication. For years, I believed that Rowland spoke to me and about my experiences, and that I understood every word. Does that sound familiar?

Surviving a background of abuse, I believed in the new 'soul' vision, I needed it. I believed in purity and honesty. I knew about passion and in always striving. For so long there was little else for me, except Dexys. Imagine how I felt the first time I heard *Soon*, and being Anglo-Irish, *Knowledge Of Beauty*. It goes on.

I have many memories of the early-eighties, often traumatic, and sometimes uplifting and precious. The later mostly concern Dexys and Rowland, who were a mainstay in my life. I perceived them as kicking against the machine, and they became a catalyst for all my rage and confusion. Yes, despite my deprivation, I was privileged to be around then.

But such narrow devotion eventually twisted my perception and lessened me. For too long I was made to feel embarrassed by the shallow success of *Too-Rye-Ay* and *Geno*. Don't get me wrong, I knew every note and word of the records, but others would ridicule my obsession, failing to see beyond the various images. In my weakness, I found it

127

difficult to articulate how original and different Rowland and his music was, and remaining misunderstood, I became angry, immersing myself further into the music, refusing to see beyond the mystique of the group and the great man.

It pains me to think about how I was both frail and naïve, and pompous and arrogant, then. I now realise that the ignorant ones were wrong, as I was wrong, but you must understand, that's how I lived. It was necessary to be that way. The only consolation now, is the memory and reality of my devotion, and how good the music still is.

For years after Dexys mid-eighties demise, I felt betrayed by Rowland. Such was my trauma, and my imagined relationship with the man, I took Dexys failure personally. I viewed *The Wanderer* as a feeble and cliche-ridden sell out, in comparison to the originality and spirit of Rowland's previous incarnations. I believed that Rowland should have lived for his art, should have continued to demonstrate the Dexys ideal through his music – for me.

You see, I had nothing to show for my adoration and faith. I wasn't strong enough to stand alone, and I became bitter. In an attempt to purge myself, I destroyed the cuttings, the posters, the interviews, tapes and tickets, *almost* everything. Yet, some of those records remain treasured possessions – it seems that, despite my denial, the truth of my faith was too powerful to allow me to discard everything. And yes, I regretted it, even in the seconds immediately after I destroyed all the memorabilia. But I just could not believe in my soul.

Now, like you, I see Kevin, for what he is: flawed, failed and full of contradictions – exceptional and normal. That is his strength and his beauty. He represents the unpretentious potential of pure feeling and a poor education. No wonder I believed so fiercely.

And the power and continuing legacy cannot be assailed by the ignorance of critics or the masses, or indeed by my doubt. Not reading the music press, I was not aware of how Rowland is beginning to be treated with the reverence he deserves, and that *Don't Stand Me Down* is finally being appreciated. How ironic such revisions of music history are. Although such changes in attitude are satisfying, it makes me sick.

Now I understand from experience that Dexys were simply a unique and powerful phenomenon, that they were and are about feelings, truth and image, and I am immensely proud of my belief. I always sensed that, of course, but such was my condition, I didn't understand it. Now I know.

But this letter is not just an excuse for the rantings of some dispossessed old soul rebel, I hoped I could contribute to your work in some small way, with a few suggestions that occurred to me in my reading. I apologise if they are impractical, inappropriate or just obvious.

Firstly, there is the question of what soul music really is. I always believed that Rowland held the key to this dilemma. Can music only be real and pure if the artist lives out the ethos of it? Can a projected lifestyle be enough? Did Dexys ever live up to this? Was it necessary that they did?

The tension between producing true, honest and intelligent music, whilst addressing the demands of commercialism has always fascinated me. Is it worth debate in the fanzine? Should you encourage the subscribers to expand their personal reminisces and explore the true extent of Rowland's impact? Would they be interested?

I think that Rowland's place in music is still underestimated. Shouldn't those of us that believe take up the banner of new soul? Even after all these years, it's still relevant – Now, more than ever. Just look at the way music has gone. We shouldn't leave it to the hacks to justify his place.

Am I taking this all too seriously? I don't know. Reading back, it is apparent to me that Dexys fed me and bred me, so it's all Rowland's fault! But whatever, it is heartening to know that there are others who also care. Through you, this has become evident.

Finally, and on a lighter note, I once played on a bill with a group who called themselves *Baksey's Midday Joggers*. They were crap, but I thought the pun was excellent. Perhaps you can suggest that Andy Leek steals that name instead. It would be more appropriate.

Yours Sincerely,

James McMurtry, Southampton

DEXY'S MIDNIGHT RUNNERS

SINGLE
DANCE STANCE

'STRAIGHT TO THE HEART TOUR'
with THE BLACK ARABS

JANUARY
19 AYLESBURY Friars
25 LONDON Music Machine (Warm up gig)
28 EDINBURGH Tiffany's
29 PERTH City Hall
30 GLASGOW Technical College
31 ABERDEEN Fusion

FEBRUARY
1 ST. ANDREWS St. Andrews University
2 DUNDEE University
4 ABERYSTWYTH University
5 SHREWSBURY Music Hall
6 WOLVERHAMPTON Polytechnic
7 KENT University
8 NORTH STAFFORDSHIRE Polytechnic (Stafford site)
9 HUDDERSFIELD Polytechnic
10 NORWICH University of East Anglia
11 NEWCASTLE-UNDER-LYME Tiffany's
12 NUNEATON 77 Club
13 SHEFFIELD Polytechnic
14 WARWICK University
15 KIDDERMINSTER Town Hall
16 MIDDLESBOROUGH Rock Garden
18 SWANSEA Circles
19 CARDIFF Top Rank
20 BRISTOL Romeo & Juliet's
21 PENZANCE Demelzas
22 BATH University
23 MANCHESTER Polytechnic

MARCH
1 LONDON Electric Ballroom

Dexys Midnight Runners

INTENSE EMOTIONS CIRCLE

February 1982   Newsletter 5

Hi Cats,

It's me again. Seb initially volunteered to write this newsletter, but what with his busily living up to his "hardest working man in showbusiness" title, and the rest of the chaps airing a unanimous "nothing to report", it was obvious that I should be the chosen one.

Well there's no good news I'm afraid to say. In fact for me it's been a pretty disappointing year. It seems ironic that Christmas should find Dexy's Midnight Runners in pretty much the same position as they were a year ago, with "Liars A to E" becoming 81's "Inferiority Part One". Oh I know this group is twice as good as the last one and I'm confident this year will be a totally different story, but the fact is we made hardly a dent in the B.B.C.'s popular music listings. I suppose it could be argued that we were only warming up, but still made good records. In the case of "Plan B" I would agree; it's presently my favourite record, but it sold very little when compared to "Show Me", which incidentally, was a pile of shit. "Liars" I'm not sure about.

Anyway, that's showbusiness, but what about Circle business? It occurred to me recently that "The Intense Knitting Circle" might have been a better title, with special emphasis on nervous breakdown and suicide patterns. The odd tearful letter I can take, but the final straw came a fortnight ago when one bright and cheerful morning I arose to find a sweet perfumed letter waiting on my doormat. I hastily opened the package (being careful not to spill my cornflakes) and began to read it. It began "Dear Kevin, Why do you hate me so much?" - (this from someone I've never met). The letter continued on this theme for the first four pages. I turned over the sixth leaf to find the first of many drops of blood concealing the frantic prose. The next four pages were covered in blood, with the correspondent signing off, "I have no more blood left to give you". It was about this time that I first began to wonder if the Circle is all it should be.

P.T.O.

Oh I know, most of the letters are interesting, honest and sometimes inspirational, and for those I thank you; but I could also do without the "I'm glad your last record didn't get into the charts" nonsense. The fact that our last record was a flop is something I'm not at all proud of and I have no intention of wallowing in the "too good for the charts" bullshit. Oh, and by the way, I have no intention of committing suicide or having a nervous breakdown.

Well, that dealt with, It only remains for me to tell you of our latest daring venture int the world of showbiz. Seriously, a strong belief that The Midnight Runners should always be a challenging and powerful force, coupled with the fact that every time I turn on the radio these days I hear a brass section as well as every dick head and his brother going on about soul, passion, etc. Anyway, what I'm saying is we're changing. The new single is in a totally different direction, it has a Celtic feel and little in common with our old records. You'll hear it soon enough I'm sure.

Be seeing you,

Kevin Rowland.

Please note our new address....
"The Intense Emotions Circle".
York House,
27, Tenby Street,
Birmingham B1 3EE.

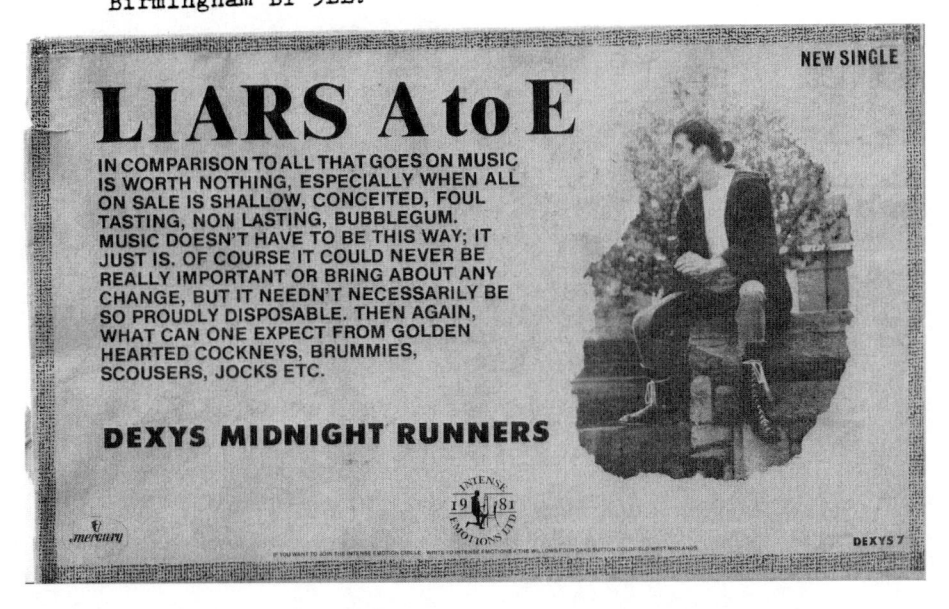

NEW SINGLE

LIARS A to E

IN COMPARISON TO ALL THAT GOES ON MUSIC IS WORTH NOTHING, ESPECIALLY WHEN ALL ON SALE IS SHALLOW, CONCEITED, FOUL TASTING, NON LASTING, BUBBLEGUM. MUSIC DOESN'T HAVE TO BE THIS WAY; IT JUST IS. OF COURSE IT COULD NEVER BE REALLY IMPORTANT OR BRING ABOUT ANY CHANGE, BUT IT NEEDN'T NECESSARILY BE SO PROUDLY DISPOSABLE. THEN AGAIN, WHAT CAN ONE EXPECT FROM GOLDEN HEARTED COCKNEYS, BRUMMIES, SCOUSERS, JOCKS ETC.

DEXYS MIDNIGHT RUNNERS

mercury   INTENSE EMOTIONS LTD 1981   DEXYS 7

Dexys Midnight Runners

Dear Clive,

you got a mention in the newsletter, I hope that Mick put down the right thing. I expect you've had loads of letters by now from circle members.

The Nottingham shows went well but it could have been better. I'm afraid it wasn't as good as we have done. Edinburgh was far better, if only they'd filmed that instead. Still it should be broadcast on ATV around November but other than that I'm afraid I don't know any details. They've given us 27 minutes so it was really difficult cutting down the show and choosing the songs to use as we did 1½ hours with encores.

We've just recorded some songs for the next single so hopefully it should be released in about a month. Record companies always seem to take a month *from the final recording to release date.*

Thanks anyway

Billy

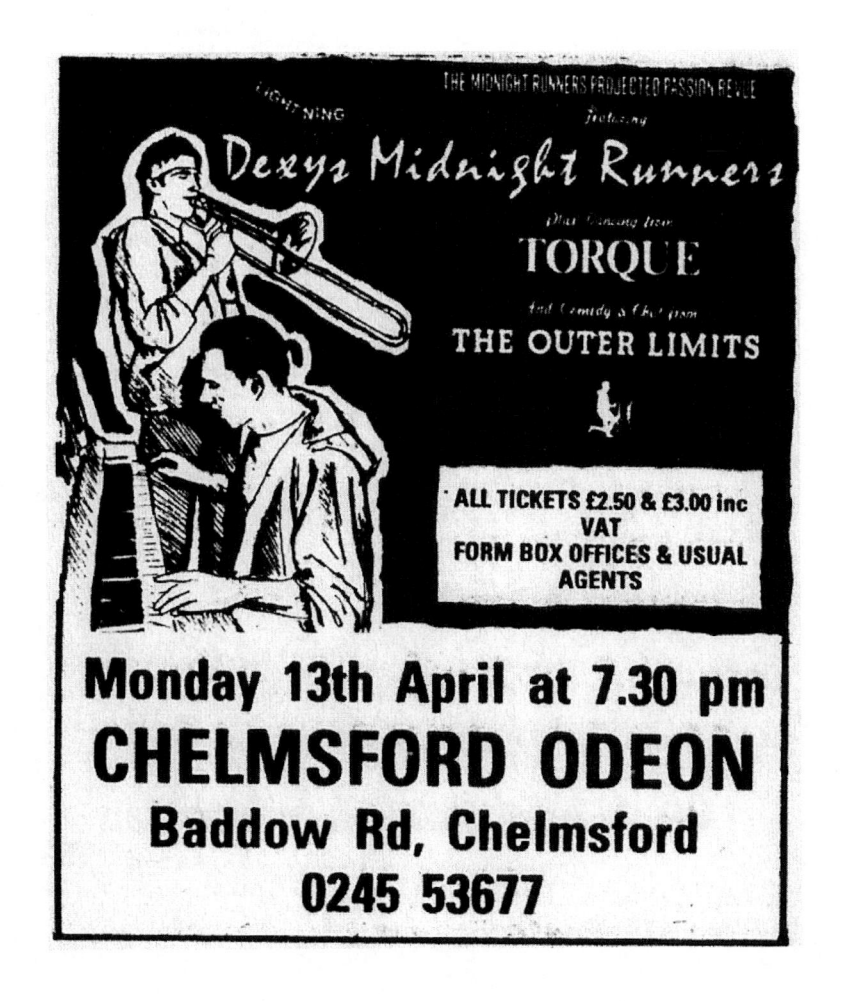

LIGHTNING
THE MIDNIGHT RUNNERS PROJECTED PASSION REVUE
featuring
Dexys Midnight Runners
Plus dancing from
TORQUE
And Comedy & Chat from
THE OUTER LIMITS

*ALL TICKETS £2.50 & £3.00 inc VAT
FORM BOX OFFICES & USUAL AGENTS*

**Monday 13th April at 7.30 pm
CHELMSFORD ODEON
Baddow Rd, Chelmsford
0245 53677**

THE PEOPLE

August 25, 1991 FRANK • FEARLESS • FREE 45p

EXCLUSIVE
ANGIE'S BACK IN EastEnders
Page 4

EXCLUSIVE
THE A-Z OF SEXUAL BLISS by ANNA RAEBURN

FREE! The BIG Magazine section

WIN A YEAR'S SUPPLY OF THAT RED HOT ICE CREAM!

So the Party is over for Gorby

HUMBLED Mikhail Gorbachev last night quit as head of Russia's Communist Party — amid speculation that he will later dissolve the party altogether.

He also set up a special committee to run Russia in the wake of the failed coup against him, to replace his discredited cabinet who were said to have backed the plot.

The dramatic developments came as:

● **TWO MILLION** Russians lined the streets of Moscow to salute the heroes who died in the coup.

● **GORBACHEV** aides admitted his wife Raisa was ill, in answer to rumours that she is in hospital after having a heart attack.

● **RUSSIA'S** leader Boris Yeltsin recognised the independence of Baltic states Latvia and Estonia — and the Ukraine broke away too.

● **AN EX-SAS** commando was behind an amazing plan to rescue Gorbachev during the coup.

Ex-paratroop officer Jim Shortt was flown to the Crimea to train rebel KGB officers to storm the Soviet president's dacha and get him out alive.

Shortt, a 38-year-old freelance military adviser, believes the KGB men knew TWO

● Continued on Page 7

DEXY STAR FINDS SECRET DAUGHTER

A great PEOPLE Exclusive

THAT'S MY GIRL: Kevin hugs his daughter Alethea-Jane

By DANNY BUCKLAND

ROCK star Kevin Rowland, lead singer with Dexy's Midnight Runners, has had an emotional meeting with the 17-year-old daughter he had never seen.

Kevin, 38, was an unknown shop assistant when he left the girl's pregnant mother. He headed for worldwide fame while the young mum made a new life far away from the glare of showbiz.

Rowland, whose hit Come On Eileen was Number One for four weeks, always knew he had a daughter.

But his world was turned upside-down when Alethea-Jane England traced him.

"There is no one prouder than me," said Kevin happily holding his new-found daughter tight.

"These past few weeks have been an incredible jumble of emotions."

Alethea-Jane, who was brought up by her mother and the man she later married, said: "I knew I had a real dad but I had no idea it was Kevin Rowland."

READ THEIR FULL MOVING STORY See Pages 4 and 5

HAVE YOU WON IN THE £1,000,000 SUMMER LOTTERY? See Page 29

Your personal number — Cut it out and keep it

THE PEOPLE AUGUST 25, 1991

How Midnight Runners singer found her again after seventeen years

COME ON ALETHEA!

Joy as star Kevin hugs his long-lost daughter... on Platform Five

By Danny Buckland

ROCK STAR Kevin Rowland, lead singer with Dexys Midnight Runners, has had an emotional meeting with the 17-year old daughter he had never seen.

Kevin, 38, was an unknown shop assistant when he left the girl's pregnant mother. He headed for worldwide fame while the young mum made a new life far away from the glare of showbiz. Rowland, whose hit Come On Eileen was Number One for four weeks, always knew he had a daughter. But his world was turned upside down when Alethea-Jane England traced him. *"There is no one prouder than me,"* said Kevin, happily holding his new-found daughter tight. *"These last few weeks have been an incredible jumble of emotions."* Alethea-Jane, who was brought up by her mother and the man she later married, said: *"I knew I had a real dad but I had no idea it was Kevin Rowland."*

POP STAR Kevin Rowland has tasted fame and fortune as the lead singer with Dexys Midnight Runners. But nothing can compare to the moment he was able to wrap his arms around his slender daughter for the very first time.

Platform Five at London's King's Cross station was the unlikely setting for the most emotional moment of their lives. And there, walking nervously towards the father she had never met, was a mature, confident 17-year-old on the threshold of womanhood.

It could have gone terribly wrong. They hadn't shared the magic moments and growing pains which shape a close family relationship and were, in effect, total strangers.

But, as Kevin hugged Alethea-Jane, the years melted away. And they became what they both desperately wanted – father and daughter.

Kevin, 38, whose band were at Number One for four weeks with *Come On Eileen* and now sing the theme song to the hit TV comedy *Brush Strokes*, said *"Nothing compares to this. No success, no Number Ones, no fame – absolutely nothing. This is the best thing that has ever happened to me."* And throwing a protective arm around Alethea-Jane, he said: *"There is no one prouder than me. It is incredible. I had never seen my daughter and we have missed so much of each other's lives, yet we are so close. Meeting after all these years could have been a disaster but it is just brilliant and I am a very lucky man."* Alethea-Jane said: *"I was nervous about meeting him but I knew it was what I wanted. We hit it off straight away and it was marvellous. It was automatic love. I don't care that he is a famous pop star – that is not important. I am proud of his success and what he has achieved but what matters most is what he is now. He is my dad and it is wonderful to be with him. I can hardly believe how well we get on and how much we have in common."*

Kevin, who has remained single, was just a boutique assistant when he was pitched into an emotional minefield. His girlfriend, who lived on the same street in Liverpool, became pregnant. Kevin was 20, she was 18 – and their future was doomed.

"*We had a relationship but I wasn't ready to settle down,*" said Kevin as he clasped Alethea-Jane's hand tight. "*I decided that I couldn't settle down. It was a hard decision to pull away but it was the only decision I could make. Had I stayed, three lives could have been ruined. It has worked out well but that is not down to me. It is down to God and most important of all Alethea-Jane's mum and her other father bringing her up so well. I always wanted Alethea-Jane to know about me and that she should be told who I was when she got to 16. It was hard to walk away but it was made easier because I had never seen her.*"

Kevin moved from Liverpool back to Birmingham. He made an early attempt to contact his baby daughter but her mum refused. "*I understand why. She was in a stable family and me appearing could have rocked the boat,*" said Kevin.

Soon he had drifted into the booming Midlands music scene of the late Seventies. And Dexys Midnight Runners became one of many groups on the gruelling clubland circuit. The band had a moderate hit with their first single. But they first got to Number One in 1980 with *Geno*, a tribute to soul legend Geno Washington.

As more hits followed and the Runners shared European stages with David Bowie, Alethea-Jane started school in Cornwall – where her mum had married and set up a happy home. Kevin and his daughter were worlds apart and, it appeared, destined to stay that way.

Then, in 1982, the band released *Come On Eileen*, a speculative country-rock single co-written by Kevin. Incredibly, it zoomed to the top throughout the world and became Britain's biggest-selling single of 1982. Even now, it can fill a dance floor within seconds of the distinctive opening violin chords. And it helped a new compilation of Dexys hits make the Top Ten album charts just two months ago.

One of the millions who bought the original single was an elfin-faced eight-year old with a keen ear for music who had no idea that her pocket money was buying a slice of her father's life.

Alethea-Jane said: "*I remember buying the record – I think everyone in the country did. But obviously I had no idea it was by my father. I knew he was out there somewhere but I never knew who he was. Having two dads was never an issue. I love them both. But I always wanted to find out who my real father was and it finally came out in conversation one night. I was determined to contact him but it took me months to pluck up the courage. I had no idea what his situation was. He could have been married, settled down with children. Would he want to hear from me? Would I just get in the way?*"

She traced him through a record company and then, with trembling emotions, began to write the hardest letter of her life. It arrived at Kevin's two-bedroom flat in North London two days later, together with a passport-sized photo.

Kevin takes up the story. "*I opened the letter and there it was, a picture. It was the first time I had seen her face. It was a shock and a delight. After 17 years I finally knew what she looked like. I was really excited. She looked beautiful, she had my nose, my features and she was my daughter. You would have to live through something like that to know my feelings. I wrote back straight away hoping against hope that she would visit me quickly.*"

A whirlwind of correspondence and phone calls followed and a meeting was arranged. They hadn't clapped eyes on each other in 17 years but the isolation was broken in just seven days. Kevin, who still sports jet-black hair, pencil-thin moustache and a goatee beard, said: "*One minute I was blissfully ignorant of what she looked like. The next I was

waiting at King's Cross for my daughter's train to pull in. A million things were going through my mind. But all the doubt vanished the moment I held her in my arms."
Alethea-Jane added: *"I was really nervous on the way down. I did not know whether I should kiss him, shake his hand or just say hello. But it all came naturally. I just gave him a kiss and a cuddle. It was a wonderful moment."*
Dad and daughter are now catching up on all the details they have missed over the 17 years. Alethea-Jane is studying the performing arts at college in St Austell. But she has been working as a waitress in Scarborough to save money for auditions in London.
"I have missed a lot but I can share her ambition now," said Kevin with natural parental pride. *"She is very artistic and talented and I'm sure she will succeed. My career is really important to me and I am making great strides but it does not compare to this feeling. If anything this has made me even more determined to succeed. I thank God it has all worked out so well."*

Picture PEOPLE

HAPPY: Kevin with his daughter, Alethea-Jane
United in harmony
PICTURE of the week has to be pop star Kevin Rowland with his new-found daughter, Alethea-Jane looks so much like him — and so happy.
— C Bremner, Buckie, Grampian
● A bottle of bubbly is on its way to Mr Bremner and our photographer. Tell us YOUR favourite People picture.

TOGETHER AT LAST: Kevin can hardly believe he's finally met his girl Alethea

KEEP ON RUNNING
ISSUE 13 JUNE 1999

"Well, you know the kind of people that put creases in their old Levis? The type that use expressions like tongue in cheek and send-up? I don't like these kind of people..."

THIS IS WHAT SHE'S LIKE (November 1985)

Reminisce Part Seven

For me, Dexys started back in about 88/89 with Too-Rye-Ay. My Father often played it in the car and my interest started then. To be honest at this time I thought Dexys were a 'One hit wonder'. It was only when I went into a record store one day that I discovered the album Geno. Then this took over from Too-Rye-Ay on the cassette deck. Next after that came the release of The Very Best Of which I immediately rushed out and purchased.

What annoyed me most about all the albums I had was that not one contained sleeve-notes, fan-club address etc. In about '92 I discovered another record shop, out of curiosity I went in, I approached the assistant - "Do you have anything by Dexys?" At this point I was expecting him to say no, but he showed me a selection of both seven and twelve inch Dexy records. I couldn't believe it! Neither could the assistant when I brought nearly every Dexys single, the only reason I stopped was because I had no money left! From then on every time I went into Southampton from that day on I always go and have a look in that shop to see if anything new has come in.

I now had two addresses of fan-clubs, I must have written to them both umpteen times but to no avail. This annoyed me somewhat as I wanted to know more and more about the band but I was having no success at all. I thought that was it of the Kevin. I found this very disappointing. Then while looking through Record Collector one day in the fanzine section I noticed the words 'Dexys Midnight Runners' – I couldn't believe it, I was overwhelmed, at long last a fanzine dedicated to Dexys. I will say it again – I couldn't believe it – I had to keep looking to make sure it was true. That is the best thing I have seen in ages. I am really happy that you give up your time and effort for all us fans. I wish my life away really hoping Kevin will be back soon.

Daniel Ford, Southampton

DEXYS MIDNIGHT RUNNERS

INTENSE EMOTIONS CIRCLE.   NEWSLETTER 6   MARCH 1982

Hello,

It's Seb Shelton........with newsletter six.

Without doubt the most obvious newsworthy item at the moment is our latest single - "The Celtic Soul Brothers" - which was released a few days ago. Written by Kevin, Jim and Mick and directed by Clive Langer and Alan Winstanley, this is a very different sounding Dexy's Midnight Runners.

Although we'd used strings on "Liars A to E" and at the Old Vic theatre last year, we weren't convinced that this was the right blend of sounds. However, on the new record cellos have been replaced by fiddles and Paul plays flute, Billy plays banjo and Mick plays piano and accordian. This mixture has given a much brighter, fresher sound which we're all pleased with.

As well as the new instruments, this record also features some new faces. I'd like to introduce you to Helen O'Hara, Steven Brennan and Roger Macduff - The Emerald Express - who added their own brand of Celtic fiddles to the title. We're hoping that they'll accept the invitation to play on future records by the group.

I know from your letters that the greatest points of interest are, and have been for some time, the forthcoming L.P. and live shows. The good news on these fronts is that we are in the middle of recording the L.P. right now. This means that it will be released in early June.

Regarding live performances, please disregard whatever else you may hear, we have no plans to play until all of the recording is finished and the L.P. released.

Some time ago the projected Passion Revue was filmed for I.T.V. at the Theatre Royal, Nottingham. This hasn't been shown yet but we're been told that it will be screened by T.S.W. and Channel T.V. on 27th March and London weekend T.V. sometime in April. The programme to watch out for is called "Video Sounds".

Closer to home, I must admit to being more than a little disappointed by some peoples' response to the lateness of newsletter 5. I'd have thought that there were more important things to do than grumble amongst yourselves or to us about that ! Let me explain about the circle; It's organized and run by us with help from Paul Burns. It's done this way to make and keep it as personal as possible so we know exacltly what's going on. Believe me, this takes care and time. Occasionally, Circle projects have to be delayed, either when we're let down by outsiders, or when there are other group projects which must come first. The intense Emotions Circle was never intended to be a slick business concern, but a personal means of contact between you and us. While we're so personally involved in the Circle, little hold-ups from time to time are inevitable - I think it's worth it !

It's been our intention for some time now to expand the straight forward newsletter format of the Circle, with us doing all of the talking, to include more participation from you. I forget who's idea it was now, but I got a letter a few months ago suggesting we circulate contributions from Circle members with the newsletters. We're not quite certain how this is going to work out yet but if you've got anything you feel that you want to say - a poem, a short story, or information about your area or yourself, (you might, for instance, play an instrument and want to form a group) then send it to us, typed out if possible.

O.K. that's all from me for now. I think you'll be hearing from Giorgio next. Till' then take care,

Sincerely,

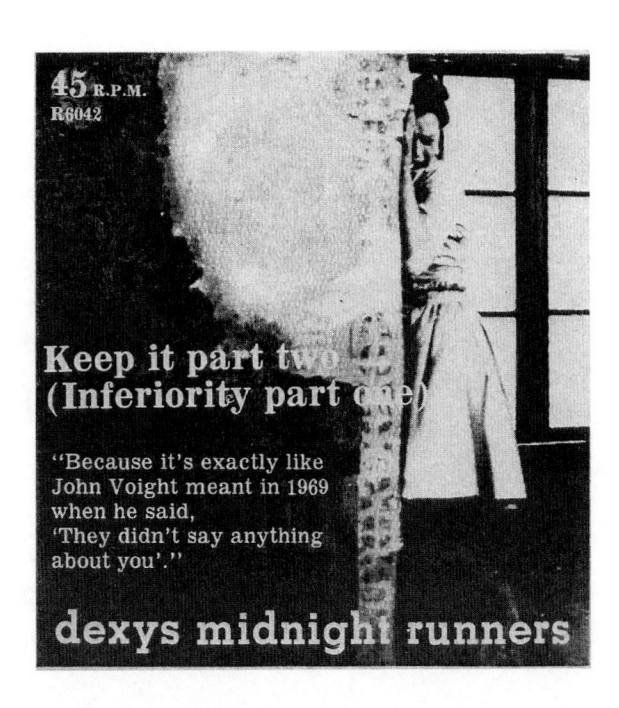

45 R.P.M.
R6042

Keep it part two
(Inferiority part one)

"Because it's exactly like
John Voight meant in 1969
when he said,
'They didn't say anything
about you'."

dexys midnight runners

Dexys Midnight Runners

Dear Clive,

Thanks for writing Kevin read your letter and thanks you for your encouragement.

With the Circle, we'll be composing a merchandizing list soon, as soon as we've ordered more t-shirts.

We still haven't signed to a record label, so the single is still waiting to be released.

We're doing an In concert on the 20th May, so it will be going out at 6-30pm on 30th May.

Ok! Thanks for writing Clive.

Jenni

INTENSE EMOTIONS LTD, 4 The Willows, Four Oaks, Sutton Coldfield.

I don't believe you really like Frank Sinatra...

Van Morrison – Jackie Wilson Said
Rumours abounded in 1982 that Van Morrison was involved in Dexys' sessions for Too-Rye-Ay. According to some reports he supplied backing vocals – well down in the mix – on the cover version of his Jackie Wilson Said. Whatever the story, Dexys stood on no ceremony with this, although Van did actually sing with Dexys when they recorded it, Kevin said - "What we were doing was an interpretation and there just seemed no point in using his voice." This was the token cover on the second album and was to be Dexys only cover single release (UK 5). The production of Too-Rye-Ay has been criticised for thinness – not here. Compared with Van's original version, this cooks. Barnstorming brass, a feast of fiddles and Kevin's usual passionate delivery belie the fact that he considered Jackie Wilson Said to be an album filler track. Probably best listened to live – the Newcastle version ("The In-A-Tent Emotion Revue) is a killer. Having been familiar with Van Morrison's version from St Dominic's Preview since it's release, it was difficult to comprehend how the Runners surpassed it's power and beauty. And of course Kevin didn't need any tea in his cup compared to Van who preferred coffee! And what about the Top Of The Pops appearance? Jocky Wilson indeed! Along with RESPECT, a demon cover.

David Innes

Jackie Wilson said it was Reet Petite...
'Reet Petite' was originally released in November of 1957 where it reached Number 6. It was re-released in November of 1986 where it entered the charts at Number 40, entering the charts one position higher at the same time was Dexys Midnight Runners with 'Because Of You'. 'Because Of You' went on to reach Number 13 and 'Reet Petite' went to Number 1. 'Reet Petite' holds the record for taking the longest time ever to get to the top spot at twenty-nine years and forty-two days!*

Neil Warburton

* Since the original issue of Keep On Running 'Is this the way to Amarillo' by Tony Christie now holds the record for the longest time ever to get to Number 1, originally entering the charts on 20th November 1971 and making Number 1 on 20th March 2005.

I'M TOO DEXY...

(NME Interview 27th March 1993)

Graham Poppie, Miles Hunt, Dele Fadele – they've all come over tired and emotional, about the soul power notions and angry young man ideas of that ol' Celtic Soul rebel, KEVIN ROWLAND. With the storm and spleen of classic Dexys Midnight Runners still fresh in mind, STUART BAILIE tracks down the righteous brother, and finds him enjoying a new lease of songwriting life after a few years in the wilderness. Kev rules OK: PENNIE SMITH

Wednesday night at the Smashed Club, North London, where rockers and writers meet to buy beer, share stories and gas on about the music that turns their heads and shakes their souls.

And often you'll hear them talking about this particular singer they love, who's apparently wandered off into the hinterland. He last released a record in the summer of '88, but that interval hasn't lessened anybody's admiration for the guy. Not at all. Kevin Rowland is high up there in the pantheon of screamers, strummers, emoters and speechifiers – and wherever you find a gathering of music fans, there's gonna be a mention of Kevin in the course of some emotional, meandering conversation.

Over in the corner of Smashed! is Graham Poppie. He sees Kevin Rowland as the touchstone of all the stuff he found thrilling about music when he started on this trip – Kevin's records with Dexys Midnight Runners were among the first he bought, and he was heavily affected by the angry young man idea.

Graham liked the way that Kevin would spit as he tried to get all the words out – the way the music was intensely laboured over, his famous clashes with record companies when Kevin would hijack master tapes or pay musicians out of his own funds to make sure the records were just the best. How Kevin was confident in his beliefs, and how the whole operation was so fanatically, indisputably precious. Many of the NME set here tonight – like Miles Hunt across the way – were too young for punk, but they got into later Jam and 2-Tone and Dexys for their fix of storm and spleen. They got the brass, righteousness and aggro of 'Young Soul

Rebels', and followed it through the raggle-taggle glory of 'Too Rye Ay' (a big Wonder Stuff influence), and most of 'em hung out through the epic folly of 'Don't Stand Me Down'. Now when they meet Kevin it's like confession time...

"The first time I saw Kevin was in this club in London," Graham Poppie enthuses. "He seemed like a sociable chap, so I shook his hand and told him how he'd changed my life and all that stuff. He looked pretty bemused at the sight of this drunken git with orange hair telling him this, but he was OK about it. But it must be quite an achievement to inspire that feeling in so many people."

MATHEW FROM Dodgy met him backstage at the Brixton Academy after a Primal Scream gig. He gushed to Kevin how 'Don't Stand Me Down' was an all-time great, but the singer was a bit grouchy. "I was off my face, so I told him a joke. I said, 'What does the snail say when he's on the tortoise's back? Answer: 'Wheee!' He just stared at me. I met him a while later and we got on better. But Kevin's like Paul Weller; he didn't always get good press at the time, but now everybody realises how great he was." And so it goes with practically everybody in the bar. Masses of journalists here have all got squiffy, fallen at Kevin's feet and told him how everything changed for them after 'Dance Stance' and 'Geno'.

Dele Fadele once told him that it was his life's ambition to write a song as good as 'Old', and Kevin smiled at him, strangely.

Beyond that, every act on the ultimate fan label, Heavenly Records, has rated him as a big inspiration. There's been a soundalike band called Pele, while a huge chunk of the book *Something Beginning With O* celebrates Kevin as a classic British soul boy, a super-cool individualist.

In brief, Kevin is more of a hero than ever. Even his records that were slagged off at the time – 'The Wanderer' and especially 'Don't Stand Me Down' – are subject to passionate arguments and revisionist debate. So when you eventually meet up with the singer, this phenomenon – the lionisation – is top of your schedule. What does it feel like, you ask, to be subject to this kind of admiration?

"Well, it doesn't happen as much as it used to. But it's crazy, really – no-one could change anyone's life. The thing about music is that it reminds people of something deep down in themselves, you know? Something they've lost sometime...

But I don't think that music really is the thing. And I think it's crazy to look up to musicians. I'm not saying all these people do, but I think that's mad."

And what about the name-dropping, how people use your name to summarise passion and commitment – is that alright? "Yeah, that's a nice thing."

I MEET Kevin in a little recording studio in a friend's house near Kensington. And there's Big Jimmy Paterson with him – the guy who played trombone with the first Dexys line-up and then developed into a fine songwriting partner, co-authoring some of Kevin's best songs. They met again three years ago, and Kevin says he realised how much he needed someone to help him: "I started to realise that I just can't do it on my own."

Kevin is fingering a piece of paper which lists the titles of the songs that I'm about to hear. Beside each title is the position that the tracks will take on the album – an LP that hasn't been recorded properly, but which already exists as an entity in Kevin's head. They're running through 'Manhood' just now, tweaking little bits of the song, getting psyched up for the revived Dexys forthcoming turn on Jonathan Ross' *Saturday Zoo*, their first sighting since they broke up in '85. They're working on the end section of the tune, on which Kevin and Jim trade lines, asking the old poser 'what is a man?' as the notes swirl and dance in a familiar way – a fresh take on Kevin's awesome Celtic soul vernacular. It sounds tremendous.

"We've been revising things a lot over the last couple of years," he figures when it's done. "In a lot of ways, this will be like the first LP. We've had all these years to write these songs, and we've taken them through lots of different stages. We weren't ready to make an LP a couple of years ago, a year ago, even."

Another song title, 'My Life In England (Margaret)', lends itself to all sorts of speculations that Kevin may have been biding his time through the last half of the '80s, waiting to set his definitive on the doorstep of Baroness Thatcher. Yet the storyline takes us back to 1965, with Kev in Harrow, completely choked on a childhood infatuation. Rowland is at his best here, dropping fierce degrees of remorse, memory and desire into the mix. The love song ends in a completely weird (but not un-Dexys) manner, with a call for the withdrawal of troops from Northern Ireland. "*You're doing no-one any favours and you're gonna leave some day,*" he mouths alongside this sweet tune. Wow.

"I don't know why I put that in," Kevin muses. "I just threw it in, really. It doesn't have anything to do with the rest of it. But I think you can put anything in a song, really. There's no rules. I just believe in peace, you know?"

After there's a playback of 'You're The Rose' and 'If I Ever' – the former a tribute to Kevin's mother, the second piece lush, tuneful and tantalising abrupt. But all of them lovely songs, the sort of thing a major label would just about die for. They must be forming queues all the way down your street, Kevin. They're not? Are you kidding?

"**WE DON'T** want anybody to feel sorry for us," he stresses, "and I don't want this to come out negative – that we're down and out, 'cos we ain't. Obviously, things could be better, there's been some rough times. We just want to find the right deal, really."

A tricky subject, this. Kevin's departure from Phonogram after the release of 'The Wanderer' in '88 was a calculated move. What wasn't anticipated was that the label who had tempted him away would suddenly change it's mind. There was a flurry of legal action, but ultimately, Kevin was left without a record deal.

And that's when the rumours began, that he'd be coming back with Heavenly or with Go! Discs, or whoever. Some stories (coming from the same kind of people who would badmouth the unsigned Paul Weller until it became politic to say he was fab again) made it seem worse than that – that the companies were scared of Kevin's reputation as a strong-willed artist, that they couldn't handle the grief or the financial risk involved, and that Kevin, along with Julian Cope and such artists, was destined to languish out there in No Bands Land.

Kevin says he's been offered some deals, but turned them down, because they inferred that he'd wind up as the company's "eighth biggest priority". Some company (he won't say who) is paying for these new demos, but if that's not a success, then Kevin figures he'll blast on anyway, doing the imminent TV show, touring in the autumn, and then, if needs be, heading off to America to vibe them out over there. So at the end of the day, Kevin, is your history a help or a hindrance?

"I don't think about the past much. That might be a problem, though. But people shouldn't expect Dexys to be like the old band – it's completely different. Whatever we're doing now is based on the future and new material."

What people still remember about the old times is the fanaticism that the band evoked –

the fitness regime of Dexys in '81, the angry condemnation of the 'hippy-press' in early ads, the use of unusual venues, no-alcohol policies at gigs – so many things that excited the devotees but pissed off the cynics completely. How does Kevin view those times now?

"Well, we were trying to make it interesting for ourselves, and make it exciting. We were very, very committed to doing something good – and that was both good and bad. We definitely suffered eventually, it was fucking hard work. I don't know how a group can keep doing it except play less... Or else have a different attitude, maybe. I stand back a bit now. In the old days, we knew we had something and we knew what we had was close to us, and we had to hold on to it because it was the essence of the group. We would get paranoid about it to the extent that if you listen to our old records, you'll find very little echo or reverb, 'cos we wouldn't let the producers do anything. It would have been alright half the time. I think we were obsessional, really. Believe me, we took it to ridiculous extremes – way beyond the call of duty."

BUT THAT'S where we came in, isn't it? That the spiky style which Kevin Rowland demonstrated, that his mission to go way beyond the norm, to cultivate his anger and hurt was what blew away so many impressionable young souls and ensures that the *mythos* endures in late night London clubs and way beyond that. You can't want to change that, can you, Kevin?

"It's all a matter of how it comes out really. But I'd say that what we got right earlier on, is what we're getting right now. It's about getting the music from inside us on to the tape. It's not about a certain guitar or a certain beat or a certain kind of lyric. It's nothing as academic as that."

It's about soul power, right?

Isn't it fantastic to be able to entertain an old school notion like that again? And isn't it a thrill to catch him banging away on form once more?

Ladies and gentlemen, a green light please, for the Celtic Soul brother.

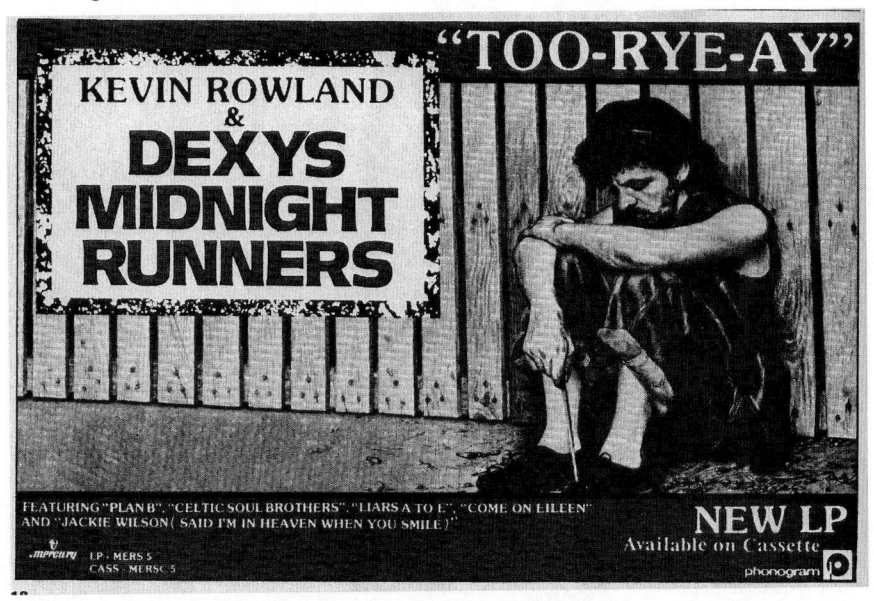

DEXY'S ROCK STAR VINCE KILLS HIMSELF

Overdose on 4 bottles of pain killers

By ANDY COULSON

TRAGIC pop figure Vince Crane killed himself by swallowing FOUR bottles of pain killers, it was revealed last night.

Vince, 45 — who had hits with Dexy's Midnight Runners and 70s rock band Atomic Rooster — was found dead by his ex-wife Jean in his North London flat.

His body lay slumped over his bed beside a suicide note saying "I'm sorry I've let everybody down. I'm sorry for all the pain I caused".

Vince — real name Vincent Chessman — played keyboards on Dexy's 1982 chart-topper Come on Eileen.

He wrote songs for a host of stars, including Kim Wilde.

In 1971, he had two Top 20 hits as lead singer of Atomic Rooster.

But despite his chart success, he was haunted by depression.

Curled

Jean, 40, who was divorced from Vince three months ago after 12 years marriage, said last night:

"Vince was a manic depressive for 20 years. He hung on for as long as he could.

"When I saw him curled up in bed I knew he was dead.

"He looked more peaceful then than at any time in his life.

"He was loved by a lot of people, but I don't think he ever knew how much."

Vince and Jean stayed good friends after splitting and lived in separate flats in the same street in swanky Maida Vale.

A close friend said: "They were still in love but Jean couldn't face his depressions.

"He used to disappear for weeks at a time and then turn up with a girl on his arm.

"When he got over the depression he would tell the girl to leave.

"But Jean was the only woman who understood him.

"Sadly, just a few days ago Jean said that they were getting on really well again."

Dexy's lead singer Kevin Rowland, 36, will be at Jean's side at Vince's funeral next week.

An inquest is expected to open on Monday.

ANOTHER Sun EXCLUSIVE

Vince Crane... used to disappear for weeks at a time suffering depression

Kim... Vince wrote her songs

Vincent Crane – The story:

Vincent Crane, real name Vincent Cheesman, was born in Reading, Berkshire on 21st May 1943 and grew up in Battersea, South London. He attended Westminster City Grammer School, and at the age of fifteen, taught himself to play the piano. At eighteen he attended the Trinity College of Music in London where he graduated in 1964, and while studying classical music there he also played blues and jazz at the **Marquee** and the **100 Club** in his spare time. After graduating from Trinity he decided to drop the classics and formed the first of several short-lived bands.

In 1965 Vincent lived in a shared house in Fulham where he met **Arthur Brown**, three months later **The Crazy World of Arthur Brown** were formed and originally started out with just improvisation, and after a year touring Britain, they played their first of many gigs at the **U.F.O. Club** in London where most psychedelic bands of the 60s started their careers.

Two years later they were signed to Track Records, the same label which signed **Jimi Hendrix** the year before, and that same year The Crazy World of Arthur Brown's first album went straight to Number 1 in Britain and many other countries, as did their single "Fire" which, amongst other songs, Vincent co-wrote.

During their tour of the U.S. the band had a number of management and contractual problems and they split half way through the tour, and it was also during this time that Vincent's latest psychiatric problems first became a problem in the form of bizarre manic escapades, followed by long periods of depression in hospital. On returning to Britain **Vincent Crane** and **Carl Palmer** decided to form a new band, with the name **Atomic Rooster**, which was taken from an LP by an American band **Rhinoceros**.

Atomic Rooster Mk 1 consisted of: **Vincent Crane** – Hammond organ and piano, **Carl Palmer**, later of **Emerson, Lake and Palmer** – drums, and **Nick Graham** – bass and vocals. They recorded their first self-titled album for **B&C Records** in the U.K. between late 1969 and early 1970, and was released in February 1970, reaching Number 49 in the charts. A track from this album was released as a single - "Friday 13th" but failed to make the charts.

By June 1970, Carl Palmer had left to join **Greg Lake** and **Keith Emerson** to form **ELP**, and **Nick Graham** had left to join a band called **Skin Alley**, but by the autumn of that year, Vincent had recruited guitarist **John Cann**, and drummer **Paul Hammond**. With this line-up, Atomic Rooster recorded their best-known album "Death Walks Behind You". The album was a big success, it also provided them with their first top twenty single, "Tomorrow Night" - reaching Number 11 in the U.K. charts, and gave them a good base on which to release their biggest ever hit - "Devil's Answer", reaching Number 4.

Vincent Crane (right) in Atomic Rooster

In 1971 the band signed to **Pegasus Records** and recruited **Pete French** on vocals, and then recorded the album "In Hearing Of" which reached Number 18 in the U.K. charts of July that year. Once again this line-up disintegrated, just after the second album was recorded, with John Cann and Paul Hammond leaving to form **Hard Stuff** and were signed to **Deep Purple's** own record label on which they released two albums, and Pete French left to form **Cactus** and **Leafhound**.

Vincent reassembled Atomic Rooster, this time with **Chris Farlowe** on vocals, **Steve Boulton** on guitar, **Bill Smith** on bass (for one track only), and drummer **Rick Parnell** who had previously joined the band when Carl Palmer left. This time Rooster signed to **Dawn Records** and released their first album for the label in 1972 titled "Made In England". Unfortunately, neither the album or the singles taken from the album charted. The band replaced Steve Boulton with guitarist **Johnny Mandala** and the following year released the album "Nice and Greasy" which again failed to make any sort of impact. Not surprisingly, Vincent disbanded Atomic Rooster.

In 1980 the so-called NWOBHM (or New Wave of British Heavy Metal) was reason enough for Vincent to reform the band, with **John DuCann** (note the slight change to the surname!) again on guitar and vocals and **Preston Heyman** on drums. The band were quickly signed to **EMI** and an album was rush recorded and released, with a single "Do You Know Who's Looking For You?" taken from the album. Once again the album and single made no impact on the national UK charts, although for several weeks it was high in the heavy metal charts of **Sounds**, but despite this, and a heavy touring schedule, EMI dropped the band.

Vincent seemed determined to resurrect Atomic Rooster, and recruited original drummer **Paul Hammond** again, and this time the band were signed to **Polydor**. This classic line-up recorded two singles, "Play It Again" and "End Of The Day", and sadly, once again they made no impact on the UK charts despite showing well in the heavy metal charts, and once again they were dropped by the label.

Somehow, Vincent bravely continued, and in 1983 was signed by **Towerball Records**, despite John DuCann leaving the band again. Braver still was Vincent's attempt to modernise the sound of Rooster – gone were the heavy Hammond organ-dominated riffs, and in it's place were piano and synthesiser compositions, with the Hammond well back in the mix. Also recruited for this album were Pink Floyd's **Dave Gilmour** and **Bernie Torme** on guitars. Despite this quite acceptable attempt, and Dave Gilmour's trademark guitar, the album, and single taken from the album, yet again failed to chart. This seemed to be the last straw for Vincent Crane and he once again disbanded Atomic Rooster, and in February 1984 Vincent joined **Dexys Midnight Runners** for their album "Don't Stand Me Down" and subsequent tour.

In late 1988 it was rumoured that Vincent was once again going to reform Atomic Rooster, but on February 14th 1989 Vincent committed suicide at his home in Maida Vale, London.

Vincent Crane 21st May 1943 - 14th February 1989 R.I.P.

(Source unknown)

TBA INTERNATIONAL PRESENTS

DEXYS MIDNIGHT RUNNERS
"COMING TO TOWN"

EDINBURGH PLAYHOUSE · Friday 1st November
NEWCASTLE CITY HALL · Saturday 2nd November
MANCHESTER APOLLO · Sunday 3rd November
NOTTINGHAM ROYAL CONCERT HALL · Monday 4th November
SOUTHAMPTON GAUMONT · Thursday 7th November
BRIGHTON CENTRE · Friday 8th November
BRISTOL COLSTON HALL · Saturday 9th November
LONDON DOMINION THEATRE
Mon 11th/Tues 12th/Wed 13th November

Tickets: £7.50 £6.50 (London £8.50 £7.50) available from the Box Offices: Edinburgh 031-557 2590, Newcastle 0632 320007, Manchester 061-273 3775, Nottingham 0602 472328, Southampton 0703 29771/2/3, Brighton 0273 202881, Bristol 0272 291768, London 01-580 9562 and all usual agents.
LONDON ONLY: CREDIT CARD HOTLINE 01-741 8989.
No support – show starts 8pm.

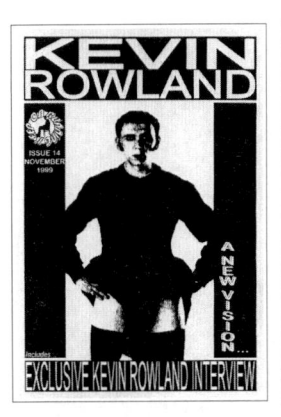

KEEP ON RUNNING
ISSUE 14 NOVEMBER 1999

"Because of you, these thing's I do

Because of you, because of you

Oh, and you love nature, you love nature

You love nature don't you

Anything you want me to do, baby I'll do for you..."

BECAUSE OF YOU (No. 13, November 1986)

Rowland: midnight stunner!

Former Dexys Midnight Runners frontman **KEVIN ROWLAND** has announced his return to the music scene with a bizarre national poster campaign depicting him in make-up and women's clothing whilst hitching up his skirt to show his pants.

A spokesperson at Creation Records, Rowland's label, said that the posters were not promoting any new release as such, but were to let people know he was "on his way back".

Rowland sent a fax to label boss Alan McGee to explain his new look.

He states: "I am not dressing up as a woman; I am not wearing women's clothing or trying to be a woman; I am wearing dresses because I choose to (who's to say I can't?); I'm wearing MEN's dresses; I had them made for me, I designed them myself; it's NOT a gay thing; it's NOT a transvestite thing; it's me as a man expressing my soft sexy side; in all the pictures you can see there is a strong sense of masculinity. This is important; I'm dressing like this because I intend to look amazing when I'm performing; I'm saying, 'I can wear whatever I like as a man'."

He concludes: "Please communicate the above to all the people who will be working on my project at Creation. It's really important we all know what we're communicating from the outset. And the above is as clear as I can put it. My plan is to sing great and look amazing like a total star."

Rowland releases an as-yet untitled single in September followed by an album, 'My Beauty', in October, the first new material he's released for more than 11 years.

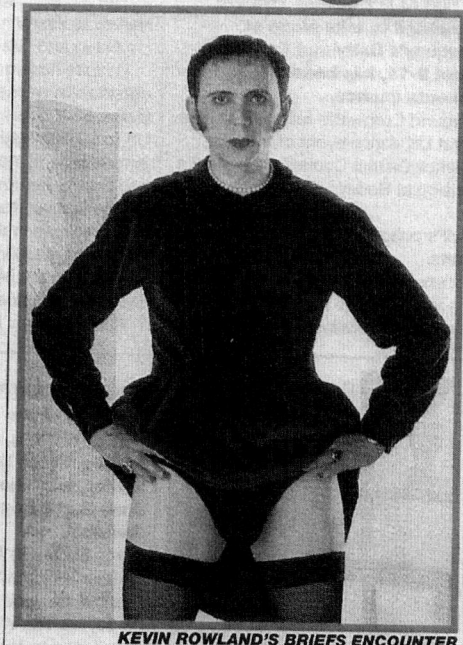

KEVIN ROWLAND'S BRIEFS ENCOUNTER

Of the new 12-track LP, he says: "People will say it's a covers album. Yeah, it's other people's songs. But I don't see it as a covers LP. It's more personal than that. These songs happened to speak to me at a particular time in my life, at a crisis point... it was hearing these songs that made me realise how far I had come, how fucked-up I had really got."

He concludes: "With this record, I feel like I've finally come home... I've got a feeling I'm going to be fucking massive."

153

"A Severe Mid-Life Crisis"

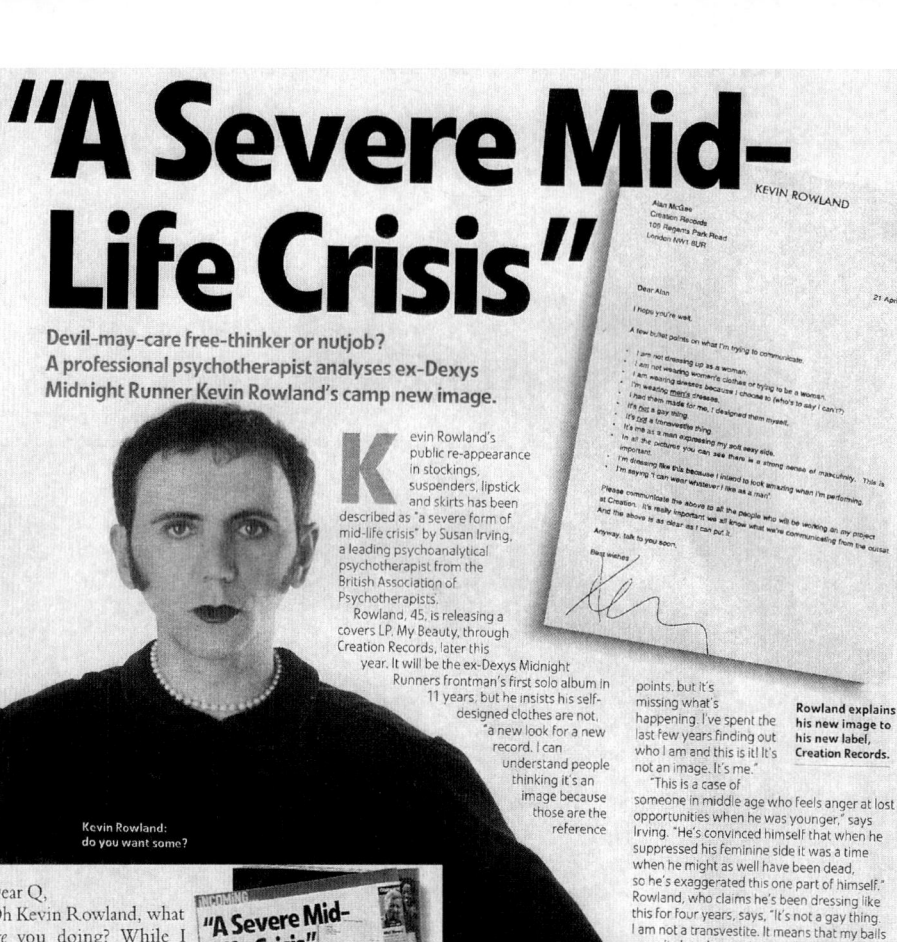

Devil-may-care free-thinker or nutjob? A professional psychotherapist analyses ex-Dexys Midnight Runner Kevin Rowland's camp new image.

Kevin Rowland's public re-appearance in stockings, suspenders, lipstick and skirts has been described as "a severe form of mid-life crisis" by Susan Irving, a leading psychoanalytical psychotherapist from the British Association of Psychotherapists.

Rowland, 45, is releasing a covers LP, My Beauty, through Creation Records, later this year. It will be the ex-Dexys Midnight Runners frontman's first solo album in 11 years, but he insists his self-designed clothes are not, "a new look for a new record. I can understand people thinking it's an image because those are the reference points, but it's missing what's happening. I've spent the last few years finding out who I am and this is it! It's not an image. It's me."

Kevin Rowland: do you want some?

Rowland explains his new image to his new label, Creation Records.

"This is a case of someone in middle age who feels anger at lost opportunities when he was younger," says Irving. "He's convinced himself that when he suppressed his feminine side it was a time when he might as well have been dead, so he's exaggerated this one part of himself." Rowland, who claims he's been dressing like this for four years, says, "It's not a gay thing. I am not a transvestite. It means that my balls aren't closed in, as they would be if I was wearing trousers."

ROWLAND ADMITS he was addicted to cocaine between 1987 and 1996, when he lapsed into a miserable routine. "Taking drugs on my own was sad and desperate. I'd just draw the curtains, get into bed, take the coke, pull the covers up over my head and lie there dreaming. Then the rest of the week would be a massive comedown."

"He's trying to make up for lost time," Irving continues. "But you can't. Because of the drugs he wasn't properly conscious for years and that time has gone, it will never return. You can grow a ponytail in your 50s but it's not like having a full head of hair in your 20s. He's not allowing himself to mourn his lost years because the sadness is too great. There's a sense of desperation about him because he's hiding from a terrible depression about what he has lost."

Rowland isn't alone in getting in touch with his feminine side. Ex-Judas Priest frontman Rob Halford, 47, came out as a gay man in 1997 and took to wearing heavy make-up. Meanwhile, Robert Forster, 42, one half of The Go-Betweens, made a belated return to his '80s flirtation with lipstick and Max Factor during recent gigs in England and Australia.

"It's a signal to people that they may be in their 40s but there's something that's still displaced and unusual about them," believes Irving. "It's no different to a middle-aged man trying to stand out by buying a Porsche."

Dear Q,
Oh Kevin Rowland, what *are* you doing? While I appreciate the right of anyone to dress how they like, why on earth would you choose the sort of frock my mother used to dress me in to go my posh relatives' house in the '70s? David Beckham just about got away with wearing a sarong because he didn't choose to shop in Laura Ashley.

Rowland claims he's expressing his "soft, sexy side"? I suppose beauty is in the eye of the beholder.

Rowland claims he wants to "look amazing" when he's performing? Is he sure he doesn't mean he wants to see "looks of amazement" from the audience?

It's all so sad. Perhaps he would be interested to know that on London's Old Kent Road, his was the only poster in a row of about 10 or 15 that had been defaced. Someone had ripped the crotch out.
Melissa Cavendish, Deptford, London

Kevin Rowland: Do you think I'm Dexy?

INCOMING...

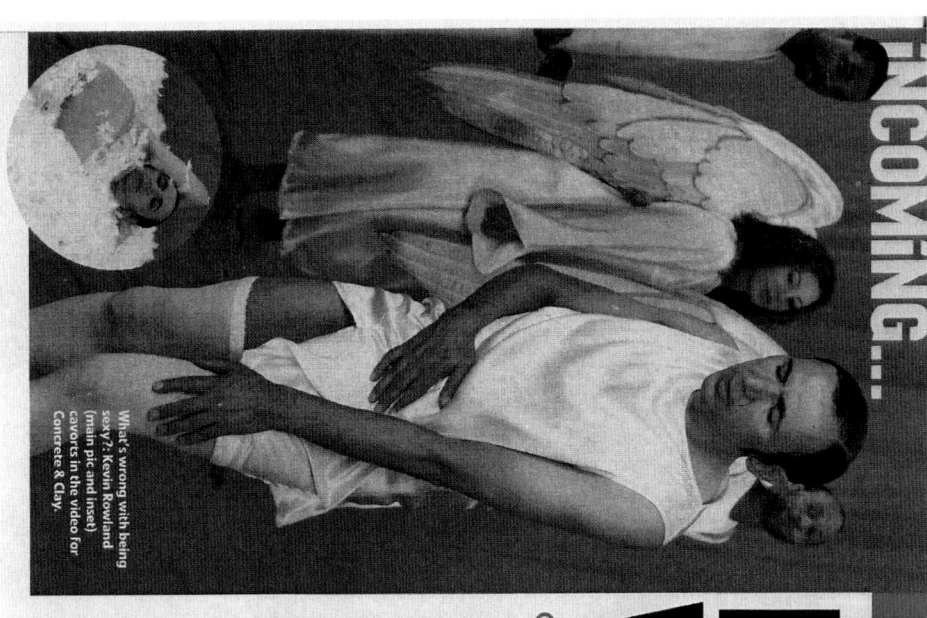

What's wrong with being sexy?: Kevin Rowland (main pic and inset) cavorts in the video for Concrete & Clay.

It Gets Worse!

Creation split over troubled singer's creepy video

Label boss Alan McGee has admitted that Kevin Rowland's video for his comeback single, Concrete & Clay – in which he parades around in a short dress fondling the front of his white bikini briefs – has upset some staff at Creation Records.

"In sixteen years, not even Primal Scream in the heroin days or Kevin Shields (*My Bloody Valentine*) when he was slowly bankrupting us, managed to divide the record company this much," McGee told Q. "Either people enjoy it for what it is: a forty-five year-old man in a skirt being true to his sexuality, or the other reaction is people in our record company think the video is disgusting to the point where they won't work with Kevin Rowland."

Rowland, who has a history of drug problems, has been given complete creative freedom by McGee, who describes him as a "genius".

At press time, the video had yet to be shown on TV.

"The Geri Halliwell video is more revealing than mine and I saw her on TV a couple of weeks ago," says Rowland. "Why should it be acceptable for a woman to show her covered crotch and bum and not a man? Any discrimination of that nature is sexism against men."

KEVIN ROWLAND – MY BEAUTY

Rowland's forthcoming album: put them away, love.

Kevin out to beat stage fright

Former Dexy's Midnight Runners star Kevin Rowland — who grew up in Oldbury — is to sing live for the first time in 14 years, overcoming stage fright which forced him to give up performing.

The Come On Eileen singer, who is relaunching his career after bankruptcy and drug problems, will play at Reading and Leeds festivals next month.

However, he said: "I want to stress that it's not a proper gig. I'm singing only three songs to a prerecorded backing track – I don't want anyone to be disappointed."

With Dexy's, Rowland notched up a string of hits and Come On Eileen became one of the most enduring songs of the Eighties. It sold more than a million copies in the UK in 1982, topping the charts both here and in the United States the following year.

KEVIN ROWLAND
EXCLUSIVE INTERVIEW

It was August 1999, yeah there must be something special about the month of August (apart from it being Kev's birthday), it was the last time I met him two years ago. And here we are in a hotel In Kings Cross, London. It's the morning after the promotional party for Kevin's single *Concrete and Clay* which included a large cinema-screen viewing of the promo video – the applause after each of the two showings was rapturous. As well as many journalists there that night and personnel from Creation – Alan McGee included, Kev's daughter was in attendance and I also spotted Glenn Tilbrook from Squeeze. I was hoping to see Helen and Billy there, but no such luck.

Anyway, it's about nine o'clock in the morning, we've just finished our breakfast and we're walking along the corridor of the hotel to the lounge to conduct the interview. Kev's wearing a sarong (I didn't really think about it at the time, but later, after reading another interview where James Brown from Loaded magazine had interviewed him, he wondered if Kevin's sarong would raise any eyebrows when walking along the south coast of England – it didn't) and as we're walking to the lounge we're talking about the Wolves – Kev's number one football team (but you knew that right?), someone working in the hotel who looked looked like a painter and decorator or maintenance man, overheard our conversation and came over and joined us and we're having a good old chat about the Wolves. But the thing was, here was this man in paint stricken overalls and there was Kevin in his sarong and actually looking quite smart and cool, and this man just didn't seem bothered about what Kevin was wearing, it was as though he didn't notice. The same thing happened during breakfast also, and there was quite a few people in there. Maybe, at long last, people of this country are beginning to realise that people can do as they like and it's got fuck all to do with anyone else (after being in Holland for a year I've really seen the cultural differences).

So, how has Kevin been finding recording again after being away for so long?
I've found it really stressful, I found it difficult but great at the same time. I found working with people very difficult. I found that all my less pleasant characteristics came out, like being a bit of a bully and blaming people for things and not trusting people and all those things came out, but ultimately I think I made a great record. I did find it very difficult but very rewarding – it's great to be back.

And you're enjoying it?
Yeah, sometimes I am, it's very stressful. Today I feel great because last night was such a great night and the video was great and it went well.

Yeah, and I was surprised to see Billy Adams on the video. He didn't play on the album did he?
No, not at all, he just played on the video. We needed someone to stand in, because Neil Hubbard, the guitarist, didn't want to do the video, and I said to Billy, "We need someone who looks like he can play the guitar," and that was it.

So, Billy's made a guest appearance. What was the reason for Big Jim leaving?
About half-way through he walked out, and I still don't really know why. I mean, we had a lot of arguments but we'd had much worse ones than we had on the day he left. I was being a bit of a drama queen and he just upped and left, he said "I'm off," he took his computer and he was off. I think he'd just had enough really, but I don't really know and we've not really spoken since. I was going to try and get him back, but a friend suggested to me to just let him go, and I'm glad I did because I found someone else who did the demo-ing for me as good as Jim did it, and also I had to take more responsibility. I realised that I'd been hiding behind Jim.

And so this is more your album, than had it been if Jim was working with you throughout?
It was always going to be my album and Jim was just helping me get my ideas across, but I realised I'd been hiding behind Jim, like when Pete Schwier who engineered and co-produced the album, and said to me, "Kevin, what do you think?" and I'd pass it onto Jim, "What do you think Jim?" I was hiding behind him.

In the last issue of 'KOR' I spoke about all the lies, the stories behind Helen O'Hara and 'Come On Eileen'. Did you do this to make things more interesting? (I first have to remind him of the 'Eileen' story!)
I said Eileen was a childhood friend? I just made it up really. I don't think I was consciously trying to make it more interesting, I think I was a bit of a liar really and living in fantasy land. Then, the one time, I was at Radio One and they were talking about the single and Helen O'Hara and they wanted an interesting story to go with a news-beat, and I just thought about the bus-stop thing on the spot and they thought it was great, and it stuck.

And what would you say to all the fans who've followed you from the early days and now feel a bit disillusioned about all the lies and the *Too-Rye-Ay* sound coming from Kevin Archer?
I can understand how they feel but... welcome to the real world. I'm not a God, I'm not a fucking Saint, I've done things wrong, I'm only human. Maybe some people look for too much from me as a pop singer, I'm a pop singer – that's my job, I'm not anyone's saviour or anything. People buy the records if they like it and that's it. I understand people feeling disillusioned and I do feel bad about some stuff. But people who have followed me from the early days, it's nice that they've followed me but that's up to them, they don't follow me because of doing me a favour, they follow me because they like the music, it's a trade-off, I make the music and if they like it they buy it. I haven't got a fan club – I don't run a fan club, I'm not saying I'm this person and I want you to be my fan. I make the music and if they like it that's it, and that's where the relationship starts and ends really. I'm not a football team that you support. I have mixed feelings, on the one hand I'm sorry that

people do feel disillusioned and I do feel sorry about everything, but on the other hand I don't want a kind of relationship that feels unhealthy to me whereby people are obsessed about me or Dexys. It's like I'm up on some fucking pedestal and if I make a mistake then they're disillusioned and I don't need that kind of relationship with an audience. If that's how they want to take it, fine, but I'm not going to be any part of that.

Kevin comes back to this question at the end of the interview (throughout the interview it did seem as though when Kevin was answering one question he was still thinking about his answer to the previous question).

Yeah, it was wrong of me to mislead people about the Helen O'Hara thing, but it was light-hearted really, but it was wrong, I'd rather I hadn't done it. Kevin Archer – definitely. About the people who have followed me from the early days and now feel disillusioned, I do feel that that's a bit of a guilt-trip, that question in itself is a bit of a guilt-trip for me, I feel like a guilt-trips been put on me. It's like these people have followed you from the early days and now you've let them down. Well, I'm selling music, I'm not selling a Saint, I'm not a code of ethics, perhaps these people are looking for too much from me – far too much.

You've all read in the music press, ever since *The Wanderer* really, how one minute Kevin's saying he'll be back as a solo-artist and then the next that he'll be back as Dexys. Can he now say 100% that there will be no more Dexys?

I can't say that.

It would be difficult for you going back to Dexys now?

Very difficult, I don't know under what circumstances there could be a Dexys. I don't know how that would work. But cant say 'never' because someone would turn around to me and say, "Oh, you said you wouldn't do that again," I change my mind, what can I say, I change my fuckin' mind, some days I'd say "Yeah, I want to be in Dexys," some days I want to be a solo artist. I change my mind, I'm entitled to. It's like you, you might have a girlfriend and then you think it's not worth it – I'll try another one, or I'm not going to have a girlfriend or I'm going to be solo, y'know what I mean?

But this album started out to be a solo album and then I thought, 'Right, the next one's a Dexys album,' because it was written with Jim, but when Jim left I thought, 'I can't do it as a Dexys album – be ridiculous,' so it will be a solo record, it just happens to be that Jim wrote a lot of the songs with me. So it will be a solo record and I realise that I'm a solo artist now, I think I've got the confidence now in being a solo artist – I can write with anyone who's good. I don't know if there will be another Dexys, who knows what's going to happen, it would have to be the right creative reasons. I would hate to think in five years time that I'd be so skint that I'd do a Dexys reunion – I'd hate that to be honest, although be better than going back to the factory. I don't think I could enjoy it, but who knows, that's how I feel now. I've often been offered big money to reform and go and do a couple of festivals, BIG money, when I needed it. I'm interested in doing something that's now, of now, not of the past. If I'd played a festival now they'd all want to hear *Come On Eileen* and I don't want to do that.

Kevin said on the recent internet interview that *The Wanderer* was not a high point, does he now class *My Beauty* as the beginning of his solo career, and would he rather forget about *The Wanderer*?

Yeah, I'd like to forget about *The Wanderer*, but I suppose I can't, because it's out there. What do you think of it?

(Shit, he's put me on the spot now!) I think that although the actual songs are fine, I just feel that the sound wasn't too good – the production and mixing. It sounds like you're singing with just a tape playing behind you (shall I go home now!). But I think the production and everything on *My Beauty* is far superior, the way it's been produced and mixed – it sounds much more of a complete album.

Yeah, the guy who done the sound and is responsible for quite a lot of the production, my co-producer in the end – Pete Schwier, he mixed *Don't Stand Me Down* – he's a great guy. I think the reason I didn't work with him after *Don't Stand Me Down* was because I was intimidated by how good he was, I don't know why that is, I just felt like 'How good is he?' Yeah, *The Wanderer*, I'd like to forget about it really, but you can't can you? When people hear I've got a new solo album out I don't want them to hear that, I'd like it to be deleted actually, but I know what Phonogram's like, if this one's a success they'll probably re-release it.

As well as being acquainted with Norman Cook (Fatboy Slim), Kevin is also a big fan of his music. I wander if Kevin's ever thought about asking him to mix any of his material?

I thought about that, he's a great re-mixer, but I don't know if I would really. I wouldn't do it at the moment. If it was an extra thing to add to a record... but he's such a powerful re-mixer, I probably wouldn't work with him because he would put his... not his sound, but it would be such a powerful thing that it might overshadow it, so I don't think I would, but he's great.

When I met Kevin a few years ago in Brighton, he talked of searching for beauty. Has he now found beauty, or what is his idea of beauty?

Have I found beauty? No, but I do find it sometimes in music and art and I love it when I find it. Beauty is a bit of a God to me in a way. My idea of beauty is...

To love yourself?

I think having beauty in my life makes it easier to love myself, if I've got beauty in my life and I'm inspired by beauty then it's easier to love myself. Without beauty the world is a pretty grim place for me – so we need beauty, and I'm glad to put out some beauty. I'm really happy with this record.

***The Greatest Love Of All*, is this about you finding beauty?**

Yeah, I think it is. It's about me finding beauty at a time of my life, in 1990, when I first heard that song. I know it came out in '77, but I never heard it, well I heard it but I didn't listen to it, I thought it was middle-of-the-road rubbish. Then in 1990 when I was in real despair, I'd brought a soul compilation tape by George Benson from '77, I put that song on in the car and it just made me cry, I didn't realise what a beautiful song it was and how much I'd lost. I didn't know at the time but that was the starting point for this album.

***Labelled With Love – I'll Stay With My Dreams*, where it kicks in at the end, is this saying that there is light at the end of the tunnel?**

Not really, that was about expressing the pain, the light at the end of the tunnel comes in *Reflections Of My Life*.

What about *You'll Never Walk Alone*? This spoke to you and is this your message to other people?

No, it's a message to myself, I'm not giving a message to anyone else. I sung that song to me when I was eight-years old, I pictured myself when I was eight and I sang that song to me. That's how I got in touch with the feeling for that song. It's a message to myself, be my own self, try and love myself, give myself some encouragement.

From all the songs on the album, is there any one song that has touched you the most? Made you think like 'Shit, I've got to sort myself out'.

The Greatest Love Of All, when I played that I was in floods of tears. *The Long And Winding Road*, I was in rehab when I heard that, someone played it on the guitar and I was like 'Shit, what a beautiful song' – all the beauty that I lost long ago.

Why *Concrete And Clay* as the single?

I just thought it was a great summer tune, and it was to owe Unit Four Plus Two back.

***Concrete And Clay* was partly responsible for *Come On Eileen* wasn't it?**

We got the rhythm, the drum beat, the samba. When we wrote *Come On Eileen* we got the beat for the Der D D. (Listen to *Concrete And Clay* closely and you will hear the resemblance.)

Kevin's new image is getting quite a response from the music press, throwing a spanner in the works yet again! But what does he say to those people who are saying things like 'He's gone mad' and 'He's having a severe mid-life crisis'?

Two words, the second ones 'off' (a favourite saying of Kevin's at the moment!), no three words, the second one's 'off' and the third one's 'wankers'. How fuckin' dare you say that about me. How do you know what's going on in my life, without knowing about my childhood? How can you say that to people? How can you analyse me? Two or three years ago that might have really damaged me because I was in a fragile state, but now I can deal with it, but I think they're wankers, complete toss-pots. I think I look great in a frock, I dress however I want and fuck them. I think they're intimidated by it... I don't know if they are or if they're not.

If *My Beauty* is not a success, will you still go onto record the next album?

Ouch! I hate that thought. I'm not sure, I'll have a good break. I can't think about that yet, I've got to try and make this a success and then I'll talk about that.

Do you think that you're now stronger to deal with success? You've said before that you find it difficult to handle.

I find it difficult now, some days I'm great, I'm great today and yesterday I was OK – at the end, after the party. The day before the party I was in a terrible state – so nervous before the party and last week I was bad.

You're scheduled to perform at the Reading and Leeds festivals, why such big events to start off with?

You know me, all or nothing. I don't know. I did a fund raiser recently for a self-help group to about three-hundred people and that was great, then I went to The Fleadh and I saw Ronan Keating do a fifteen-minute set, and I started to think, 'Hold on a minute, I could do that'. But before that I thought I could do a guest appearance with somebody. Then I thought, 'What the hell, I'll just do this,' so I'm gonna do it.

So that was it and I think it actually went quite well – I'm not a journalist y'know? I'm just a fan. Sure, there were other questions that I could have asked but I didn't have much time to prepare and it was about nine o'clock in the morning! I don't know if Kevin was taking it a bit easy with me (you know his reputation for interviews!), but I was a bit surprised and also relieved as to how smoothly it all went. Kevin seemed a bit surprised at the end - "Is that it?" I thought about saying 'That's all there ever was!' but I thought I best not!

Anyway, it's the day of the eclipse, y'know that special event to some people that only happens about once every seventy-years where the moon crosses the sun (and I had an excellent view from Marble Arch!).

"So, what you up to later Kevin? Be watching the eclipse?"

"I don't know, they say that you're not supposed to look at it don't they? How you supposed to see it then? Y'know me, if they say 'don't do it,' I'll do it... maybe I'll just look with one eye!"

During the party the night before, well-known music critic Johnny Rogan was being interviewed on the stairs, and it was quite interesting as to what he had to say. They had no objections as to me taping the tail-end of the interview. Here it is -

"The only two groups from the eighties who I respected were *The Smiths* and *Dexys Midnight Runners*. If you want to see what Kevin Rowland means then when you see him today, when he's promoting his new record, everything that sums up Kevin Rowland is there yet again, he is a man unto himself, he always has been, he always will be. He is the point essential character of Rock Music that I've ever seen. I think that one of the greatest albums of all time is *Don't Stand Me Down* and it will always be recognised as that. The tragedy was that when that record came out that people completely dismissed that record, myself included, they was so comatosed about it, and now everyone thinks that it's such a great record. And what Kevin is doing now is unbelievable, as it always was, and Kevin Rowland must be seen today as one of the most important things, in my mind, of the last twenty-years and if you don't see that then forget it."

- Johnny Rogan

READING FESTIVAL

Festival news extra

KEV BRAVES BOTTLES

Former **DEXYS MIDNIGHT RUNNERS** frontman **KEVIN ROWLAND** made his first live appearance for 14 years at Reading Festival last weekend, only to be pelted with bottles, cans and toilet rolls by the crowd.

Rowland took to the stage in a sarong and denim jacket and announced he would sing only three songs to a backing track.

The missiles started to fly halfway through his opening number, a version of 'You'll Never Walk Alone'. Then, accompanied by two female erotic dancers, Kevin whipped off his sarong to reveal a white silk mini-dress and stockings for his current single, a cover of Unit Four Plus Two's 'Concrete And Clay'.

The bottles continued and, during the final number, a cover of Whitney Houston's 'The Greatest Love Of All', Rowland was hit on the head and, visibly shaken, he stopped singing and said: "I'm standing here trying to sing to the best of my abilities. Who wants to hear me sing?" After a portion of the audience cheered, he continued, only to be pelted by an increasing number of objects.

Despite many comments that Rowland's act was no better than watching karaoke or a sideshow at a Soho strip joint, he remained defiant: "There was nothing indecent about the show. By the third one, when a couple of people threw things, I started feeling really uneasy and it got to me. I thought, 'How can I go on?' I had to say something because if I didn't, I'd just feel like an idiot, that I was being abused. I was standing there thinking, 'Kevin, you're a fool and you shouldn't have done this.'

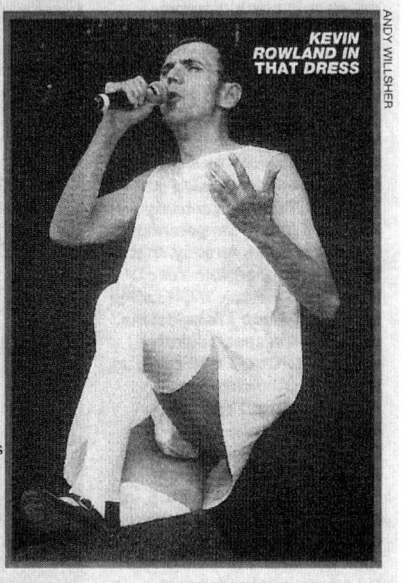

"But I realised when I said, 'Who wants to hear me sing?', there was a big surge in the middle *(of the crowd)* and I thought, 'Yes, Kevin, you did it.' It's so hard not to take it personally. But people do throw things at festivals, don't they?"

KEVIN ROWLAND IN THAT DRESS

ANDY WILLSHER

KEVIN ROWLAND: OH DEAR

The bottles start coming almost immediately. **KEVIN ROWLAND** walks onto a stage for the first time since the last Dexys tour in 1985, says, "I'm a nervous wreck," and begins the most bizarre 15 minutes of 'entertainment' we've ever witnessed. First, 'You'll Never Walk Alone' with a backing tape, and the wild bravery of a middle-aged man in a skirt singing glorified karaoke to a not-entirely sympathetic mob is quite, quite moving. He appears baffled, saddened and angered by the boos and missiles, that only multiply when he rips his skirt off to show a shiny mini-dress and stockings, introduces two writhing lapdancers, and sings 'Concrete And Clay' while licking one of their bums. As the song ends they're fondling Rowland and hitching up his dress to show his pants.

Next, a rant about not being played on the radio that shows that his blazing single-minded ambition remains. And then 'The Greatest Love Of All' – *"No matter what they say about me, they can't take my personal dignity"*. By then, of course, it's too late for 'them' to get anywhere near it.

It all reeks of tawdry shock tactics, but in a way it works, inevitably overshadowing **THE DIVINE COMEDY** as the traces of Neil Hannon's foppishness barely register in Rowland's wake. The deal here is simple: old songs = good; new songs = bad. Hannon behaves nowadays like he's trying to normalise himself, to make a presentably bland pop star out of a bookish eccentric. But, of course, it's not quite working.

Still, they're far superior to **FUN LOVIN' CRIMINALS**, men preoccupied with the concept of cool as only the profoundly naff can be. Now we can get a fix of funny mobsters – mercifully without the lumberingly unfunky funk-rock backing – by watching *The Sopranos*. Which makes Huey

WHOSE BEAUTY?

TITLE	ARTIST	YEAR	POS
The Greatest Love Of All	George Benson	1977	27
Rag Doll	Frankie Valli	1964	2
Concrete And Clay	Unit Four Plus Two	1965	1
Daydream Believer	The Monkees	1967	5
This Guy's In Love With You	Herb Alpert	1968	3
The Long And Winding Road	Ray Morgan	1970	32
It's Getting Better	Mama Cass	1969	8
I Can't Tell The Bottom From The Top	The Hollies	1970	7
Labelled With Love (I'll Stay With My Dreams)	Squeeze	1981	4
Reflections Of My Life	Marmalade	1969	3
Thunder Road *	Bruce Springsteen	1975	LP track
You'll Never Walk Alone	Gerry and The Pacemakers	1963	1

(* Withdrawn from 'My Beauty')

George Benson is best known as a solo artist, but prior to his own success, he was a session man and producer. He's renowned as one of the finest contemporary jazz guitarists in the U.S.

The Four Seasons were led by **Frankie Valli**, of course, and enjoyed two spells of stardom. Rag Doll is from their early 60s success period, when they had hits with Sherry Baby and others. The disco boom of the mid 70s saw Frankie and the boys rack up more success with The Night and December 63 among others, and you've all heard Frankie Valli, where? From the soundtrack to 'Grease' of course!

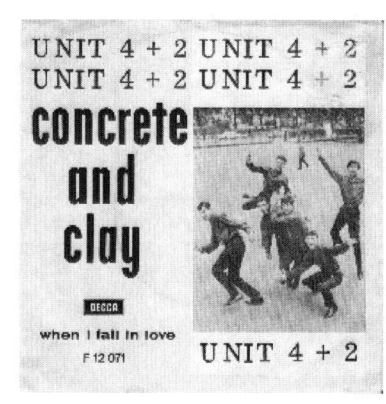

Unit Four Plus Two included Rod Argent in their line up. They failed to trouble the upper reaches of the charts again. Rod's band, imaginatively titled Argent hit paydirt with Hold Your Head Up in 1972, and had a later minor hit with God Gave Rock n' Roll To You.

I'm a believer, everyone knows about **The Monkees**, don't they? Even had their own TV show, which I used to get up especially for on Saturday mornings back in the 80s.

The initial letter of **Herb Alpert's** surname is the 'A' of 'A&M', the record company whose name is spat defiantly by Johnny Rotten at the end of album track 'EMI'. Herb and his band Tijuana Brass, had instrumental hits with Spanish Flea and Tijuana Taxi prior to this laid-back ballad from 1968. Aberdeen's premier soul cover band, The Jive Bombers, have a horn section called Marijuana Brass, in some sort of tribute. Marijuana? See any pattern here?

Ray Morgan? To the surprise of many, The Long And Winding Road was not a hit single for The Beatles. Although a Lennon/McCartney composition this was actually a minor hit for the man in question. Its status as McCartney's swansong was cemented only after Phil Spector had been brought in to make some sense of the box of tapes that comprised the output of The Beatles final sessions. 1970s Let It Be was the result. Sir Paul has not spoken to Phil Spector since, feeling that he overproduced the material given to him by the other three. Who's Ray Morgan? You may well ask.

Mama Cass, nee Cass Elliot, was one of the heavenly-voiced quartet that was The Mamas and The Papas (Monday Monday, Creeque Alley, California Dreaming). It may have been Kevin's old chum Danny Baker who claimed that two rock n' roll deaths might have been avoided had an anorexic Karen Carpenter eaten the sandwich that Mama Cass choked on.

The Hollies, in my book, are forever associated with saccharin pop like Jennifer Eccles, Carrie Anne, Bus Stop and so on. Those were the early hits. After the departure of Graham Nash (to CSN/CSNY), latter period hits like I Can't Tell The Bottom From The Top proved that there was a bit more substance than first impressions told. The Air That I Breathe, He Ain't Heavy and Long Cool Woman In A Black Dress are testimony.

Squeeze snuck out of the South London post-punk woodwork once the initial amphetamine and solvent driven energy buzz had given way to songs and craftsmanship. Difford and Tillbrook and pals never made it to the top of the Premiership, but have always been handily placed to turn out flawless performances. Their songs get better and better. I recommend Cold Shoulder and Some Fantastic Place from their later canon. Perhaps Kevin would like to...?

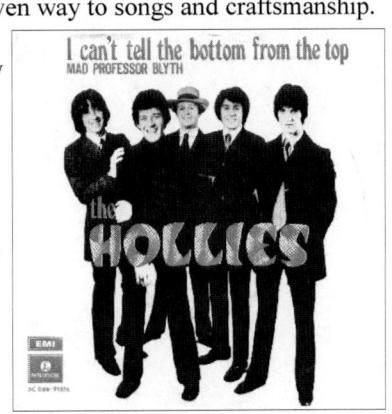

Marmalade, probably most notorious for hitting the upper reaches with pap like Ob-La-Di, Ob-La-Da, but there was a more serious side to the golden-hearted Jocks. Reflections Of My Life and 1973 rocker Radancer gave some deserved cred to a previously-maligned outfit. And why is marmalade not just called 'orange jam'? Apparently it was given its name when Mary Queen of Scots was a girl living in the French court. When she was ill one day (Marie Malade), she was cheered up by having orange jam on her Hovis. Probably.

Thunder Road, eh? (For those fortunate enough to hear it!) Is from **Bruce Springsteen's** 1975 album Born To Run, its widescreen homage to blue collar American life is as typically Bossular as it gets. No facts needed about Bruce, but a great story once told by Billy Bragg as a link between songs: "I was playing in a little club in New Jersey and the rumour is that Bruce Springsteen is in the building. I was quite excited. After my set, I was taking a slash when Bruce came in and stood next to me. 'Great songs, Bill', he said, 'But what about writing about cars?' So I took his advice. This one's called 'From A Vauxhall Velox'."

Does You'll Never Walk Alone need any introduction? We all know it's a show tune from Carousel given the **Pacemakers'** treatment, later adopted as a terrace hymn by fans of the editor's favourite team. Pink Floyd sampled the Kop giving it the full Otis for one of their albums (answer anyone?), and it was used as a fundraiser following the Hillsborough tragedy in 1989. A sweet silver song. Sung like a lark by Good Old Kevin.

David Innes

The Boss Says "No"

Springsteen nixes Kevin Rowland's Thunder Road "interpretation".

Bruce Springsteen has refused to allow Kevin Rowland to release a lyrically-adapted version of Thunder Road, despite a personal letter from the 45-year-old singer introducing himself and asking for permission. As a result, the track was pulled from Rowland's solo album, My Beauty, at the last minute.

Bruce Springsteen

18 August, 1999

Dear Bruce,

My name is Kevin Rowland. I was in a group called Dexys Midnight Runners who had a hit with "Come On Eileen" in '83. I've covered "Thunder Road". I've done an album of songs that helped me out of my drug addiction. I've been completely free from drugs for nearly six years now. I'd done "Thunder Road", because it helped me in my early recovery. I've sung each song to myself, visualising myself at different ages as I sung. This was the greatest thing I could give myself. In order to communicate truthfully, I changed words where they didn't fit my own experience and I've changed a few on "Thunder Road". All of these songs are completely relevant to me. I needed to sing them. It's not a cash in, it's my story told through these songs. These are my interpretations, how I hear them.

Please allow me to sing this song, my way. I love your version but this is my version. I was told your management won't allow me to have it on the album as it stands. But I can't change it. I makes artistic sense as it stands to me. Please listen to it and listen to your heart.

Best Wishes,

Kevin Rowland

ALBUMS

Soul model

Rowland: aiming for the heavens

KEVIN ROWLAND
MY BEAUTY
Creation ★ ★ ★ ★ ★
Long-lost Dexys' leader returns with show-stopping covers collection

KEVIN Rowland claims these songs showed him his definition of beauty, that he needed to record them before he could do anything else. They're not "covers" to him: he feels he's lived inside every line (he's altered several lyrics to make them even more personal). True soul singers do this, make the clay their own. When you hear his delivery of certain phrases, you'll understand.

Learning to love and stop punishing himself has been a convoluted process for Kevin, whose previous self-destructive tendencies and obsessive traits have been well documented. Drugs and depression stole several years of his life; making this record has blessed the last few. He's back, and this is big. People may focus on the clothes; I'm going to talk about the music. I was fortunate enough to hear this in March, before the photographs became a talking point. It made my heart burst then, and it does now.

Those of us who feel Dexys made the most richly passionate records this country has produced since the Seventies naturally have high hopes for Kevin's comeback. Rest easy: he aims for the heavens here and strikes sparks off them. *My Beauty* is a grandstanding masterpiece of confessional crooning, as epic and luxurious in execution as it is ambitious in intent. It proves that lo-fi doesn't equal truth any more than cynicism equals suss. Get that orchestra in! Get those choirs in! Then sing like a god, like the only singer who counts . . .

After an initial flurry of disorientating whispers and shouts from deep within Kevin's psyche (*"Remember that time;" "Fuckin' heavy, ain't it?", "Forget it, baby"* and even *"Mum!"* trip over each other: this is no everyday opening), Fiachra Trench's gorgeous strings swoon in and "The Greatest Love Of All" begins, spoken at first. Then, everything *whooshes*, and *"I decided long ago, I didn't wanna walk in anyone's shadow"* is sung with such startling conviction it takes two layers off your skin. Kevin sets out his new manifesto here: he was in a lonely place, but, no matter what, he'll live as he believes and they can't take away his dignity. In context, the corniest songs can be revitalised. Not with irony, nor with piety, but with that rarest, most radical of qualities: unqualified sincerity. The same bristling pride infuses "This Guy's In Love With You", "The Long And Winding Road" and "You'll Never Walk Alone".

In a nine-minute assault on The Four Seasons' "Rag Doll", Rowland lends umpteen layers of meaning to *"One day you'll be understood"*, before introducing an endless refrain of the word *"shine"*. *"A beautiful choir,"* he tells us/her/whoever, *"and they're all singing for you. That's yours. Belongs to you. It's great. It's telling the truth and the word. It's over – the bad stuff's over. Here we go . . . "* Devotees of the let-me-testify Dexys set-pieces will be licking their lips already . . .

"Concrete And Clay" and "Daydream Believer" are pop's charms in clover; "It's Getting Better" relishes in *"Once I believed that when love came to me/ it would come with rockets, bells and poetry."* "I'll Stay With My Dreams" is Squeeze's "Labelled With Love" transformed into a long dark cocaine night, while Springsteen's "Thunder Road" is strangely shorn of Americana. The production and musicianship throughout are sublime (Hubbard and Newmark, of late Roxy, among others, have the deftest touch), while the vocals are always on a pitch of controlled intensity seldom heard in the Nineties.

The unlikeliest sources provide the platform for perhaps the two pinnacles. The Hollies' "Can't Tell The Bottom From The Top" becomes on-your-knees gospel (*"How do I feel? I don't know! I just can't go on . . . just fuckin' confused. y'know? With fear, and . . . "*), while Marmalade's "Reflections Of My Life" is granted incredible profundity (*"The world is a sad place, a mad place, an awfully hard place to live – oh, but I'm afraid to die"*). We'll see the mountains tumble before Kevin Rowland does something conventional or predictable, before he ceases to confuse, enlighten and inspire. I'll play this record for the rest of my life.
Chris Roberts

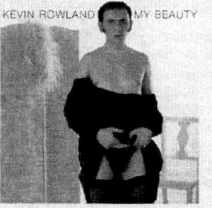

KEEP ON RUNNING
ISSUE 15 APRIL 2000

"You to me are sweet as roses in the morning

And you to me are soft as summer rain at dawn

In love we share that something else

The sidewalks and the streets

The concrete and the clay..."

CONCRETE AND CLAY – KEVIN ROWLAND (1999)

MY BEAUTY

A mixed bag of reviews, "a commercial disaster," and one of the top albums of the year! KOR looks back on the year that was...

"A Commercial Disaster"

Alan McGee stands by Kevin Rowland after pathetic album sales.

Kevin Rowland's comeback album, My Beauty, has become one of the year's biggest disasters after failing to reach the Top 200 during its first two weeks of release. One leading retailer has sold only 13 copies of the album nationwide. Based on the chain's market share, Q estimates the L.P has sold less than 500 copies.

Rowland's label boss, Creation Records' Alan McGee, told Q "I don't give a fuck if it's a commercial disaster because it's one of the most beautiful records I've ever been involved in. It is difficult for Kevin. I think the problem is the image. It probably is difficult to buy if you're a heterosexual male, but that's their problem, not Kevin's."

Did YOU buy My Beauty? Did you like it? Or not? We want to hear from YOU. Send your views to Q marked "The People Vs Kevin Rowland".

McGee and Rowland: money scores another victory over sense?

Music

Preview

TV hell

Kevin Rowland shows us his beauty.

Oh Lord. *Why* did I volunteer for this? As you are no doubt aware, the former leader of Dexys Midnight Runners has made a comeback which involves dressing in slutty women's clothing, giving self-flagellating interviews about his drug and poverty hell, and covering MOR songs that 'showed me my definition of beauty'.

Since hearing the 'My Beauty' album, I've been drowning in a well of Kev confusion. Half of me remembers the impact Dexys had on my youth, respects the integrity of his motives and wants to give thanks for some good old-fashioned 'ridicule is nothing to be scared of' pop star behaviour. The other feels that one of my heroes is humiliating himself in a misguided quest to reclaim his self-esteem, and

> 'Someone from his record company should stop him before he loses every shred of dignity.'

that someone from his record company should stop him before he loses every shred of dignity. I hadn't made a decision until I read the reports and saw the pictures from his recent Reading Festival appearance. A middle-aged man in make-up does a couple of songs before bringing on two young girls to cavort around him in cheap lingerie. He kneels on the floor and, tongue waggling like a beached cod, simulates licking one of their arses. So much for a 'definition of beauty'.

But, no matter how many dimensions and complexities any record arrives with, it is basically asking you to part with cash for music you will enjoy listening to, hopefully more than once. On that level, we can immediately dismiss a whole set of songs – 'You'll Never Walk Alone', 'Daydream Believer', 'Concrete And Clay', 'The Long And Winding Road' and 'This Guy's In Love With You' – because songs so overexposed can only be covered by investing them with something new musically, which Rowland doesn't or can't. Moreover, Bacharach tunes like 'This Guy…', need a crooner's technique to negotiate their subtleties, which is why all the versions you remember are by great interpretive singers. Rowland, for all his unique and passionate pop-soul strengths, is not any kind of interpretive singer.

It's the horrifying 'Songs Of Praise' choir at the beginning of the Four Seasons' 'Rag Doll' that provides the most extreme example of the album's major problem. Like everything here, the musicians play like a cross between the Ronnie Hazelhurst Orchestra and the cabaret band at your cousin's wedding reception. This, no matter the choice of the song or the standard of the singing, is *bad music* – trebly, leaden and almost laughably twee.

Opener 'The Greatest Love Of All' is the album's only real triumph, or the album's most embarrassing disaster, depending on how much you hate the George Benson/Whitney slush-fest in the first place. On one hand, the wince-inducing 'Mum! Fuckin' heavy ain't it?' spoken-word intro, the saccharine arrangement, and Kev's nasal vowels. On the other, the genuinely moving sincerity Rowland brings to a set of pseudo-religious platitudes. He really seems to believe that, not only is learning to love yourself the greatest love of all, but that no one has ever really thought about it before.

In fact, Kevin transforms a couple of sow's ears into silk purses. The Hollies' 'I Can't Tell The Bottom From The Top', with its Beatles strings, funny/sad ad libs and disconcerting blend of jaunt and angst, is almost in 'Don't Stand Me Down' territory. And on Marmalade's 'Reflections Of My Life', Kevin again invests another banal song with an almost beautiful pathos, even if the backing does keep reminding you of the theme from 'Red Dwarf'.

But the clincher is 'Labelled With Love (I'll Stay With My Dreams)', the Squeeze country pastiche with lyrics changed to describe Kev's descent into cocaine hell (but with gender unaltered). So desperate is he to chronicle the details that rhyming and scanning are dismissed. And it works, in an odd way, not allowing you to turn away from the uncomfortable picture that's being thrust in your face. But, yet again, it's an overfamiliar tune with a Daniel O'Donnell arrangement, turning something designed to be harrowing and cathartic into something unintentionally funny. And there lies our path through the bullshit. Because bad music can be just as powerful, in its way, as good; it perverts the most noble of sentiments.

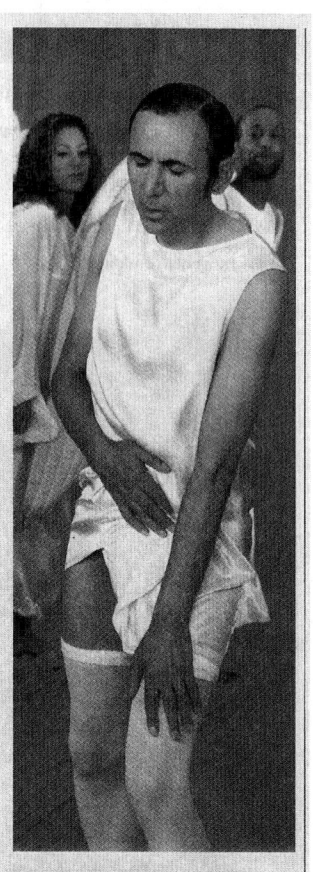

Still, it must be *sooo* exciting for the record company to encourage the follies of such a *crrrazeee* guy! Let's hope they remain as enthusiastic when 'My Beauty' bombs, and Kevin Rowland realises what he's done to himself in public. *Garry Mulholland*
'My Beauty' is released on Mon Oct 11 on Creation.

Old boots and panties

The songs that make him feel like a natural man, the clothes that make him "feel sexy". By **Glyn Brown**.

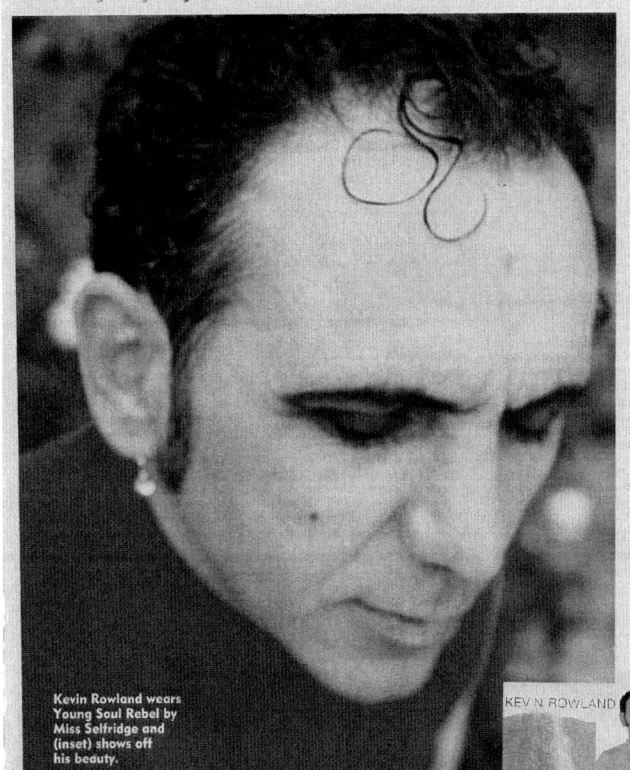

Kevin Rowland wears Young Soul Rebel by Miss Selfridge and (inset) shows off his beauty.

Kevin Rowland
My Beauty CREATION

Eleven years away, he's been bankrupt, coke-addled and label-free. He's back. And showing his knickers.

KEVIN ALWAYS was one for image. We had the Mean Streets look when he was a young soul rebel. We had the gypsy string-vest look of Too-Rye-Ay days. He's been on a few peregrinations since then. According to recent interviews, he's been troubled for ages; now he's finally embracing something he'd hidden deep inside. The manifestation of it... well, he's plucked his eyebrows, shaved his legs (how else do those elasticated stockings stay up?) and, though he says he's not gay and he's not a transvestite, he refers to himself in at least one track here as "she".

This comeback album, first of a three-record deal, is a set of covers, mostly '60s and '70s classics, certain words of which have been radically changed so everything now pertains to Kevin. Some songs are very good indeed – a slowly jazzy This Guy's In Love With You, a warm and sexy take on the Cass Elliott hit It's Getting Better; others are karaoke atrocities – The Long And Winding Road with its chug-a-chug syncopation, Rag Doll's cheesy, Mike Sammes Singers choir, I Can't Tell The Bottom From The Top, featuring Kevin crying.

Musicality, though, is almost a side issue. From any angle, this looks like a man still clawing his way out of a breakdown. There are frequent whispers of reassurance ("It's OK, it's OK. Bad stuff's over now"), which are either self-indulgent or, if they're earnest, appallingly tragic. And any moments of unintentional humour (Daydream Believer's "homecoming queen" takes on a whole new slant) get wiped out by a harrowing new version of Squeeze's Labelled With Love. Between hiding under the sheets and sniffing coke, our heroine (for it is he) is "a frightened old witch/With pure panic she shivers/Sweats like a pig/And the neighbours she sickens". So: unwise, on the whole, or very brave? Too self-revealing, or necessarily cathartic? Music was never such therapy.

Some words with Kevin Rowland.

How did the deal with Creation come about?
"I'd met Alan McGee in about 1992, and we talked about doing something, but we didn't. I bumped into him again in the summer of '95. I'd had the idea for this record, but I was umming and ah-ing. Alan said, 'Are you feeling like you wanna do music yet?' And I said, Not yet, no. He said, 'When you do, give me a shout.' Six months later, I called him."

Why return, after all this time, with covers?
"Yeah, I know. I'd already written new stuff – I got signed on my own material, that's the next album. But I had to make this one first. Why? These tracks comforted me, they seemed pure, and it felt like the right thing to do. This album's as relevant and personal as anything I've done, and every one of the songs, in my new awareness, brought a tear to me."

New awareness? Was it a feeling of confidence?
"Quite the opposite. It was an awareness that my life was completely fucked up, and it had to change. I didn't like the way I was, and I didn't like how closed down I'd become: my world was just minute. This is about opening up, really. I still keep closing down, but you have to keep pushing yourself. I had a voice coach, too, because my voice was shot away, it was tiny. And it's always a struggle with nerves for me: you get tense, your voice closes up."

You've altered lyrics to make them personal and at times you sound like a man *in extremis*. Were you attempting to exorcise something?
"I just needed to put it all down. Everything that's happened to me is in there – happiness, too. I'd sung every song to myself, at different ages, so on the first track, The Greatest Love Of All, I was talking to me in 1990. I was pretty ravaged at that point. Rag Doll – that's me as a kid. Up to Labelled With Love – a period of disaster. And then finally, change."

Your new look seems to have upset some.
"What, the macho geezers who used to like Dexy's? I've had a lot of this, and it's terrible. People wanted me to come back as I was 10, 15 years ago – certainly not as I am now."

Some people wonder if you've cracked up a bit.
"Is that what they're saying? (*Slight sigh*) Yeah, but you're right, I've noticed it myself. It's wearing me down, to be honest. But I don't know what it all means – I haven't got a fucking clue, and I'm sick of trying to analyse it. Now I feel fucking worn out, actually (*resigned laughter*). But I made the record, I did what I needed to. And I'm pleased with it."

Kevin Rowland
My Beauty
(Creation)

The body of the corrupt cop sinks slowly into the mire of trash and slime. "He was some kind of a man..." intones Marlene Dietrich, "what does it matter what you say about people?" The close of Orson Welles' *Touch Of Evil*, it's a plea for generosity of spirit, for recognition of mankind's resilience in the face of doom.

"*No matter what they say about me/ They can't take my personal dignity*", sings Kevin Rowland on his cover of 'The Greatest Love Of All'. You hope he's right, because this is no quiet plea, no everyday flaw. This is someone who still sends grown men starry-eyed and giddy, who has made his comeback amid satin, suspenders and no little mockery, who has chosen to bend his talent to some of the most overplayed, contempt-breeding songs on the planet. He's down-scaled his search for the young soul rebels to a quest for his own place in the world, producing a record that's poignantly addictive, troubled and troubling.

However you see it, the fact remains this is a collection of songs that the semi-mythical Dexys Midnight Runners frontman claims helped him regain his sense of self after years of substance abuse and mental dereliction. Never mind that tunes like 'The Long And Winding Road' and 'You'll Never Walk Alone' are more often linked with pushing people over the edge in nasty lift muzak incidents, the whole concept is akin to rifling through the minutes of a self-help circle. Rowland still inspires the sort of goodwill that could be banked in offshore accounts, and nobody would doubt his right to make this record. Whether it should be released for widespread consumption is another matter. The unease just grows.

Sure, he often sings beautifully, even making the ghastly Jonathan Livingston Seagull nonsense of 'The Greatest Love Of All' perversely brilliant in a 'Hey! Let's do the show right here!' kind of way. Fleeting moments glint with the legendary steel; the scared muttering that starts the record, the melodic coughing on 'Daydream Believer', the sudden vocal clutch at the end of 'Concrete And Clay' – yet unless you have a Val Doonican fixation, this LP could chill the fiercest ardour.

Never meet your heroes, runs the advice, for they can only disappoint you. Never patronise them, either, for both sides deserve better. Whether noble failure or tragic relic, 'My Beauty' is the sound of a collapsing perspective, a judgement shattering.

But what does it matter what you say about people? Kevin Rowland. He's some kind of a man. (6)
Victoria Segal

CROSS-DRESS PURPOSES

The Dutch know what they're talkin' about...

('My Beauty' review from Dutch daily-newspaper 'De Volkskrant', 28/10/99. Translated for KOR by Wim Bakker)

Kevin Rowland moves us with record filled with covers

After world-wide success in the early eighties with Dexys Midnight Runners (hits: Geno and Come On Eileen) it went downhill fast with Kevin Rowland. A widely acclaimed but unsaleable Dexys album Don't Stand Me Down and a flopped solo-record brought Rowland almost literally in the gutter. He became addicted to cocaine, unemployed and swore never to sing another note again.

We have Creation-boss Alan McGee to thank for the current comeback of Rowland, one of the greatest pop-singers of the British islands. McGee has invested a large sum of his fortune he earned with Oasis in 'My Beauty', but it seems unlikely he will see some of that money back.

Rowland does exactly what every marketing-expert would advise against. He makes a record filled with songs everybody knows (Whitney Houston, The Beatles, Herb Alpert) and he puts a portrait of himself in lingerie on the cover. Because, so tells Rowland, before he can write new material, he had to record the songs that tell something about him. The eleven songs on 'My Beauty' (For the twelfth song, Springsteen's 'Thunder Road' he got no permission) are sequenced in such a way, you can follow how Rowland regained himself.

In this context, 'Rag Doll' gets a whole new meaning and Rowland re-wrote a few lines from 'Labelled With Love', to change the topic of the song from alcohol – to cocaine addiction.

This makes this record interesting, but more important is the way in which Rowland approaches this album. He sings with a passion you'll seldom encounter. Much work has been put in to the arrangements; sometimes bombastic, but always just not too much. Rowland crawls into the songs and makes them his own in a way you could loathe because of so much vanity. But Rowland deserves admiration; in a time of fabricated marketing tricks, he dares to be himself. His 'This Guys In Love With You' is the most moving song that has been put on record this year.

The People Versus Kevin Rowland

The verdict is in.

Stocking filler: Kevin Rowland at Reading '99 and (above) as his fans see him.

Kevin Rowland has responded to Q's estimate that his My Beauty album has sold less than 500 copies after failing to make the Top 200.

"In answer to your article where you say My Beauty has sold less than 500 copies," he writes, "it sold 729 copies in its first week of release. Admittedly sales have been disappointing. I disagree with Alan McGee, image isn't the problem, complete lack of airplay is.

"The single, Concrete and Clay, received one solitary play on Radio 2, zero plays on Radio 1 or any other well known stations, and there were no peak time TV performances or showings of the video. Very few people can be expected to buy a record without hearing any of it."

Meanwhile, the postman has been grumbling about the high volume of correspondence received in response to our appeal to those who purchased Kevin's My Beauty. Among some 50-odd letters – some written in crayon, some enclosed with interesting portraits, but mostly positive – only the cover image of Kevin in a dress proved to be a point of discomfort. Matthew Priest from Dodgy also rang Q, explaining that he too enjoyed the album.

Here, then, is a selection from The People Versus Kevin Rowland mailbag. Verdict? The people like Kevin Rowland.

"My wife took the CD to the counter to pay and the guy shows it to his mate, waving it, saying, Look at this bloke in women's get-up. If I was there, I would've beat the shit out the fucker."
David Blake, Wellington, Somerset

"If less than 500 people have bought this record then that is a real shame, but I am proud to be in the minority."
Dave Nicholls, Birmingham

"When I went to my local branch of Our Price, they said that they had only taken delivery of one copy on the day of release and that they had sold it."
James Blake, via e-mail

"I knew there was a problem when my ears began to bleed."
Craig Mullin, London

"Kevin's version of Daydream Believer is my five-week-old daughter's favourite song ever, ever, ever."
Kevin Rota, via e-mail

KEV WINS!!

BIG JIM PATERSON EXCLUSIVE

Jim & Kev on the run in '81

WHY DID HE DO A RUNNER FROM 'MY BEAUTY'?
KOR FINDS OUT...

Dear Neil,

Thanks for asking me to explain my reasons for quitting the making of Kevin's LP 'My Beauty', almost half way through the recording. It's been almost two years since I walked out, and because it was such a bad way to end our working relationship, I feel justified in telling my side of the story.

I'm sorry to say that my reasons for leaving were nothing to do with musical differences. It wasn't because I didn't like my job or couldn't do it. Unfortunately it was because of the humiliation I felt on a few occasions when I was at the receiving end of some of Kevin's tirades. He insulted me once too often, so I reacted the way I thought was best for me and left. It's an indication of the state of our relationship at the time that he was not aware of doing anything out of order in the first place. I know it's best to sit down and talk things through, but we had already tried that after the first time I had to walk out because of impossible working conditions. We did manage to sort things out, and everything was going well and we were all enjoying it, but as time went on, things got a bit tense again and sometimes unpleasant.

I think I have enough experience and am a good enough musician to know that I was doing my job well and I was fully aware that it was Kevin's solo project and not a Dexys LP. I was always behind him 100% and also felt proud that he'd asked me in the first place. Being involved in something as big as that, working with Pete Schwier and all those brilliant musicians was nerve racking in the first place. I'm not a producer by profession, so a lot of things were new to me, which made the job even harder.

The final straw came when Kevin sat down next to me in the control room, having just done a lead vocal take of 'It's Getting Better'. He turned to me and accused me of not giving him enough support and letting him down. I managed to keep my temper but I got very angry and my first sensible thought was to get out and calm down, but he wound me up even more so I packed up my keyboard and left. The next thing I knew, I was trying to flag down a cab on the Fulham Palace Road with my keyboard stuck under my arm. I couldn't get one so I got the tube at Hammersmith and then had a twenty minute walk. It was a cold February day, but by the time I got home I was sweating and shaking like a leaf.

I just felt so hurt that he could have said that to someone who had joined the band in 1978 and was still there with him in 1998. I had been working with him on his LP for about two years, sometimes spending three or four days in Brighton, sometimes writing out scores for possible string arrangers, or parts for musicians for twelve hours a day. I was doing my best to make Kevin's record as good as possible. I really enjoyed my job and had the great pleasure of working with Pete Schwier who is one of the nicest people I've ever met. He's also probably one of the best at his job in the world. He was a true professional and showed incredible character under some terrible pressure. During the recording he also suffered from a personal tragedy and I only have the greatest of respect for him.

Before we had even started recording, Kevin and I both agreed that nothing would come in the way of our recoveries. In order for me to stay well, I have to put myself first, therefore when it came to a point when I had some thoughts of sabotaging my sobriety in some kind of desperate attempt to get out of the situation I was in, Kevin and the LP became a threat to me and I quit before things got out of control.

Kevin has said that he was being a "drama queen" but couldn't understand why I left, well I can handle him being a "drama queen" but I don't have to take personal insults as well. I may have over-reacted, but I have to think of my own well being above all else. Recovery is an on going situation, it never stops, so I have to have control over my life. I can't afford to let anybody use me any more. There quite often comes a time in your life when you have to say enough is enough and end a relationship which has become unhealthy. I deeply regret having had to come to that decision because Kevin and I have been friends for a long time, and we have made some great music together, but I feel he didn't show me the respect I deserved. He was given a chance to make a personal LP about his pain and the dark times he went through and I was more than happy to help him do that, but I was going through my own recovery, and have only so much to give.

I had almost walked out on another occasion. I had come back from my brother-in-laws funeral in Sandwell. My wife came with me to the studio, I didn't want to leave her on her own. I ate a lot of sweets, especially mints in those days, sugar can be a big problem when you stop drinking. I had only just stopped smoking as well, for about two months, so you can imagine I wasn't in the mood to be insulted. Kevin came into the room where my wife and I were waiting, he saw a bag of mints on the table and came over and smelled my breath. My wife and I were horrified by his insensitivity, she has been a good friend to Kevin for almost as long as I have, she has been with me throughout all my bad times, so knows about addiction. We both realise that you have to be single minded and sometimes ruthless to achieve success, but you shouldn't lose sight of what's really important in life. You just shouldn't do that to anybody and he of all people should have known that.

I am still angry as you may detect, but I can look back and say that I was right to walk away because you cannot reason with someone who is not prepared to see the other point of view or doesn't care for anyone's feelings. I took the addition of the words "when he got involved" on the LP sleeve notes as another little dig, two years was longer than most of the others involvement. I think he must have a short memory. If you add up the amount of hours I put in, compared to the money I was earning, it should be me who's moaning.

'My Beauty' should have been fun, it should have been a celebration, it's not every day you come back from hell. We did have some good laughs, it certainly wasn't all arguments and tension, and the thrill of listening to some of the best musicians in the country still made it an experience I will always remember with great joy.

I've bled for Dexys and loved every minute I was in the band, so I think I deserve a little bit more respect from a man who was supposed to be my friend. I'm not upset that Kevin got his deal with Creation with songs I co-wrote, I've never had a problem with that. It's just a shame that it's all come to an end in such sad circumstances. I understand the pressure he was under to make the LP, but it's all relative, every time he took it out on Pete and I, he made us feel like shit and put us under pressure.

This has probably turned into a character assassination but it's certainly not meant to be. I know you are a huge fan of Kevins Neil, and I think you have good taste in music, but unfortunately I came to a point in my life where I could no longer communicate with him, so I think it was in everybody's interest, and for the sake of the album, that I quit. It took a spur of the moment decision to walk out on that final day, but I

Jim and Kevin back in '80 in a sweaty club

177

carefully thought about my future and my recovery so I have no doubts that I have to look after myself first, and I cannot be there for someone to take his "drama queen" outbursts out on. Kevin is a Pop Star, I'm a musician, that's all right because that's what we chose to be. There is no way I can begin to understand what it's like to be a Pop Star, but I know what it's like to spend fifteen days in detox, then almost six months in rehab.

At the moment I'm co-writing songs with, ironically, Kevin's brother Pete and a girl from Coventry called Amee Panchal. She's a really good singer, looks great and has a brilliant character. I think she's going to be a star anyway, whether it's with my music or not, I can only try my hardest. I'm also practising my trombone again, I would like to get back to the standard I was at when I left college in 1977. I have a lot of things I have to do for myself now, I learned to swim aged 39, now my wife wants me to learn to drive at nearly 44. I'm probably more contented than I've ever been and I intend to keep it that way.

I'm sure that Kevin and I will probably bump into each other somewhere down the line and I won't ignore him, but I won't treat him as the friend he once was because I have lost my respect for him. Most of all, I'm sad that he didn't even mention my wife in the list of people who have been there for him in the past when he needed a friend. If anybody deserved a thank you on the LP sleeve it was her. She helped him as much as anybody, and I feel it is a snub because of our soured relationship.

I hope you understand my point of view Neil. I wish I'd left because we couldn't agree on a bass line or drum pattern, then I may not feel so bad about it all. At the end of the day he got his LP and that was the most important thing and when I did my job I did it properly. I can listen to it and say I am proud to have worked on it.

If this reaches you before Christmas, I hope you and your family have a nice time and I wish you all the best for 2000.

PS. The very first person to quit the band was Kevin and it was me who ran after him and persuaded him to come back, although I doubt if he had any real intention of leaving.

KEVIN ROWLAND
MY BEAUTY

New Album Released 11.10.99
Creation Records

*Issue 15, April 2000 was to be the last issue of 'Keep On Running'.
From there things went a bit like this...*

David Innes welcomes the long-awaited return of
Kevin Rowland and **Dexys Midnight Runners** in 2003.
(originally published in Songbook magazine 2003)

Awaking, in an untidy bundle of bedclothes and, undoubtedly, with a hangover - such were the times - my hand reached out automatically to switch off the radio alarm. I was awake and I had only seconds to hit the button and silence the babbling inanity of the DJ. Was it Noel Edmonds? Mike Read? Any other interchangeable 'zany' personality whose views, opinions and outlook I had no desire to hear?

But too slow, the next song had already begun. Strident sub-Memphis brass, impassioned singing and, through the medium-wave white noise, was that a mention of Laurence Sterne? Not what was expected on Radio 1 in November 1979. Finally, amid the banal chatter and grating DJ sound effects between songs, it was revealed that this was (barely-controlled DJ mirth) Dexys Midnight Runners' 'Dance Stance'.

I'd heard the name before. Weren't they on 2-Tone? This wasn't ska, was it? Only in future years was I to realise how close I had come to seeing Dexys in the flesh and at their most impassioned and raw. In November, 1979, I was privileged to be part of the beery, sweaty mob which witnessed the 2-Tone tour in Aberdeen, featuring The Selecter, The Specials and Madness. After their Aberdeen date, Madness left the tour having been signed by Stiff. The replacement act, from 15 November, two days after the gig I witnessed? Only Dexys Midnight Runners.

Then the press coverage began, aided by main man Kevin Rowland's uncompromising, contrary stance. Anti-music biz, anti-everything but Dexys own vision, articulated in the vitriolic energy-laden debut album *Searching For The Young Soul Rebels*. The close-knit gang philosophy, the single-minded belief that his was the most important act on the planet. Pretentious, some thought initially, including me. But suspicions of shallow superficial style over substance were forgotten when in interviews, Rowland and sidekick Kevin 'Al' Archer cited influences. Anyone, I decided, who rated Zoot Money's 'Big Time Operator' to be a lost UK soul icon, and had the chutzpah to take it on as part of his live show, was someone special. And the flight of second single, 'Geno', to the Number 1 spot coincided with Aberdeen's first League Championship win in twenty-five years.

Dexys aggression and passion-laden live shows, their venomous antipathy towards the mainstream music press, and their cantankerous insistence that not one other contemporary act mattered meant that column inches were filled with polarised opinion. Was Rowland and Archer's singular New Soul Vision artistic bluff or wholesale life commitment?

The start to finish full-tilt power of *Searching For The Young Soul Rebels* saw to it that a formidable army of believers in Dexys' manifesto was assembled. The debut album is as strong a rallying call to Britain's disaffected, disenfranchised young masses, suffering the first wounds inflicted by Thatcherism, as anything offered by the punk explosion of three years previously. The clever inner sleeve band biog and the cryptic notes against each song title served to offer reference points to supplement the Rowland/Archer twin-pronged vocal attack. Songs of alienation, isolation and frustration accompanied by the Blythe-Spooner-Paterson sonic brass attack makes *Searching For The Young Soul Rebels* as powerful a debut release as has ever been committed to shellac.

After further chart success with dilettante-baiting 'There There My Dear', Dexys suddenly split asunder, Rowland's seeming need to control all around him proving too much for all but Archer and the ever-loyal trombonist Big Jimmy Paterson.

As the dust settled, news filtered through of a change of direction. Rowland, always keen on style and image, but backed up with unswerving commitment to outstanding material and fanatically-honed playing, led his reconstituted Midnight Runners in a strict training regime, to cement further the gang mentality. 'And Yes, We Must Remain The Wild-Hearted Outsiders', the B-side of 'Liars A to E', itself an attack on the shallowness and parasitic nature of journalists, summed up the seemingly-deliberate distancing of Dexys from their contemporaries and the cosy incestuousness of the music world.

As the group (on-sleeve 'essays' denied that they were 'a band') adapted its stance but remained true to the vision, rumours circulated, backed up by tapes, that the sound was changing, although the signature brass frenzy was still evident in 1981's 'Show Me'. Rowland was now experimenting with strings and, as he admitted only years later, he stole wholesale the fiddle-based string sound being honed by the now-departed Kevin Archer.

Archer's fledgling Blue Ox Babes' nascent down-home rustic image was also an influence on Rowland, and with the release of single 'The Celtic Soul Brothers' in spring, 1982, the transition to gypsy chic had been completed. No doubt the adoption of this image was also in some way due to Dexys studied contrariness and desire to distance themselves from the style crimes of 1980s New Romanticism.

Too-Rye-Ay was Rowland's latest manifesto. Still searching for truth and strength throughout its song cycle, his approach was less strident. Where *Searching For The Young Soul Rebels'* desire to paint the new soul vision had seen vitriol and contempt as vehicles, *Too-Rye-Ay* was more reflective. Rowland was still in pursuit of his vision, but through purity of emotion, filial unity and inner strength.

Acoustic instruments dominate, with Helen O'Hara and Steve Brennan, credited as The Emerald Express, on twin fiddle attack featuring heavily, with sublime interplay between the strings and Dexys ever-present brass section. The difference in approach and emphasis did not obscure the umbilical link with *Searching For The Young Soul Rebels*. *Too-Rye-Ay* was just the next logical piece of the complex Dexys jigsaw. Such was its impact on me that I was impatient to get home from a holiday in Paris, number two only to Keith, Banffshire as the world's finest location, to get *Too-Rye-Ay* back on the deck.

Commercially, this was the Runners' zenith. 'Come On Eileen' was a multi-million-selling world-wide hit and that pop success has often obscured the musical excellence evident in this Dexys incarnation. 'Come On Eileen' is often bracketed with 'Hi-Ho Silver Lining' as a wedding reception singalong floor-filler. On its own, it is still a first class song. In context of *Too-Rye-Ay*, it is proof that Kevin Rowland possessed not only inspirational visionary qualities and an eye for distinctive style, but also had finely-tuned pop sensibilities.

Further success came with singles 'Jackie Wilson Said', the mellow 'Let's Get This Straight From The Start' and a re-release of 'The Celtic Soul Brothers'. Televisual highlights were a curtailed *Tube* session in November, 1982, and a feature in a festive show where contemporary acts played well-loved Christmas songs. Amid the predictable Spector covers, a family-friendly 'Mary's Boy Child' and someone's none-too-original 'White Christmas', Dexys take on fellow-Midlanders Slade's 'Merry Xmas Everybody' stood out. The *Too-Rye-Ay* line-up, augmented by The Brothers Justice (George Chandler and Jimmy Thomas) made the song their own. All Dexys fans I know have poorly-taped copies mic'd straight from the TV speaker and guard their copies jealously. Video copies are much prized.

Then there was silence. Throughout 1983 and 1984, there were very few snippets of news about Rowland or Dexys. Even though the *NME* had become self-indulgently unbearable by this time, we still bought it every week, in the hope that a scrap of information about a single, an album, a tour would be included. Our only solace was EMI's attempt to cash in on Dexys Mercury success by repackaging singles, B-sides and selected other tracks on the compilation, *Geno*. Apart from that, nothing.

Some, desperate for a fix of something as powerful as Dexys, looked for substitutes. The thumpy but thin singles by Jo Boxers never quite hit the mark. The Smiths quickly reached iconic status, but were merely a distraction, albeit with substance. The Faith Brothers, shouty, passionate and brassy, were lightweight in comparison with what Dexys followers were really waiting for. The Big Heat momentarily warmed me with their Elvis Costello-produced slab of soul 'Watch Me Catch Fire', but we were still waiting for the main event, for the visionary's return from the wilderness.

Initial lazy journalism invited Dexys comparisons with Poguemahone, although Shane MacGowan was dismissive. He correctly pointed out that Dexys were a soul act who had embraced Rowland's Irish musical heritage whilst his own band were an Irish roots band who had embraced the irreverence of punk.

In mid-1985 there appeared full-page ads in the press, of a be-suited Rowland, shorn of wild black curly hair, but no text, no information. Album release dates were rumoured. Release dates were extended. Production difficulties. Disagreements over the sleeve. Reluctance to release a single as a promotion. But only industry words. None from Rowland.

When *Don't Stand Me Down* landed, critical acclaim was not universal. Fans, however, considered it Rowland's finest effort yet. Again the themes were linked to the previous two albums. The search for truth, beauty and self-fulfillment. In delivery, there are passages of bewildering beauty, with some of Rowland's strongest-ever singing in evidence. The backing, much of it provided by respected session musicians, is crisp, direct and restrained and allows Rowland to express himself fully and impressively.

Don't Stand Me Down is a collection of striking contrasts. The brass-driven swagger of 'Listen To This' and passages of the twelve-minute *tour-de-force* 'This Is What She's Like' are complemented by the gentler, reflective country-tinged subtleties of 'Knowledge Of Beauty' and 'The Waltz'. Kevin's contempt for the shallow and superficial is still evident though as he savages the complacency and hollow emotions of his targets, the middle class peasants with their home bars and hi-fi's and the so-called socialista. "Still burning," as he admitted on opening track 'The Occasional Flicker'.

Kevin Rowland has admitted since that his personal insecurities prevented him from promoting *Don't Stand Me Down*, a work of which he is still intensely proud. There was no single from the album apart from a hastily-released extract from 'This Is What She's Like', and only a short UK and European tour before the silence descended again.

On a personal note, I was unable to realise my ambition of seeing Dexys live on this tour, but my new-born daughter was with me when I bought *Don't Stand Me Down* on 5 September, 1985, even though her arrival and early infancy prevented my attendance at any Dexys show. There was some compensation in October when Kevin led the band through 'Listen To This' and 'Kathleen Mavourneen' on *The Tube*.

Nearly three years elapsed before Rowland's solo album, *The Wanderer*, saw light of day. During that time, only tiny snippets of information came the way of Dexys expectant public. Stories of street fights with journalists and production work with Adam Ant were given publicity, but it seemed that Rowland was guarding his privacy ever more fastidiously.

Only the theme tune for BBC sitcom *Brush Strokes*, 'Because Of You', made it into the public domain and the charts. Desperate for any aural product Dexys-linked, some fans (okay, it was *me*) even bought Tanita Tikaram's debut album which featured Helen O'Hara on fiddle. Recognising similar Rowlandesque passion in their refusal to compromise, Dexys fans also seized upon the recordings and the frenzied live shows of The Proclaimers, whose second album *Sunshine On Leith*, released just after *The Wanderer* in 1988, credited Kevin Rowland as an influence.

The Wanderer is a significant departure for Rowland, but as he has often claimed, his removal from the public eye for substantial periods means that we are not party to the gradual changes that take place in his outlook and craft. What Rowland allows us to see are snapshots, and often these are beginning to date in the lead time between recording and release.

The 1988 solo album was produced by Eumir Deodato, and his electronic influence is obvious throughout with programmed drums and samples underpinning some impeccable playing from sessioneers, although loyal lieutenants Billy Adams and Helen O'Hara receive sleeve acknowledgements. Rowland is in much more mellow mood, even avuncular on the single 'Young Man', taking in a Harlan Howard song and offering Jerome Kern's 'The Way You Look Tonight' as a bonus track on the twelve-inch release of 'Walk Away'.

The more laidback groove was no surprise to Dexys collectors who had feasted on B-sides, where Dexys explored simple structures and semi-autobiographical, conversational pieces. This was Kevin the crooner, the overt passion laid aside, but still working out and articulating his view of the world for those of us prepared to listen. Old habits die hard, however, and there is still a sideswipe at the rich in 'Tonight', although Kevin's contempt is spelled out rather than spat out. The Forrest and Heller remixes of 'Tonight' in twelve-inch format were a small concession to the times.

Once again, silence. No album-promoting tour, nothing after the album-derived singles. There was news of some sessions being recorded, but no releases. Rumours of bankruptcy abounded. Tabloid hacks picked up on Kevin's reunion with a daughter he had never met. Stories began to circulate about cocaine use and a slide into dependency and addiction. At one point, the man who had presided over a Premier League act which had sold millions of discs across the globe was rumoured to be claiming state benefits.

A brief reappearance in 1993 on a Jonathan Ross TV show showcased two songs from demo sessions Rowland was recording with erstwhile Dexys members Billy Adams and Jimmy Paterson and, although there was talk of a new album, nothing was delivered. The record companies, meanwhile, were cashing in on the absence of new product. A series of poorly-compiled Best Ofs and Greatest Hits found their way into the shops.

Much more welcome was 1993's CD release of a Radio 1 Newcastle performance from July 1982, showcasing the *Too-Rye-Ay* line-up in scintillating form. It certainly sounded better than my cassette version, taped straight from the medium wave. 1996 also saw the 1980-82 Radio 1 sessions made available, with Rowland-penned sleevenotes. It is a demonstration of the majesty of the Runners' early live performances.

It seemed that Kevin Rowland and Dexys were to be consigned to history, a footnote in the reference tome of ground-breaking UK acts, remembered by the shallow for hit singles, but revered by followers. Only a brief war of words between Rowland and the *NME* saw his profile raised at all during this barren period.

Some comfort was provided by the emergence of *Keep On Running*, a Dexys fanzine produced and edited by Oldbury stalwart and self-confessed Dexys obsessive Neil Warburton. It was heartening to find that there were many others (I would say thousands, but Neil would probably produce the circulation data) who suffered, like me, a nagging hunger pang in being deprived of Rowland's latest take on the new soul vision. It was also a happenstance coincidence that Peter Innes's *Fit Like New York?* appeared at the same time, containing practically the same memory of 'Geno' and Aberdeen's 1980 League win as my 'Reminisce' article for *Keep On Running*. We're not related, and up until the book's release, Peter and I had never met. Neil eventually tracked Kevin down in Brighton and produced a charming interview in the pages of *Keep On Running* as a result of spending a day in Rowland's company. Good old Kev. Good old Neil.

When Rowland finally made his reappearance, it was to promote his comeback album, 1999's *My Beauty*. He admitted in stark interviews that he had been at the bottom, largely as a result of cocaine addiction; that for months on end, he had stayed in bed shunning the world; that he had been close to suicide in his despair. His inner strength, however, a constant reference throughout his musical journey, had seen him find rehabilitation and the wherewithal to endure the withdrawal pains and guilt.

Alan McGee of Creation, always a Dexys fanatic, provided Rowland with a deal to record *My Beauty*, as well as the re-release, on CD, of *Don't Stand Me Down*. This re-release was, of course, greeted with critical hosannas and Kevin's own sleevenotes confirm that for Rowland himself, it was a career pinnacle.

My Beauty contains no new Rowland material. It is an album of songs that helped him through his addiction and rehabilitation. It is, at times, a harrowing listen as he articulates his pain through the songs of others. From the opening 'The Greatest Love Of All', through a jaw-dropping 'Rag Doll' and via 'I Can't Tell The Bottom From The Top' and 'It's Getting Better', Rowland makes the songs personal to him.

By the time he has re-written the words to 'Labelled With Love', replacing the subject's descent into alcohol addiction in Difford and Tilbrook's hit with stark references to cocaine abuse, and ended the set with 'You'll Never Walk Alone', the listener has been on a nightmare journey with the man, has felt some of the pain, but is grateful that the outcome has been successful.

My Beauty reviews were mixed, sales were disastrous and the 'Concrete And Clay' single bombed. How much of this was due to Kevin's comeback image of choice cannot be quantified, but it is probably safe to say that a fickle public were reluctant to buy an album whose cover and promotional material showed Kevin dressed in female clothing.

Perhaps this was not the wisest of images with which to promote a comeback, and there can be no doubt that the adverse crowd reaction to Rowland's subsequent short appearance at the Reading Festival, performing three songs from *My Beauty* was in no small way due to his attire. If nothing else, it showed that he was still independent of mind. That was always the way. Had it been any other artist, chances are that that might have spelled the end. Not for Kevin Rowland.

In summer 2003, to confirm rumours gathering credence, a Dexys tour was announced. Interviewed by various sections of the media, Rowland has poured scorn on the idea that this is another 1980s repackaged greatest hits cash-in show. This tour, he has said, will be a tour that re-evaluates classic Dexys songs which will be performed theatrically, using arrangements that bring them up to date.

Rowland is an artist who has constantly revisited previous material, questioning its relevance, and his back catalogue is liberally littered with Part 2's and Part 3's and re-recordings of songs. The 2003 re-appraisal is wholly in keeping with his previous way of working. The hits will be performed, but Dexys were always much more than those, and there will be new material too.

As I write this, two songs previously unreleased, but which have always been available to the strong devoted, will be tracks on a definitive *Best Of* released in September, 2003. One of these, 'Manhood', will be released in single format at around the same time as the album. The other, 'My Life In England', classic autobiographical reminiscing on Rowland's early life, will also be a single later in the year.

It is the 2003 tour, however, that has galvanised Dexys Midnight Runners' followers. For many of us, we are realising a twenty-year-old ambition. We will be witness to the man who has soundtracked a large part of our lives bringing the message to us again. London's Festival Hall show was sold out shortly after tickets were made available.

A corner of a Dexys website, named *Where Are You Going With That Suitcase?* after Dexys aborted early-80s album, has been set aside to allow fans to tell others which venues they will be attending. Old friends will meet and some will introduce themselves as Soul Brothers and Sisters of Scarlet for the very first time, having corresponded via sundry media for the best part of two decades. This will be a joyful celebration of devotion.

As the dates I am attending draw nearer, the CDs are ever-present in my car or on the system at home. The messages they bring have scarcely seemed more relevant. In a world where madness is abounding, Rowland's kind words, echoing down the years comfort me that the only way to change things is to shoot men who arrange things, that vendors of charisma have rarely been so busy and, for some, including my football team, their winning day was long ago. It's okay to be still burning, to get angry, to attempt to kick back against the dumb patriots, the purveyors of hollow sorrow and those who are secure in their habitat familiar. Emotion does not date or grow old.

That's why, when he takes the stage at Aberdeen Music Hall at the beginning of November, I will be closer to tears than I have been at any time since the birth of my children. The man, the band, the Plan is back. The time, the place and the mood is right, and good old Kevin's gonna be all right.

Truly my bombers, my dexys, my high.
Let's make this precious.
Like this ....

David Innes, 2003 *(Re-produced for 'KOR' with kind permission of David Innes and Dave White)*

'Living the dream...'
by Ian Jennings
('The Gathering 2004' programme)

I was in Spain when the dates for the Dexys 2003 tour started to come through, Andy 'The Kiwi' Purcell was frantic, 'What a fucking stupid time to go on holiday' was the general thread of his emails throughout my summer break. Tickets were purchased for several shows and plans were made. Without going into too much detail, certain events dictated that I needed time away from work which coincided with the Dexys tour... coincidence? I needed to get away from everything and the Dexys tour appeared to be the perfect therapy, so I decided to do the whole tour, every single UK and Ireland date.

For many years I harboured the dream of following a band on tour, being part of the 'gang'. I recall telling a work colleague once that if I could go back in time I would have loved to come across Dexys rehearsing back in 1978/79 and becoming friends with the band and subsequently joining them on tour. When Steve Spooner told me the tale of 'Tommy' I realised somebody had already lived my dream, 'Tommy' even lined up with the band on Top of the Pops 'playing' the trumpet!! One regret from the 2003 tour was that I didn't get to meet 'Tommy', or Darren to give him his real name, at the Coventry gig he attended.

Anyway, doing the whole tour was something I just had to do and so the long drive from North Yorkshire to Portsmouth started the adventure. Throughout the next twenty dates I saw many things, visited many places and met many weird and wonderful people. Apart from missing the first two songs of the Basingstoke show due to a a car crash, (actually I would have missed only one song but I was in the bar having a brandy and a pint at the insistence of the venues manageress who I had told about my mishap...), I witnessed every chord change, every stroke of Lucy's violin and every beat of Crispin 'The Pump' Taylors' drum, I listened to every word sung and every ad-lib spoken, I saw everything... but I'm no music critic, all I can say was that to me every show was different and equally enjoyable.

My tour highlight was definitely the time spent with the band. Due to my involvement with The Bureau reunion, messrs Paul Taylor, Pete Williams and Mick Talbot did their best to make sure that I was on the guest list every night which certainly helped with finances. Steve, who worked for the promoters, had great fun in putting my name down as something different every night. The first I became aware of this was in Aberdeen when I saw that I was listed as 'Ian McJennings'... Newcastle was 'Ian Geordie Jennings' and Leicester the rather grand title of 'Ian De Jennings Montfort'... there were others and probably some I wasn't aware of, Steve was a top bloke, really looked after me (and The Kiwi during his eleven dates of the tour). I was always made welcome backstage and a can of Stella was quickly thrust in my hand with The Pump and Mighty Mick Talbot in charge of the fridge on most evenings.

I enjoyed some tremendous evenings in the company of the band members in which I include Kris the tour manager. Kris and I enjoyed a love hate relationship during the tour, everywhere he turned I seemed to be there, I haunted the man!! However, we have stayed in touch and look back on the tour with great fondness. On the rare occasions when the band stayed overnight in a hotel you could forget rising early in the morning. Newcastle, Manchester and Belfast in particular were special evenings spent in a relaxed atmosphere with wonderfully generous people. My did the Guinness flow in Belfast...

The Belfast gig, although poorly attended, did bring about the funniest heckle of the tour, if you can call it a heckle. At the front of the stage a trio of young male fans were enjoying the performance when one of them shouted, 'Kevin, I want you to have my babies!' to which his friend responded, 'That's just fucking disturbing...', you had to be there, it was funny, trust me. One of them even stole the cushion which Pete dropped to his knees on during 'Until I believe in my soul' although this was quickly retrieved by The Kiwi.

As for me and The Kiwi, I suppose apart from stopping Neil KOR from falling to certain death after he jumped from the balcony in Dublin (that was a bigger drop than you thought eh Neil? Credit to The Kiwi though, he carried on filming the show as Neil was pulled to safety) the day and night spent in Milton Keynes was the most bizarre part of the tour. We arrived in this Americanised monstrosity mid morning after a sleepless night in a flat in Enfield after the London show and took our clothes to a launderette due to the grubby night bus journey through London the previous night (5am we both finally hit the pillow). The Kiwi found the shopping centre extremely disturbing, lack of sleep and the 'Logans Run' type look about the place freaked the hell out of him. To make matters worse he hadn't realised it was November 11 and so at the 11th hour the bells chimed and everybody stopped. The Kiwi lost it, not helped by a person continuing to walk whilst all around stood rigid.. The Kiwi simply shook his head and asked 'what the fuck is going on?!!!' It was a surreal moment... and this was just the beginning, the story of that night's gig, which was equally bizarre and ended with a text message to Pete Williams which read 'the Anzacs won the day,' will be left for another time. Won't even mention the whip Andy... not yet anyway.

So, for now, that was a short insight into my attempt to live the dream. I also flew over to Sweden to take in the Stockholm and Gothenburg shows but it had to end somewhere and the warm handshakes and hugs I received at Stansted Airport when it was finally over meant so much to me... I was part of the gang, I had lived my dream.

Dedicated to The Kiwi, Andy, two weeks of memories, a lifetime of friendship.

Ian Jennings (aka Kendo), 2004
(Re-produced for 'KOR' with kind permission of Ian Jennings)

Neil 'KOR' Warburton, Andy 'The Kiwi' Purcell and Ian Jennings, Dublin 2003

'Time to Reflect (The Greatest Love of All)'
by Neil Warburton
('The Gathering 2004' programme)

The New Year is soon upon us.
What a year 2003 was! A life-long ambition was achieved in October, after having the worst year of my life the previous year.
2003 brought me 'The Greatest Love of all', it happened in two weeks during October and November. 'Big G' had planned it.

Amsterdam airport (9 in the morning). Two men with 'Hold all's' enter Irish Pub, en route to Bristol (via Heathrow) - 'The Long and Winding Road' welcomes us!

Bristol Colston Hall (about 6pm) - 'The Doc'! Yates Bar - 'CRANNIE'!, the fab 'Brothers Grace, Mr Rose, Helen Terry...
We STORM the venue chantin 'Now that I'm fit to show it...'. Straight to the bar! Few more beers! Announcement! "Dexys Midnight Runners will take to the stage in 5 minutes." I began shaking, tears comin' to my eyes, I'd waited so long... a young bar person stood laughing, how could she understand? 'DON'T YOU KNOW HOW IMPORTANT THIS IS?' - I couldn't go in, I'd waited so long! I think eventually it was Wim and Crannie who pulled me in. I really would have been happy enough that night, just sittin' outside the door. 'The Waltz', 'Old', that was my Mother's favourite, a tear came to my eye. 'Let's Make This Precious', I had to get up now! "Sit down" I was ordered! After a brief argument with security I sat down - but only for about 30 seconds! Some nice girl (who were you?) came and took my hand and WE MADE A STAND! Now security had no choice as everyone stormed to the stage!
All these people singin' and dancin' to 'MY GROUP'! I'd waited years for this! Some waited for autographs after the show, I couldn't take any more! And the Brothers Grace pointed me out the nearest takeaway! I'll never forget that night.

Next up was Cambridge. 'The Cow' - www.dexys.co.uk! Dave Hill. Tales of 'Rag Doll' at New Years Eve parties! But it didn't compare to the previous evening at Bristol - subdued crowd. When they eventually decided to storm the stage ('Eileen'?), I rushed to the back! I wanted a different view! All these people singin' and dancin' to 'MY GROUP'! The beauty...
In the foyer/bar after show, I was introduced to 'Kendo'. He WAS my long lost brother.

Guildford 'Sports Bar' - STOKESEY! James! John! What happened to the 'hooded tops' we'd planned!?

Glasgow 'Station Bar'... Nah! It was only me and Wim who found it! EDDIEEEEEEEEEEEEEEE!

Despite countless telephone calls we had to meet at the venue! David Innes, who had previously helped me enormously with 'KOR', I met for the first time, and found that we were actually seated together! 'BIG G'! Myself, David and Wim, just practisin' steps and keepin' outta fights as 'Geno' roared! Never thought it would happen!

Newcastle. Enter Mr Peter Innes! 'KIWIDEX'! David was unsure if he'd make it, then came a knock at the window! ...Archie!
Later that evening... "I can't eat squid!," "Thanks for the beers though Steve!"

Manchester. Vinni! Old Bros re-united. Someone said something about finding a seat! "Anyone got any spare socks!?"

Liverpool. 'The Cavern'! Accidental meeting of what had now become 'The Brotherhood'. What a precious moment. 'The Ship and Mitre' - "There's Peter!" Avoiding security to sneak down the front to share precious moments with fellow brothers. "We know where we are" - Kevin Rowland. I ended up having the flag!

Northampton. 'Rat and Parrot' - two or three girls at the bar in Dexy chic! "Excuse me please, you're standing in my space!"

London. 'Mulberry Bush' - Anthea Turner! "You goin' to see Dexys?" I ask, "No, 'The Stranglers" she replied! Bunkin Boxes...

Dublin. "Meet you in nearest bar at airport!" 'The Clock!'...
"What's the room number?" Jumpin' the barriers at train station!
A tearful farewell to brothers who I had never previously met.

Take care all and never forget 'The Beauty.'

Neil Warburton, December 2003

Ian 'Kendo' Jennings (left), Vincent Cain (centre) and myself (right) with Kevin Rowland and fellow Dexys Lucy Morgan, Crispin Taylor, Mick Talbot, Volker Janssen and Paul Taylor during the 2003 tour.

Well known music journalist and author of over twenty books, **Paolo Hewitt** told his own Dexys story at the 30th Anniversary of Dexys debut album 'Searching for the Young Soul Rebels' in Birmingham at The Flapper & Firkin, July 17th 2010.

This is a piece I've written about my first experience of meeting the band. But first of all, I want to say this from the outset...

Over the years many stories have attached themselves to this extraordinary band, the band we know as Dexys Midnight Runners, but we should never forget one thing, that is the impact, the enduring nature, the strength and the beauty, of their amazing music. Without it, everything else falls apart.

That music still means as much to me today as it did back then. With that point made, let me now say this - "Ready when you are Mr Rowland." That was the opening sentence of my first ever article about Dexys Midnight Runners - "Ready when you are Mr Rowland." It took me hours to get that line right. I remember sitting in the kitchen in my small North London flat in February 1980 writing opening line after opening line, trying to get the right sentence to kick-start the article. It was highly important to me, I had to get the piece right. Dexys Midnight Runners have that kind of effect on you.

I first came across this extraordinary group on January 25th 1980 at the Camden Music Machine. It was an unforgettable introduction. They strode on stage like stevedores and performed like warriors. The music roared at you like an angry ocean wave. They really did blow people away. I would later discover that Kevin Rowland would insist that the horn section rehearsed without amplification and this idea certainly paid off. No one, at this time, could match their intensity nor those wonderful songs about desperation, confusion and isolation, all framed in the context of a new soul vision that the singer exhorted us to welcome. They looked brilliant as well, with their wooly hats, their white tee shirts, leather jackets, the moustaches, the heavy donkey jackets. Yet this was not a band that was seeking to be loved by its audience. That night it felt like it was this band against us and the world. The singer rarely addressed the audience, and when he did, it was to tell us to be quiet during certain songs. He never joked, he never smiled, he simply expressed himself as best he could. That was his only concern, to express himself as fully as possible.

I went home after that show on the Friday night and I knew only one thing - I had to write about this band. I called their record company, EMI Records, very first thing on Monday morning and I was given a plan - "Travel to Shrewsbury, see the band play, then join them on the train heading to Wolverhampton for the next day." I did as asked. Which is how, at about ten o'clock on the morning of February 5th 1980, I first met Dexys Midnight Runners. I found them in a train carriage, all of them pretty quiet.

I noticed Kevin Rowland sitting on his own, so I went and sat next to him. "Hi, I'm Paolo from Melody Maker, I've come to do the interview," I said. No response from Rowland, nothing, silence, he didn't say a thing. 'OK,' I thought, 'let's try another line,' "Good gig last night," I said, "We don't do gigs, we do shows," Rowland replied, as he carried on looking out of the window. I sensed the guy was a little bit hesitant, perhaps he figured all writers were out to get him. Fine, time to show him I'm a fan, time to show him I knew his music. "Nice scenery," I said, "but hey, thankfully not living in Yorkshire it doesn't apply." Rowland looked at me with a flash of pity and went back to staring out of the window. I'd run out of words, I'd done my best and failed. I stood up and went to the seat opposite and didn't say a word until we'd reached Wolverhampton. Two can play your game, I thought to myself. It was a tense journey, full of silence, this was not a band seeking to be loved, the irony being of course that today, thirty years later, they are loved with more intensity and devotion than any other band from that time and that decade.

Wolverhampton was reached and we disembarked from the train. There was a slight kerfuffle over the train ticket (I believe there were quite a few in those days), which left me separated from the band. As I came out of the station I heard a shout, I looked to my left and there in the distance was a band member motioning me forward, I followed him to the gig which was a short distance away. When I reached the Polytechnic, where the band were playing that night, they were loading their gear into the hall. Kevin had just grabbed this huge speaker when he said to me - "We can do that interview now if you like?" He later confessed to me that he only liked doing interviews at this time as it got him out of lugging the equipment into the gig. We did the interview in the dressing room and later in a cafe. We spoke about many things - soul music, principles, Ireland, ideals... Rowland was absolutely certain about his view point - this was this and that was that. "To write about Irish authors as you do in 'Dance Stance' is pretty unique," I told him, "No it's not," Rowland snapped back, "for us it's normal, not for other bands maybe."

After the show, another performance full of intensity, I found myself in an Indian restaurant with Big Jimmy Paterson and Kevin. As we ordered I told Kevin that I could never quite make out the words to 'Tell Me When My Light Turns Green', Rowland meticulously wrote out the lyrics on a small note pad which he gave to me. It was a telling sign of the seriousness that he attached to anything with his music, and before you ask I've lost the note pad! Meanwhile, Big Jimmy told me all about his favourite film at the time, Roman Polanski's The Tenant. I returned home and wrote my piece. Reading it back now, I can see that I was holding back my feelings towards the band's utter brilliance. I think this was due to my dealings with the band. I was not used to be treated so off-handily. Not that I thought highly of myself, it's just that bands were so grateful then to secure press coverage. To be treated differently created a barrier, a barrier that as their musical brilliance continued was broken down.

In August of that year Dexys pulled their master stroke, 'Searching for the Young Soul Rebels', had been released to great critical and universal acclaim. It was a stunning debut album that I loved and played constantly. The band had won huge acclaim for their tense live performances and a whole lot of press for stealing the albums master-tapes and holding out EMI to ransom. Yet that was nothing compared to the advert they placed on

August 6th in all the music papers, in which they claimed they had been totally misrepresented by the 'hippy rock press', that no one was able to understand them and they would now resort to their own means of communication. I went ballistic -

> 1. My piece may have been many things, but misunderstanding them, never.
> 2. Suggest I'm not up to the job. How dare you.
> 3. Call me a 'hippy'. That's fuckin' done it now.

I called EMI Records and the girl there told me that Kevin Rowland was actually in the offices right now. "What's he doing?" I ask, "Err... he's being interviewed." "HE'S BEING INTERVIEWED? BY WHO?", "Err... The Sun newspaper," she replied. Again, I went ballistic. "Wait there, I'm coming over," I said. I could not believe this guy, I mean 'The Sun' is reprehensible now, but at that time it was the devil's bible. And this was before Hillsborough. I rushed over to Manchester Square where EMI Records were and I strode into their office. Kevin had just finished the interview and was standing by someone's desk chatting away. He wore a white tee shirt and blue cotton drilled trousers. Looked pretty good, I had to say. "Busy" I say, "Talking to The Sun eh? Too fuckin' good to talk to the music press now, prefer talkin' to fascists instead eh?" You could say I was a little angry... "Perhaps we should go in this office" Kevin suggested. "So what's wrong with my fuckin' article?" I demanded, as we sat down. "Well..." he said, "you put in that stuff about us bunking trains, I didn't like it, it kind of made us look like criminals." "But you did bunk the train," I replied. "I know, but there are more important things." "Like what?" "The music" he replied and he was right, of course.

Over the next five years Dexys would release two more outstanding albums, deliver some of the best live shows I have had the fortune to witness, create brilliant new looks and come forward with so many radical ideas. They really shone and we know this because thirty years on, we are here tonight, brought together by one thing, the music of Dexys Midnight Runners. For all of us, it carries huge meaning and a place in all of our hearts, for whatever reason that might be. This music remains alive and vibrant and wonderful and will do so for ever and ever, amen.

Paolo Hewitt, July 2010
(Re-produced for 'KOR' with kind permission of Paolo Hewitt)

Paolo Hewitt with Kevin Rowland in 1980

DEXY'S MIDNIGHT RUNNERS
Music Machine, London

THREE guitars, three brass, one keyboard and drums and we have the ... Next Big Thing. At present Dexy's Runners may not have the repertoire that such an accolade presupposes, but as a live entity they're probably one of the loudest, strongest and most convincing bands currently treading the boards.

Straight from the kick-off they seized the audience with all the panache and swing of a band that just knows it's going places — and not for one moment did they let up. Saxes blared, drums rolled, guitars clicked, and ... hey, what we're talking about here is sweet, sweaty soul music, derived from Tamla and Stax sources, imbued with passion and energy, and delivered with an almost unnerving verve and precision. Their songs didn't just beg to be danced to, they grabbed you and made a *demand*. No-one could refuse, and no-one did (apart from the bores at the back).

Their set included "Breaking Down The Walls Of Heartache" (so much better than the recent Jane Aire cover), "Respect", which was given a corny big band treatment just the right side of being kitsch, and "Hold On", which the vocalist arrogantly asserted was the best version so far (and I'm not arguing).

More importantly, the songs that the band themselves have concocted prove that they'll be no one-hit wonders. "I'm Only Looking" displayed an impressive understanding of the soul ballad; "Geno", which looks like being the band's anthem, pays tribute over a strutting, sassy beat to the long-forgotten soul artist; and their criminally under-produced debut single, "Dance Stance", mocked vinyl version.

Of course, all the time comparisons with, say, Southside Johnny & The Asbury Jukes floated through my mind — given the onstage attire of bobble hats and swinging horn section — but for the first album (they've already turned down 2-Tone) it's essential that they're given the kind of instinctive production that Steve Van Zandt gave Southside's "Hearts Of Stone" or, better still, Robert John Lange's work on one of Graham Parker's finest attempts so far, "Heat Treatment".

It's understandably depressing that the bands currently doing the business are all harking back to the Sixties for musical inspiration, instead of wrestling with the sound of Eighties — whatever that might be — but to their credit Dexy do tackle some interesting areas in their lyrics. Their current single, for example, is an angry diatribe against ethnic jokes, especially Irish ones, which is more a Gang Of Four concern, if anything. Still there's not a lot you or I are going to do about it, unless, of course, you've got your own ideas.

In the meantime, Dexy are on their way. You are advised most strongly to attend. — PAULO HEWITT.

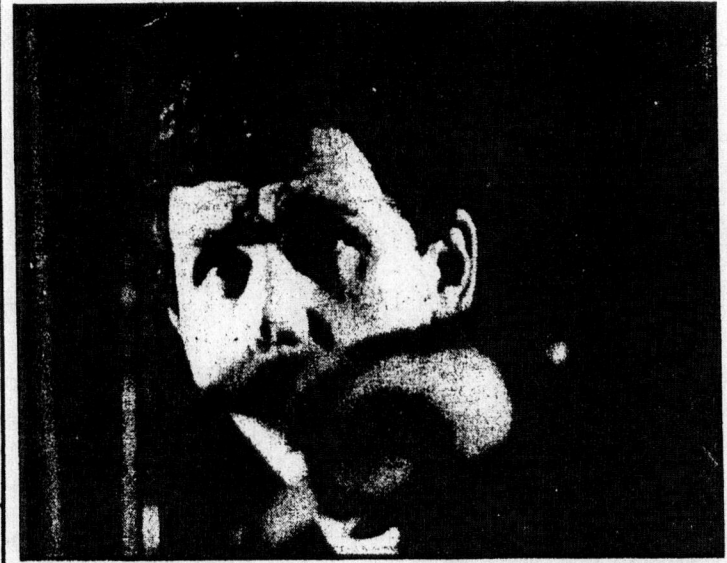

Dexy's Kevin Rowland.

The following has been written EXCLUSIVELY for 'Keep On Running' by Eddie Blower, who took the photo that appears on the front cover of Dexys debut single from 1979 'Dance Stance'. Eddie has been living in London for the past thirty years, but was originally from Bearwood, Smethwick in the West Midlands and was the keyboard player in Dansette Damage (1978 – 1981).

Before we started Dansette Damage in early 1978, I was a professional photographer and I had photographed The Killjoys at Barbarellas in Birmingham. By the time Dexys Midnight Runners was up and running I knew Kevin and Corky, who was helping them organise at the time. This was the time of the band's coloured suits. One night I went with Colin Hall (lead singer, Dansette Damage) to see them play at The Romulus on the Hagley Road in Birmingham with Joy Division supporting. The coloured suits, the soul music with punk attitude and the tightness of the band were in stark contrast to Ian Curtis and Joy Division that night, who sounded off the mark. Kev asked if I could take some photos of the band the following Sunday morning and I jumped at the chance.

I turned up with ideas of how to use all that 'colour with attitude' that was to be in front of my lens. Anyway we met at the Apollonia café on Broad Street, which has since been replaced by the hotel standing next to the Birmingham Registry Office. The band members arrived and they looked very different from the previous Thursday, with the beginnings of the look that would be associated with their first album and the 'Geno' single. The suits had gone! Kev explained to me that this was their new look and we had a quick chat about his vision for this new image and armed with his clear instructions, we started shooting immediately. He wanted a single flash blast straight into them, no fill, just as raw as was possible, which I of course found very easy to achieve! I didn't know at the time that one of the shots taken that morning in the rear of the café, by the pinball machines, would be chosen for the cover of the first Dexy's single 'Dance Stance', but one of them was. And what a great single it was!

However, looking back at the shot now, it definitely captures the new 'defiant' mood of the band, a look that would have been hard to create in the coloured suits, as great as they were.

We shot in a few locations that day, but the one I really remember was the ticket barrier jumping at New Street Station. I think this was Kev's idea (history may know otherwise), but definitely

The photo that later appeared in the music press taken by Mike Laye

not mine, as has been said by some over the years. But I do think this was the first time it was captured and it really worked. This was the end of the day's session and only about four of the band came down. Kev and Al Archer were definitely there, I'm not sure about Jim and anyway he could have simply stepped over the barriers with ease! The great thing was that the band members actually looked like they really wouldn't have a ticket (and they didn't - they practiced the shot by 'jumping' into the platform area!). What I remember was the genuine look of confusion on real Sunday afternoon passengers faces as Dexys just did it, just exploding from the crowd and over the barriers at a shout from Kev. They used this idea again a little while later, for a piece in one of the weekly music papers and the shot really worked for them and added to the public image of Dexys Midnight Runners not always playing by the rules, any rules! I still have my original copy of 'Dance Stance' given to me by Kev. I asked him to sign it for me as I was proud to have the photo that I'd taken appear on their very first record sleeve, and in his own inimitable style it proudly says "Crap photo but never mind! - Kevin Rowland."

I had one more small role to play in the Dexy's story. Kevin, along with Corky were on the hunt for a new keyboard player. If we timeline it now, it was for the "Too-Rye-Ay" line-up. With the money Dansette Damage made from the 'N.M.E' single we invested in equipment and I had taken on the role of keyboards, having never played a note in my life. I learned everything by rote and I used to have memory cards with me on stage! Kev and Corky came round to see if I was interested in playing organ and piano with Dexys and as I explained to them, if I joined, who was going to actually 'play' the keyboards to the level required!? They needed a real player and I knew the right boy for the job. A few years earlier I had been photographing a local Birmingham band called Stress and they had a great young organist who would entertain us at rehearsals by playing things like 'The End' by The Doors or taking requests for bits of Emerson Lake and Palmer etc! Now this kid could play and I nominated him to Kev and Corky as the man for the job. I think he was in another Birmingham band like Cryer by this point, but off they went to check him out and they got their man. So I retained Kev's friendship (as he would have soon tired of me and my keyboard failings) and Dexys got my excellent nomination, Micky Billingham, definitely the right guy for this period of Dexys!
Eddie Blower, 2012

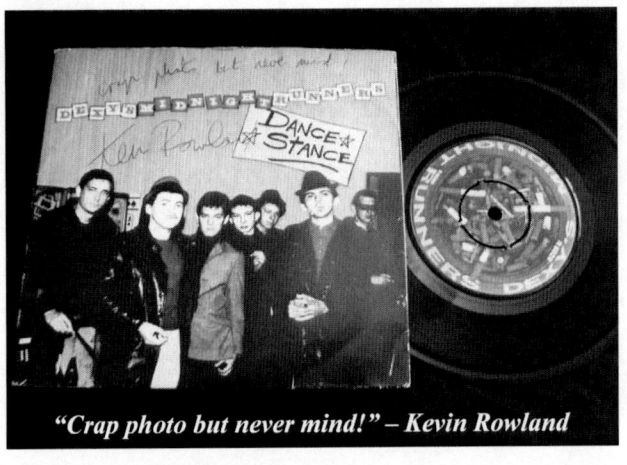

"Crap photo but never mind!" – Kevin Rowland

I first met Kevin in the late 70s (very early Dexys days) it's pretty well documented that Dexys had little to do with other bands but he's always taken the time for a chat, he came to see Dansette Damage and he told me recently how much he liked the band. I'm now working on new material and I also have a covers band called Rebel Soul (Classic Hits with a Dexys Twist) and when we met up recently Kev was well interested in Rebel Soul and liked what I was doing with it...
TOP MAN xx.
Colin Hall (Dansette Damage 1978-1981), 2012

I remember like it was only yesterday, buying Dexys Midnight Runners first single 'Dance Stance' when it was released, and from that very first hearing I was hooked. Then along came the band's debut album 'Searching for the Young Soul Rebels'. Never before had I heard such passion, emotion and honesty from a singer, who alongside his band clearly believed in every word he delivered. This included expressing his love of soul music and his burning desire to keep the scene alive. The band had the tightest brass section that I had ever heard, and straight away I knew that this band was truly something special. As Dexys evolved and grew, the fans grew with them, and many spiritually reached 'The Bridge' alongside Kevin and the band. Dexys took their fans to a whole new level, it was an emotional and passion fuelled journey. Like an old friend, Dexys records have always been around when you've needed them, and now that Dexys have reformed in 2012, that good friend is reinvented and home to stay.
Dexys are a true inspiration to many, let the magic begin once more ...
Andy Keys Clark (Solo-Artist), 2012

"When I look back on the sound of '82
There was a man and his band who knew just what to do
He searched for the young soul rebels and he sang with passion
His band was full of soul
and yes, yes, yes he wouldn't follow fashion..."

'When Dexys Ruled The World' is on the album by Andy Keys Clark 'The Prophecy' available on CD or download at Amazon.
https://www.facebook.com/andykeysclarkartistpage

The album photo to 'Searching for the Young Soul Rebels' was taken in Belfast, Northern Ireland, 9th August 1971. Featuring the picture of a young boy aged thirteen fleeing his burning home. Which was a number of houses set fire to by Loyalist Protestant against Catholic families in Cranbrook Gardens, which is in North Belfast. I discovered the next day in 1971 that the picture had been taken, when a neighbour who was in London seen the news on TV and the photo appeared in the London Evening Standard newspaper. It was not until 1980 that I found out that the photo was used for Dexys album cover. A friend of mine at work said to me "Your photo is on Dexy's Midnight Runners album." When I seen it I said "Yes, that's me." Then when I went into the record shop there was a cardboard cut out of me! I stood in shock for a few moments as all the memories of that day in 1971 came flowing back. The young boy on my left of the photo is my brother Kevin and second right to me is my other brother Gerald (half-cut out on album cover), the woman in the background is my Mother Kathleen.

As a footnote, I am proud to feel like one of the Dexys boys.
Anthony O' Shaughnessy, 2012

Dexys 80 for my coming exile: the Right band Right place, Irish anger in a post-punk new romantic England. A suitably implacable presence in The Little Nibble, Bearwood that was the first time I met 'em all, then Anthony O' Shaughnessy turning up in Europa post Ulster Hall gig with the Soul Rebels record shop display cut out of himself. 'Plan B', roaring outta 'Keep It part 2' breakdown, the (re)intro of the decade: those three boxing booted shows, it's too late for us clarifying the new soul vision to a keen fury and sanctity shows at The Old Vic. Totally into the ethos, RAN all the way from Bounds Green for the final one in the run. No ticket, just ran in the door. How did that happen? Fuelled by Dexyfied determinism, I guess.

And on and in through 'Eileen' n 'Too Rye Ay,' an interview which if I recall started with an unscheduled Van Morrison meet in Notting Hill and ended in MY bedroom in Bounds Green. The big beery beefy war-helmeted audience member at undersold Don't Stand Me Down show in Brighton there only for 'Vinnie Vinnie Vinnie,' Kevin coming to lip of stage to have words with him. What's that, what's that repeating part? 'Let's get this straight from the start': Even the long wilderness years interspersed with undersung greatness, 'My Life In England'. Always crucial, always different.

And in 2012 the story continues, take your Irish stereotype and... y'know, soar. This is a band for life.
Gavin Martin
(Music Journalist), 2012

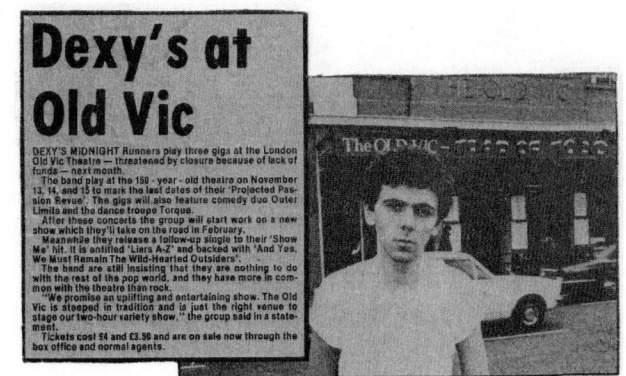

Special thanks to the following members of Dexys Midnight Runners who have written EXCLUSIVELY for 'Keep On Running'...

Paul Speare
(Saxophone 1981-82)

Paul joined Dexys Mark II in 1981, performing on the singles 'Plan B', 'Show Me', 'Liars A to E', 'The Celtic Soul Brothers', 'Come On Eileen', 'Jackie Wilson Said' and the album 'Too-Rye-Ay'. Although Paul left Dexys just prior to their huge success in 1982, he has fond memories...

When the late Phil Savage, proprietor of Birmingham's Outlaw Sound Studios, telephoned me at home one evening in December 1980, I assumed that he was about to ask me to play for a recording session at his studio as he had occasionally done in the past. But on this occasion he was recounting a brief history of a local band I'd barely heard of - Dexys Midnight Runners, who were regular visitors to his studio - leading to the point where they'd recently lost a number of band members and were looking for, among other things, a tenor saxophone player. Although I recall thinking that I'd be unlikely to be tempted away from my comfortable job as a woodwind teacher, things started taking a very strange turn and I soon found myself a full-time member of this unusual band, about which I knew little.

The events which ensued - as well as those which preceded and followed my own tenure of around eighteen months - have been documented enough not to bear further repetition. In fact, I have contributed to the telling of them at various times, perhaps a little too candidly. What is clear to me now is that, for such a short period, the Dexys experience was one which punched well above its weight in influencing my life. Joining the band diverted me from what seemed to be a predestined and unsuitable career in education (as I later found out when returning to that world for a while), and also gave me an experience of working with a group of people unlike any I'd encountered before, in a very insecure and challenging environment. This experience has helped me in so many ways since. I also learnt how recording studios work and something of the skills of music production. And it seems we even made some significant music in the process.

My time with Dexys ended too soon and I left on the cusp of the moment that the rewards for all our hard work were about to materialise. I've had regrets about that ever since, but the intense workload, coupled with the volatile personal relationships, and the fact that two of my closest collaborators - Jim Paterson and Brian Brummit - had left some months earlier, had all seemed to undermine my ability to function effectively. I looked for support in the hope of being talked out of my decision to leave but none was forthcoming.

However, all was not lost as I eventually joined forces with Jim and Brian as a freelance brass section and enjoyed a moderately successful career of recording and touring with other artists of the day, although it never felt that we were really 'part of something' in the same way. After this, life continued to develop in unpredictable but fascinating ways, probably because I'd learnt - as the current popular saying goes - to "Just Do It." Despite the intense pressure - and great disappointments - of being in Dexys, it's something I've never once regretted.

Phil Savage always enjoyed reminding me that he was responsible for my recruitment into this most unconventional of bands and I never felt inclined to disagree. However, I doubt he would ever have realised just how significant that telephone call turned out to be.

Now Kevin Rowland is back in the limelight - accompanied by Jim Paterson, Pete Williams and Mick Talbot from the early days - with almost universal acclaim from critics, both for the latest Dexys album and his live shows. Again, he seems to have found a unique approach to live performance which has caught the imagination of the press and the public. Hopefully he'll be able to handle the pressures that will come from this and find the personal rewards from success that always seem to have eluded him in the past. I wish him well.

Paul Speare,
September 2012

Dexys 1982, the dungarees were unveiled along with violins, and under Kevin's orders Helen Bevington became Helen O'Hara, Roger Huckle became Roger McDuff and Steve Shaw became Steve Brennan, and they would be known as 'The Emerald Express'.
"I can remember thinking 'thank God I didn't get the McDuff name'."
- Helen Bevington (BBC Dexys documentary 2000)

Steve Shaw
(Violin 1982-83)

KOR - "OK Steve, first of all, let's get this straight from the start..."
The George Bernard Shaw reference was a subtle way of putting across my real name being Shaw (I think?) - I remember my Dad at the time was quite narked that his work-mates had bought the Dexys single 'The Celtic Soul Brothers' and reminded him that the male fiddle player was named Brennan. Around that same time, one of my Dad's mates had a son, Steve Tong - and when he released their amazing songs with Roy White (White and Torch 'Who's Asking You'), he experienced the same difficulties at work too. Also, I have always enjoyed a good book/play with a gallon of Jacksons tea - what bliss - so there's some truth in the irony!

Steven Brennan
Steven Brennan describes himself as the "quiet, stop at home type". The young fiddler's idea of relaxation is to be tucked up by the fire reading a good play. It has been said he has much in common with his great uncle, Bernard Shaw.

The last time I met with Kevin Rowland was probably about three years ago, at a hotel in Birmingham. I remember he was making an effort at that time to catch up with people that had been in the group, as part of his recovery programme. We'd arranged to meet at the Hotel du Vin, sometime after lunch, as he was staying in Coventry, seeing his brother. Anyway, thinking back, he said to me, reasonably quickly and with clarity, "You only thought you were in the group because I lied when I said you were." As bizarre as this seems, it actually made some sense to me - as my departure from the group was pretty uneventful.

During the promotional work on 'Too Rye Ay', the group had become a core nucleus of five players - Kevin, Seb Shelton, Billy Adams, Helen O'Hara and me. That's why most of the group photos from that time include those people, and not so often the other players who took part, but were involved. Kevin told me it was down to his "own insecurities at that time" and he added that he "shouldn't have lied."

The first time I met Kevin was probably early December 1981, I was really taken in by his enthusiasm, interest, charismatic way and his clear vision on the sound our string playing would have on the group's new songs. He had a clear sense of the timbre or texture that the collaborative mix of brass and strings would make - and he was always really supportive in bringing this to fruition. We worked on it a lot - to produce a pure, simpler way of playing, that was the antithesis of the 'bel canto' playing style I was striving to harness at college. My violin lessons, spending most days alone in a practice room, or rehearsing Puccini's 'La Boheme' with Helen, who was the orchestral leader, was the only kind of music making I was aware of up to then. Kevin explained that he had a plan - to record a single soon (at Air Studios in Oxford Street), where Paul McCartney told me, "the drinks machine owes me a shilling" - and where the skills of Langer and Winstanley made my violin sound like a Strad *(a violin made by Antonio Stradivari)* - resounding around the parqued live acoustic studio. An LP planned for March or April, would hopefully follow, which would be done at a studio in Goring on Thames, then owned by Martin Rushent.

Rehearsal time for the LP was always intense and physically gruelling (by any means of interpretation - certainly by orchestral measures anyway), and driven further by Seb's 'The Sarge' commands to always "play it harder." I remember we were given parts for a song, all clearly written, with added tempo markings, key and time signatures etc; called 'James, Stan and Me' - which Kevin later explained referred to James Brown, 'Stan the Man' Van Morrison and KR himself.

As part of the sound we were striving to produce - a natural acoustic, open sound - with more of a folk element (than classical playing required), meant playing open strings whenever possible, which is never possible when a song is written in G flat! At the same time, we were also working on another song, that had the working title, 'Yes Let's!' - which was in C, but at this stage, had an instrumental chorus in E flat. Kevin worked and re-worked these ideas a lot (probably much more at home after a full day in the practice room), and at some point, these merged ideas came off the anvil as 'Come On Eileen', which was in C.

Dexys 1982 (L-R) Helen O' Hara, Kevin Rowland, Seb Shelton, Giorgio Kilkenny, Micky Billingham, Steve Shaw and Billy Adams

The musical skills, dexterity and dedication within the group - combined with incredible creativity and artistry, pretty much made my commitments to Puccini, null and void. I was completely astounded and in many ways, quite in awe – through witnessing such an emotive, meaningful creative process at such a productive level. I have probably remained so, to be honest - based on anything penned by Kevin and Big Jim.

The time we spent near Reading, staying in a small B&B pub each night, while recording during the day, was a truly insightful and uniquely privileged way to see how sublime melodic ideas become tangible fabulous songs – with a gene for historical longevity and eternal approval. There were changes taking place in the group - that I was pretty much unaware of, and would not have formulated any sense from anyway, during that period. I could begin to understand, maybe more so now, that the addition of a string section, may have signalled a rough sea change, to what was a distinctive and hugely successful hallmark sound. In many ways and probably due to this, I never got to know Big Jimmy, Geoff or Brian at all, or on any level really.

Snaker (Paul Speare), would often come over to a student flat I shared platonically with Helen - so I did get to know him and his highly articulate humour, quite well. Much later I did get to meet Geoff and Jim through Kevin Archer, who always had a positive and warm regard for both, during the time we were working on the *Blue Ox Babes* LP with Pete Wingfield.

At some point during recording 'Too Rye Ay', we were all back at the pub where we were staying and Kevin came down, during early evening, with a bin liner, full of baggy American dungarees, Tam o' Shanter berets, plaid scarfs, work jackets, thick belts etc. - all quite oversized - in fact all items were really quite comically huge. I remember there was more than a hint of anxiety and probably some misplaced humour - along with a few jocular nervous remarks, as it became increasingly clear, that these clothes would be the new look for the group. On a personal note, I was a bit disappointed - of course I was! As I'd seen the group on Top Of The Pops, only a few months earlier, playing 'Show Me' - and had been really struck by the group's hard-knock image - when the other groups, all looked pretty ridiculous flouncing aside Dexys - wearing boxing boots and ponytails, airing an unseen certainty…

So following the completion and recording of 'Too Rye Ay', 'The Celtic Soul Brothers' was released as a single - and from then on, things moved pretty swiftly and the summer of 1982 blazed and emberred, as 'Eileen' climbed high and held it's own place in the charts. During live performances, we would usually play two shows most days, often for ten or twelve days, back-to-back - with a matinee performance during the afternoon, followed by an evening show, usually around 8.30pm. I don't remember there being any doubt or reservations about the group's stamina or whether Kevin's voice was OK or would continue to hold out - or if the brass players were OK and their lips remained intact - it was just done, implicitly, wholeheartedly, unquestionably. During a period of live dates in Northern Ireland, we stayed at the well known Europa Hotel. It wasn't that unusual for some people in the group to spend such limited spare time alone - maybe to relax in the bath, phone our family or just have an early night. Billy (Kevin Adams), all too often bore the brunt of any practical jokes, but I do know all too well, that I shot like a bolt out of my bed when an alarm clock, that had been placed inside an empty Kimberly biscuit tin, danced to its shrill right under my bed, shortly after I'd fallen asleep. Incessant banging and shouting at my door carried on this disturbance, while mocking my nervous disposition. I'd always been known to have a bit of a temper, so for my fuse to ignite always caused a great source of amusement and laughter.

I have never known such a fierce intensity and synergy to life, as I experienced during events around those years - and probably never will again. But I do know, that despite Kevin telling me twenty-four years later that I had 'never been part of the group' - I did make a contribution to that sound - and I had played on those historical, fabulous songs.

Steve Shaw (aka Brennan), October 2012

Steve Shaw recently with Charlie Reid from The Proclaimers

FORWARD LOOKING MAN

Looking back from a forward looking man
Is hard, but now I'm asked
Could not decide what best to do
Want not to cry, to moan, or boast

It started off in '79
With a Geno Washington fix
Having just got off the road with same
Was recruited into the mix

I came from many backgrounds
Used them all in a special way
To design a brass homogeny
Unique still to this day

It's all about the style
Is what we quoted, one and all
But the sound style of the brass became
The most pertinent style of all

EMI signed Kev, Kev, and myself
Put all eight in a studio
Made an album that became a classic
Subdued McCartney with our hit 'Geno'

The road we started should have gone far
But got replaced by another "trend"
With brass being replaced by wood
Young Soul Rebels came to an end

I could not accept a traitors heart
Soul, Jazz, Funk, still in my blood
So split I did, I could not sell out
The dream that I still had

Now my crew is GI Blythe
Slamming album 'Lost In Space'
With Big Jim, Arch, and other friends
Hot brassy groovement in your face

Geoffrey 'JB' Blythe, 2012
(Saxophone 1978-1980)

Big Jimmy Paterson
(Trombone 1978 – Present)

Dexys... is it a drug? Is it a bird? Is it a plane?

Well, to me it's a drug, but it's not Dexedrine, the well known stimulant often used by dancers in clubs such as the Wigan Casino in the 70s. It's the group that I joined in late 1978, the group that changed my life forever. I didn't know at the time that joining Dexys would have such a profound effect on my life but thirty-four years later, I'm still playing with the group and am enjoying it just as much, if not even more, than before. I'm addicted to Dexys, the group, not the drug, although the effects may be the same. I get a buzz from playing in Dexys, I get withdrawal symptoms when I'm not playing with them. I go to sleep thinking about the next day's fix of Dexys. I wake up and jump out of bed, anticipating a day's rehearsal, or a public performance, which is my source of endorphins.

I've experienced things that most young musicians only dream of. Playing on two British number ones, co-writing one of them. Touring most of Europe, playing to an audience of 100,000 people in Portugal, meeting some of the country's greatest musicians, recording in Abbey Road and other iconic studios. The list could go on but to be honest, it's actually more about the thrill of just being part of a group that has had such an effect on so many people's lives.

Of course, I've also made some friendships that will last forever, as well as having met my wife through being in Dexys. The group transcends what would be considered a normal lifestyle. Shopping for clothes as a group, going to clubs or football matches as a group, it's about experiencing things as the Dexys family.

Then there is the music, from Kevin's incredibly honest and emotive lyrics and vocals; Geoff's brass arrangements; the brass sound itself; the power and commitment; the passion and vulnerability; it all goes to making Dexys unique in so many ways. They say that 'Come on Eileen' is played at every wedding in this country, apart from Kate and Wills probably. If that is true then I am part of something so huge, I can't really comprehend it. I certainly didn't expect that when I started to learn the trombone forty-six years ago.

I don't really have much to say about Dexys, it's all about being in a group that makes me feel alive. I wish everyone could have the wonderful experiences that I have had.

***Big Jimmy Paterson,
October 2012***

Big Jim with Kevin in 2012

Kevin 'Al' Archer

EXCLUSIVE INTERVIEW

Kevin Archer (known as 'Al' at the time) was Kevin Rowland's original *right hand man* from 1978 to 1980. Guitarist and backing vocalist, and the man responsible for writing the music to Dexys Midnight Runners horn-driven first Number 1 – 'Geno'. Rowland also later admitted in an interview with Q magazine in 1993 and then a Creation Records press statement in 1997 that he had stolen the 'Too-Rye-Ay' sound from Kevin Archer -

"I experienced hollow success with 'Come On Eileen' and 'Too-Rye-Ay', the musical sound of which, folky fiddle and texture, mixed with Tamla like soul, came from Kevin Archer and not me as I claimed. The idea and sound was his. I stole it from him hurting Kevin Archer deeply in the process. I conned people all over the world from the people close to me and the people I worked with, to the fans, to the radio and TV programmers, and I made a lot of money. To everybody I conned I'm sorry, to my beautiful friend Kevin Archer I love you, I'm sorry I hurt you. I was jealous of you and your talent, you deserved better, I hope you get what you deserve. Appropriately I felt like a total fraud, and unworthy and unable to deal with the acclaim that came my way." - Kevin Rowland, 1997

Like Rowland, Archer's story began in Wolverhampton in 1958 where he was born. He has lived in the same road in nearby Cradley Heath in the West Midlands all of his life, only moving across the road at the age of ten to the house he still now resides in. His Father was a Military Policeman in the Second World War, his Mother was in the land army. His Mother and Father married after meeting whilst they were both working delivering the post. Kevin attended his local Old Hill primary school where his friend was a kid named Mark Cole, this is where his musical journey began -

Mark was very much into music and books, he was into Bowie; Mott The Hoople; Three Degrees, just anything really. We used to walk up the road to the bus-stop together and he used to tell me about music, he'd say "Listen to this, great this is...". Most of the lads were going on about a band called T-Rex, I'd never heard of them, I never listened to the radio or watched much television. I said "I bet they're crap" and they'd say "No, they're really good, they've got a record out called 'Hot Love'." So I brought the record and I thought 'That's not bad, that's alright, I quite like this,' and I followed T-Rex from the age of about twelve up until the age of eighteen when Marc Bolan died. My brother was brought a guitar for a Christmas present when I was about thirteen, and after about a month he got bored with it and he just left it lying against the wall. I picked it up, and as I was getting into music I started to try and play along to the records. I used to tune the guitar to the records, 'Get It On' was in E, so that's how I got used to tuneing. I learned all their records, then I started to learn other people's records. I wrote poetry as well, Marc Bolan wrote poetry, he wrote a book called 'Warlock Of Love' and I aspired to be like him, Marc Bolan was influenced by Bob Dylan and I got into him later. I wrote poetry and put it to music and sometimes I'd go to Mark Cole's house and he'd record me playing and say "That was good." When I was fourteen I got my own tape-recorder and I'd record me on that. There was a drummer who lived up the road, a bass player and a guitarist, at that time it was like everyone was playing something. It was quite an affluent area around here in 1971 and I used to get them guys here and record them.

I never liked school, I wasn't an academic and the teachers asked me what I was interested in and I said "music" and that I've got my own band called Spectrum, and they told me that we could practise at the school after school hours for free. So we practised twice a week at the school, I'd be on vocals and guitar and we used to do David Bowie songs like 'Suffragette City' and The Ronettes 'Be My Baby', I was frightened to do T-Rex songs even though I knew them all. The teachers were quite impressed with us and asked us to do something for the school, so we ended up putting on a show in the main hall for the kids that were a few years below us in school. I was about fourteen-years old and a bit nervous about going on stage so I brought a little bottle of rum and I had a sip of it and then got on stage and just did it. We played for about forty-five minutes and I can remember that I was wearing a satin jacket with stars on it, along with flares and platforms as I was influenced by glam-rock. I was asked to do some songs for the kids that was my age and I wouldn't do it, my mates were heavily into Northern Soul and I was as well, but we'd seen some black kids from Dudley at a youth centre Northern Soul disco we used to go to in Old Hill, and they'd be brilliant and we just thought 'how come we're not that good?', they could do flips and somersaults. There was ten of us and we started to practise in the local park – flips and all the dance moves and by the end of the year some of us were as good as them, and that's how I got introduced to Northern Soul really, I never went to Wigan or any of the main places but it was massive locally anyway.

When did you realise that you had a talent as a songwriter?
That came later, I didn't take it serious at first. I just did it because the music I was into, they also seemed to be poets and guitarists and I was like just mimicking them, writing interesting words, I wasn't into English, but I noticed that I was interested in certain words and phrases. It was probably when I was sixteen-years old that I realised I was OK at writing, it would have been the time when punk came out. That was brilliant with punk because it was just so basic that anyone could play it really, and it was a voice for playing it. I was at Rowley Regis college at the time, after leaving school with no qualifications and I met Pete Williams there and he was playing bass in a band and they were auditioning for a talent show on TV – 'You're A Star' I think it was called. I was quite impressed that they may be going on TV so I introduced myself, told him that I was a guitarist, and he said that he needed a guitarist in his band. They practised in Blackheath Conservative Club, so I went up, there was another guy in his band Steve Marsh who was the singer and his brother Gary Marsh on drums. They'd play 'Black Magic Women' and

'The Ballad Of John And Yoko' for some reason. We later moved to a pub in Blackheath and practised in a room above the pub. There was this guy named Sid there, he was a great big fat bloke, he drank about ten pints a day, he was into short-wave radio and that shit and he said that he would manage us. He said that he'd charge twenty-pence entry on the door and he pocketed all the money! We used to get a good crowd, we used to get all our mates to come so there'd be about thirty people there. We'd play in the pub once or twice a week, we done an ACDC song called 'Live Wire' and Steve Marsh would just make the words up. Steve later left to join the fair so there was only the three of us. Punk was just bubbling under and we decided to go punk and called ourselves The Negatives. I wrote four or five songs and Pete Williams wrote two or three and we carried on as a three-piece. Steve came back from the fair and wanted to rejoin us, but we wouldn't have him back. Pete Williams seen an advert in the paper saying 'Punk bands wanted', so he phoned up and it was Pete Rowland and we organised a date for him to come down and see us. He came down to see us with his brother who was Kevin Rowland and we played for half an hour then went to the bar for a drink. Kevin asked me what my lyrics were about, and I said it's about everyday things, blah, blah, blah. I think he thought that I was bullshitting him and he asked if we could play the set again, so we played the set again. Pete Rowland said that we needed to do a demo tape, to keep the same line-up and songs because they are quality and that he'd send them to record companies. So we all clubbed together and got about sixty-pound together to do a demo tape. I said to Kevin Rowland "Where's a good studio?" Kevin was in a punk band at the time called The Killjoys who were quite established and he recommended Outlaw Studios. So I phoned Outlaw Studios and arranged to do a recording, but on the eve of the recording Gary Marsh the drummer left, so there was only me and Pete Williams left. So I phoned Pete Rowland and told him, he said "No problem, I'll get Brod." Brod was like a short haired hippy, aged about thirty-eight, whereas we were only about eighteen. So we met him on the day, learned him the songs in about two hours then recorded them. We sent the tape to Pete Rowland but didn't hear anything back, we did bump into Kevin Rowland in Barbarellas in Birmingham and Pete Williams went over and chatted with him, he was friendly enough and asked how things were going.

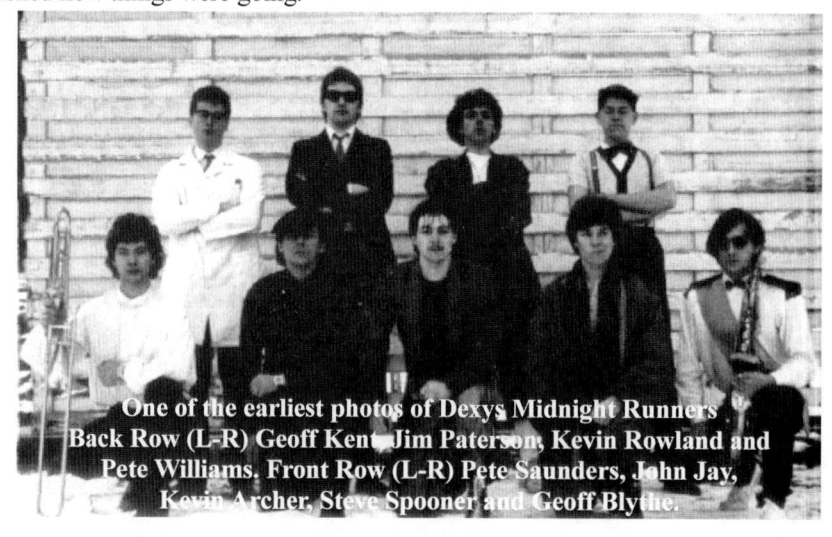

One of the earliest photos of Dexys Midnight Runners Back Row (L-R) Geoff Kent, Jim Paterson, Kevin Rowland and Pete Williams. Front Row (L-R) Pete Saunders, John Jay, Kevin Archer, Steve Spooner and Geoff Blythe.

About two months later I get a telephone call and it was Kevin Rowland telling me that he was after a guitarist for The Killjoys and asked me if I wanted to go to an audition, I said "Yes, I'd be interested," so I went to his house in Apollo Road in Oldbury. I asked Pete Williams to come with me, Kevin said "What you brought him for?" I said "Well, he's a mate." Anyway, I played him a few songs and he says "That was just average," he was really critical. I said that I'm a good guitarist, but he kept putting me down. He phoned me after this for another audition at Outlaw Studios and I was accepted into The Killjoys. I was working as an electrician at the time for BSR who made record turntables, it was like the closest job I could get to music. Kevin Rowland said that I had to give up my job, so I gave up my job and joined The Killjoys. I was with them for about three months and then they split up. I don't know what the exact problem was, but they were all middle-class, there was Mark Phillips and Ghislaine Weston (later of Motorhead Girlschool). We practised one show and I don't think the band were happy with me joining. I wrote a song and Kevin said that he'd put it in the set, and I don't think the rest of the band were happy about it because I'd just come into the band. We recorded two demos in London with a guy named Lee, he was a fat bloke, he was always drinking milk. He lived in Cambridge and he wouldn't give us the demo tapes, so me and Rowland bunked the train down to Cambridge and knocked on his door, he slammed the door in our faces. We saw him later and beat him up. That was the end of The Killjoys really. Rowland was very intense and he would lose his temper with the rest of the band, he wasn't too bad with me though. That was the end of The Killjoys anyway. A couple of weeks later Rowland phones me up to say that he's starting a soul band and asked if I would be interested in joining, I thought 'Soul, that's me'. That's how Dexys Midnight Runners started really, just the two of us.

Is it true that there were two mixes of 'Geno' and EMI wanted the faster version released?
It may have happened because EMI did that a lot, but I think you're talking about 'Burn It Down'/'Dance Stance'. Bernie Rhodes mixed it and we didn't like it and it was remixed later by Pete Wingfield. We did exactly the same with 'Geno' at another studio, the studio used to be a church and Pete Townshend from The Who was there, I think he owned it. We were there for a couple of weeks and they weren't very happy with the sound or something. I wasn't really involved that much then, even though I wrote it, it was a group effort. We hadn't got a producer and Pete Rowland suggested Pete Wingfield, so we contacted Pete Wingfield and it all changed. He came up to Wolverhampton and I had the idea of using the Geno Washington riff from his song 'I Gotta Hold On To My Love', but Pete said that it was too long and he said "Just do 'der d, der d, der d'" and we put that at the front of the song, we were impressed with it and went to the studio and recorded it. After recording we went to McDonalds and Pete Wingfield could afford a McDonalds and we couldn't, he said "Why aren't you eating?" and we couldn't afford it, even though we were signed to EMI and had already reached Number 40 in the charts with 'Dance Stance'. Bernie Rhodes had signed us to Oddball

Records and when 'Dance Stance' only got to Number 40, we broke out of that deal and signed direct to Roger Ames at EMI. It wasn't a very good deal, but at least we had singles out every few months. When 'Geno' came out I don't think anyone took it serious, I did because I'd heard it in my head, the brass riff, and I thought 'that is good'.
I remember when I took it to Kevin and the rest of the group for them to hear, Kevin was cutting Steve Spooner's hair at the time, and Geoff Blythe came up with some harmonies.

The stealing of 'Searching For The Young Soul Rebels' tapes, what involvement did you have in this and did Rowland discuss this with you beforehand?
Yes he did, he just said that he was not happy with the situation and that we should nick the tapes. It was at Chipping Norton Studios, a great studio. 'Geno' was at Number 1 and Kevin said "Let's nick the tapes" and everyone was like "What?" We did it. They didn't expect us to nick the tapes but the royalty rate was only about 7% and we managed to get the royalty rate up a bit by doing it, it was worth it in a way, it was exciting and good fun but it drained us a lot. Spooner reeled the tapes off and got them in the van, and I remember lifting Pete Wingfield off the bonnet of the van, he was shouting "You'll never get away with this." But we did! There was a lot of politics in the band which didn't work really, it was like "Do this, do that" and that spoilt it a lot, I think we would have been better musicians if we had just concentrated more on the music.

Where was the Birmingham hide-out?
There was a couple of places but we were mostly in the Apollonia on Broad Street drinking tea, we was always in there, it's where the Hyatt Hotel is now. The owner in there used to take the piss out of us saying "You'll never make it," his wife was Italian, she was really nice. The owner was always taking the piss out of us and when we made it we went in a few months later and he said "Oh, I remember you!" His wife was really nice, she made a lovely stew. We used to hatch all our plans in there in the back room, we'd sit down with our cups of tea and it was like "This is your job to phone a club in London and get us a gig." We'd send our demo tapes off to record companies and never got them back most of the time.

You sang the B-side to 'Keep It Part 2' – a cover version of Cliff Bennett and the Rebel Rousers 'One Way Love', how did that come about?
I was out of the group at the time, I was suffering from nervous exhaustion and when I came back Rowland said "I want you to sing 'One Way Love'", I said "No," he said that it would be good, so I did it. We went to the studio and Rowland said that he would play guitar and do backing vocals.

Archer (left) with Dexys Midnight Runners in 1980
Photo: Mike Laye

What were your feelings at the time when Dexys split?
It was during the month I had off and when I rejoined I noticed a split happening, it was like the rest of the group was against Kevin and I befriended Kevin. Before I left though there became a bad culture of smoking dope, Kevin wouldn't do that, so he would go in another room with his brother John and we would be in another room smoking dope all night, which is a bad culture which I regret. When I came back after my month off I just thought 'What's going on?' I was just happy that 'Geno' went to Number 1 and I'd established my name in some ways. When we finally split up in Switzerland, I just thought that I'm gonna form my own group – vocals with strings. I knew what I wanted to do with music and I had a girlfriend and I was very close with her and I didn't have time for the group really.

When Dexys first split up was you asked to join The Bureau?
Yeah, Pete Williams knocked on my hotel room door in Switzerland and said that he was leaving Dexys and forming a new group and asked me to join, I said "No." Then me and Kevin Rowland got the aeroplane to Luxembourg to do a radio interview there. Then we flew back to England and I said that I'm gonna form my own group with my girlfriend and he didn't know what to do, he didn't have a clue.

Then you formed The Blue Ox Babes?
Yeah, initially it was just me, Yasmin and Nick Bache who was a guitarist I met at social security, he knew me from Dexys and he was a big fan. He asked me what I was doing and I told him that I'm forming a new group and he said that he'd be interested in joining. He wrote the riff to 'Apples And Oranges' and then he left, I've never heard from him since. Then I got Andy Leek in on piano who took it to another level, and then I went to the Birmingham School of Music and I asked around for a violinist and everyone was suggesting Helen Bevington (O'Hara). Helen was great, we went to Outlaw Studios in October 1981 and got it all down. Our sound pre-dated what Dexys went on to do. I did say to Kevin at the time that I've got a really good violin player and that he could use her if he wanted. Helen was on a course at college at the time and she was happy with just being a session player. We didn't have enough funds for Helen to be a full-time member, whereas Dexys did. I said to Kevin "We got Helen if you want to use her," he said "No," and the next thing I know she's there on Top Of The Pops! Later on I moved to Edgbaston from Old Hill and Kevin Rowland was living around the corner and I bumped into him in a cafe and he was like "I'm sorry," he started to confess to me about nicking my sound and image. He offered me £15,000 and I said "No," and I never heard anything from him until later on when he confessed publicly to nicking my sound and gave me royalties from 'Come On Eileen' and 'Too-Rye-Ay'.

Hatching plans...

The Blue Ox Babes were formed in 1981, but it was 1988 until anything was released?
Yeah that's right, I had a nervous breakdown in 1986 and I was in hospital and I'd split up with Yasmin. I went into hospital and everybody visited me and Darren 'Tommy' Langford came to visit me, he used to hang around with us in Dexys, he said that he'd look after me and sort things out. By the time I came out of hospital I was diagnosed as paranoid schizophrenic and I'm still on medication now. In 1987 I reformed The Blue Ox Babes, I remember going to a practice room in Birmingham by the fire station and we practised there for about a year, it was freezing cold. We met up again with Pete Rowland and he got us in Rich Bitch Studios which was much better. We went to Outlaw Studios afterwards and we had Vincent Crane and Woody Woodmansey, we did some demos with them and we wrote 'Gregory Right' and a few of the other songs. But the reason it took so long before anything was released was because of my illness and the lack of money, I was paying for everything out of my own pocket. It was a slow process, we'd failed once before. Dave Robinson at Stiff Records had offered us a deal previously and I turned it down. Dave Robinson asked me who I wanted to produce us and I said Pete Wingfield and Dave said that Pete had gone off the boil, I just didn't get on with Dave. He phoned me up later on when Dexys had 'Come On Eileen' out and I remember hearing 'Eileen' on the radio and thinking 'That was my idea'. Anyway, Dave asked me again if I wanted to sign to Stiff, but I wasn't interested as it was only a contract for one record.

You later had three singles released through Go Discs, that I thought were very commercial pop songs. Why do you think that you didn't succeed?
Well, I'd written all those songs before Dexys had come out with the same sound and all the radio stations and the press were like 'It sounds too much like Dexys', even though it was me who came up with the sound. We were on tour with The Proclaimers and the record company said that they weren't going to release the album, after we'd worked our guts off on tour. We finished the tour, got back home and Yasmin said that she was leaving, then Steve Shaw left and gradually everyone left, and that was the end of The Blue Ox Babes.

You must have been pleased when the album finally got released on CD in 2009?
Yeah I was. It's sold over 1,000 copies, which isn't great but by record sales today it's not too bad. It's due to be released again in 2014.

The Blue Ox Babes

Did you do anything after The Blue Ox Babes?
I did, the last thing I did was in 1990, I did some electronic music. I did a course with Phil Savage from Outlaw Studios for a year and recorded six or seven songs. I don't have a tape of it, that was the last thing I done.

Have you heard Dexys new album?
Yeah I have, but most of the songs on there I have heard before as some are twenty years old.

Rowland used to send me his demo tapes, the songs have changed though like 'She Got A Giggle' changed to 'Wiggle'.

Where did the name 'Al' come from and did you mind your name being changed?
I didn't really mind, but I've got a cousin named Alan and he thought I was named after him! I don't know who came up with the name, they were all denying it. I did mind it later on, because it was Kevin Archer playing on the record and I wanted people to know my name and I felt I'd earned my dues by that point. But I wasn't really bothered, they'd call me Al sometimes and Kev other times.

Where did you get your wooly hats from?
A place in Blackheath, my Dad used to work around the corner. Me and Rowland wandered around the shops and we went into one shop and there was a pile of them on the counter, so we sent the shop keeper around the back to pick something else up and we done a runner with the hats! I had a red one and Kevin had a red one, but he wouldn't wear his. I stuck with mine, then we got them from anywhere. I used to have a supply of about ten in my bag and people would come up to me and ask me for a red hat!
I probably went through over fifty hats!

Rowland didn't like you wearing a red hat?
No, he didn't like it. He was jealous.

Why did you bunk the trains to do Top Of The Pops?
We didn't bunk the trains to do Top Of The Pops, but I remember Top Of The Pops sent a limousine to pick us up from Birmingham to take us down to London to do 'Geno' and Rowland didn't like the limousine. The following week when we had to go down to London again, Kevin sorted out a van. It was fun when we bunked the trains though.

What songs are you most proud of writing?
'The Teams That Meet In Caffs' and 'There's No Deceiving You'.

Kevin Archer, November 2013

Kevin Archer in 2013

Yasmin Saleh
THE BLUE OX BABES
EXCLUSIVE

I grew up with the sounds of Barry White, The Temptations, The Jackson Five, James Brown, blues reggae and my ultimate favourite was Diana Ross and The Supremes. I always loved music, dancing and fashion it went hand in hand for me. Years later when 2-Tone was dominating the charts, Pauline Black sang 'On My Radio' and Madness were one step beyond. It was around this time on a British sunny day I first met Pete Williams on my way up to Northfield motorway café with my mate Terry in Birmingham. He was my first connection to Dexys and it was through this chance meeting with Pete Williams that I was introduced to Dexys Midnight Runners, without realising at this time that Dexys Midnight Runners was a band that would have a huge influence and impact on the rest of my life to date. Pete invited us along to see Dexys play at a little club in Birmingham, it was a small, intimate, dark and warm club. Unknown to me Dexys performance would be the start of a love affair in more ways than one. When I first heard Dexys sound, from the beginning to the end of their set the music grabbed me right through the heart, I was blown away by their energy, stage presence, power and enthusiasm. The whole room was filled with intense passion and emotion. Watching Kevin Rowland sing with all his heart and the likes of Archer, Paterson and Blythe playing with such conviction and soul, giving 100%. It truly was intense energy in motion and it touched me to the core of my soul, it was the start of an intense love for their music which had a profound impact on what I would listen to. It was totally inspiring, I felt like I could relate to Dexys music and Rowland's lyrics which were sung with such heart felt emotion and unique vocals, he was also unique in his performance on stage. After the concert I met the rest of the band members including Archer, we talked and it was only by a total misunderstanding that we stayed in touch. It was 1980 and 'Geno' climbed it's way up the charts, in private Archer and I would meet and share stories about music and our lives. I was 16-years old with no permanent address, labelled Gypsy Rose Lee because of the nomad life I lived moving from place to place, I had no permanent address or home. I remember when Dexys recorded the album 'Searching For The Young Soul Rebels', the excitement behind nicking the final mix of the tapes from the recording studio, there was a lot of commotion, Archer came back full of enthusiasm and excitement, not knowing what the outcome would be or whether their plan to hold the record company to ransom whist negotiating a better contract would work, whether the police would intervene and arrest them or the record company would realise their worth and give them what they wanted and deserved, they were in a good position to negotiate as 'Geno' hit Number 1; they had a lot of bargaining power. It was a very clever, rebellious and entrepreneurial move which paid off for them. I helped Archer get the tapes from London to Birmingham but we couldn't put the tapes through the X-ray machine because we might damage them.

Archer and I became very close and he asked me to move into a house with some of the other Dexys crew. No one was ever at home except for me as they were away on tour along with Keith Allen and Alexei Sayle as supporting acts. The shared house didn't last long as the neighbours complained about the uncut lawns and the state of the garden. Just after this I moved into Archer's parents house in Cradley Heath, Dexys had already hit Number 1 in the charts with 'Geno' and no girlfriends were allowed on tour, so Archer used to call me when he could and sometimes I would go and meet him in between gigs, flights and international tours. Sometimes I would only see him for 2-3 hours before he had to grab his bag and leave again. I don't think he liked leaving too much towards the end of his career with Dexys. Occasionally I would go to a gig in the UK but Rowland had a policy set in place that no girlfriends were allowed on tour and he was not happy if a girlfriend was present, words and warnings would be expressed. Corky was Dexys manager at this point and they had their offices in Cannon Lane in Birmingham City Centre, next to a little eatery where everyone used to congregate for a bite to eat. Dexys had some pretty machiavellian characters working for them at this point. Corky used to put his finger to his thick lensed glasses, push them back, squint slightly and whenever anyone asked for money he would say "There is no money lads" even though they had a Number 1 hit. Tommy was Corkys gofer running around doing errands, they also had a bouncer called Jimmy the Con who used to stand at the front of the stage when Dexys were playing a live gig. Jimmy was built like a brick shit house, solid and compact with a bald head and menacing look on his face, no one could get passed if they tried, they didn't get far, he was like a brick wall. No one would want to try either, he looked like a character out of Snatch.

As 'Geno' made it's way down the charts it was replaced by 'There There My Dear' (written by Rowland/Archer), which didn't do as well as 'Geno' but climbed high and had a great impact none the less. Things in the band were getting a little conflicting by this point, Archer seemed to be more and more frustrated with Rowland's demands, one day on an early Saturday morning TV show appearance I saw Archer getting a little more zealous and overly aggressive kicking over speakers on live TV, on his return he said that he had had enough of Rowland who was being didactic over many petty things, one being that he couldn't wear his red hat any more, Rowland made such an issue out of his hat and he couldn't see why. It was after this incident that Archer said he wasn't going to be one of Rowland's sheep and let him order him around like a dictator "I'm not going back" he said. I was shocked and thought it was the wrong decision to make but it was his right to make a stand. Archer did the right thing by Dexys and Rowland though and stayed to help train Billy Adams (his replacement) and teach Billy about the live set and songs. Archer was a major part of the music writing team, writing the music for 'Geno' and 'There There My Dear' and many more tracks, so I'm sure Rowland must have felt some loss. My personal opinion is that Rowland and Archer both complimented each other in ideas and writing but clashed in egos.

Dexys went into their new look, boxing boots and anorak period ('Show Me', 'Plan B'), whilst Archer set out to create a whole new style of music with a new image. Archer and I travelled for a while to a few places in Europe (Spain, Greece, France) looking at different types of music and fashion. Collecting rare and old music as well as various fashion items, in search of unique sounds, instruments and ideas for fashion (looking at the different sounds of violins from the Arabic sounds of strings to the Gypsy, Irish and eventually Cajun use of strings and instruments, Jew's harp and harmonium etc). We used to spend time visiting flea markets in France where we picked up different clothes, the rag market in Birmingham where we purchased lots of old vinyl, Cajun music and Gypsy styled music with images of gypsies sitting around camp fires. We would stay up all night talking about ideas, we both had a huge amount of enthusiasm, Archer gave me a tape of The Chieftains which I loved and played all the time. Archer and Rowland stayed in touch and I got a job at Paul Burtons (Dexys new Manager who owned Browns Hairdressers). This is also where I met Pauline O'Brien who was Irish and an amazing hairdresser, she was credited with having an input into the 'Too-Rye-Aye' Dexys image. We became really good friends and after a while she also became a very good Dexys fan and their personal hair stylist. I discussed with enthusiasm and without reservation all the ideas and the things we were doing in The Babes with both Burton and Pauline who I considered to be good friends. I still love Paul Burton and stayed in touch even after I left Browns Hairdressers, he used to make me laugh and was always friendly. Pauline became really good personal friends with Rowland, I only ever saw Pauline O'Brien once after 'Come On Eileen' was released during the 'Too-Rye-Ay' period at a Dexys concert wearing a little red dress walking around the theatre, but never again after that.

When Archer first decided to put The Blue Ox Babes together he asked me if I wanted to sing, I grew up loving musicals and would have loved to sing, dance and perform but in reality my shyness got the better of me, there was no way I was going to get up in front of people to perform even though I had been part of a singing group at school and entered private singing competitions in my earlier days. I remember Archer got me to sing in front of Micky Bilingham once, I was literally hyper ventilating, I went red and mumbled into the mic, I loved singing but getting up in front of people was very daunting for me. I was more interested in working with the fashion side of things, image, I didn't want to join The Babes as a singer but Archer was persistent and gradually won me over.

Initially it was just Archer and me until Archer added a third addition, Nick Bache who lived locally in Archer's home town of Cradley Heath and he helped with the song writing. Archer used to sit there with me in his back lounge playing his guitar and getting me to sing along to what he was playing, it made life much easier for me, casually getting me to sing along, making me feel more comfortable with singing and relaxed enough to be creative in my input on backing vocals etc. I got first hand introductions to all the new tracks, I was more prepared than anyone else in rehearsals... Nick Bache our new addition was a very passive, quiet, gentle character with a homely boy image, he was sweet and polite but with a quiet sense of humour. Archer then recruited Andy Leek and Ian Pettitt, Ian used to be in a band with Pete Williams called These Tender Virtues. We rehearsed in Cradley Heath on an industrial site. To be honest, it all sounded like shit to me at first - untogether and very raw. I was very much in awe of all of these guys though and I felt like a novice in comparison it felt like I didn't belong with such talented musicians. We had a few songs and Leek was a great contributor and support for Archer. Archer went about searching for a violinist, he put an advertisement in the Birmingham School of Music which is where he found Helen Bevington (O'Hara), she was very middle class and student like. When she came into rehearsals and Archer explained to her what he wanted she was amazingly talented, versatile and creative, she nailed the sound and the style of playing that Archer wanted to suit the songs immediately .We started with a few tracks only – 'Four Golden Tongues Talk', 'What Does Anybody Ever Think About', 'Thought As Much' and 'Apples And Oranges' and we went into Outlaw recording studio in Birmingham with Phil Savage. I was not a musician and was in awe of those around me, I totally enjoyed the experience of participating in listening and watching how all the music came together, but felt a little inadequate and even embarrassed at times due to my

Yasmin with Archer

lack of musical training and experience. Both Andy Leek and Helen blew me away with their musical ability and performances, when Andy Leek picked up the harmonica on 'Four Golden Tongues Talk' it sent shivers down my spine. Andy Leek, Helen and Archer were amazing in their contributions to these first demo tapes. We could not have produced the tracks without them, brilliant musicians, song writers and very creative. I loved Phil Savage at Outlaw too, he was such a relaxed and easy going person to be around and work with. After the recording session and the final mix when I got to listen to the final sound it all seemed to have come together and for the first time it made sense. The final sound was amazing, original, energising, exciting and full of passion. All that searching, all that time trying to put something original and unique together and here it was. The first tracks were down, it was a real high when Archer brought the finished mixed demos home, I remember thinking at this point that this could be big, I always believed that we could do something but I realised that what Archer had created was a totally original style of music for this period in time. The sound was so original, unique and so different from what anyone else was doing on the music scene at the time. It felt good but we were still in the early stages, we still only had a few songs and the dress down image which was initially going to be a sort of Country & Western Cajun look (I loved 'Paint Your Wagon' musical and was taking inspiration from that style initially, I also had it in mind that I wanted to make a mini musical for a video) had now naturally progressed to a more Romany Gypsy look. I was still working at Browns Hairdressers and both Pauline and Paul Burton used to ask me questions, they seemed really enthusiastic about what we were doing as a band at the time which I was only to happy to talk about as they were my friends; Pauline was my best friend. Later after 'Come On Eileen' had been released, she became closer to Rowland and basically cut ties with me.

We did see Rowland every now and then and I used to see Dexys members in Browns hair salon quite often. I really liked Paul Burton and I had a huge amount of respect for Rowland, he was my hero and someone I looked up to, I was in awe of him, I think Archer was too in his own way.

After The Babes demos were finished Archer took them to Rowland to listen to. He came back to our bedsit one day really excited about having played his new demo tape to Rowland and raved about how Rowland loved the new songs, this meant a lot to Archer, he really valued his opinion. I was shocked that Rowland liked what we had recorded, it meant the world to me too. I didn't realise Archer gave him a copy of the tape not that it would

Key attraction!

ALL keyed up.... that's songbird Jasmin Sataha as she tunes in for a summer music extravaganza.
Jasmine, aged 26, is part of the promotion team trumpeting the attractions of Birmingham International Jazz Festival.
And she's perfectly qualified for the job. Because Jazz Ian Jasmin, from Edgbaston, is also the singer with Midland pop group The Blue Ox Babes.
The ten-day festival starts on Friday July 1, and features big names from the international jazz scene including American stars Claude Williams and Nat Pierce, Britain's own saxophone wizard Courtney Pine and top bands from Germany and Holland.

have made any difference, I kind of idolised Rowland, I respected him as a writer, musician and performer. I loved his lyrics and I even showed him lyrics I had written myself, which he said he liked, I must have been the proudest person on this planet on his response. I loved his lyrics; they were very special to me.

We continued to go about creating more music and focused on finding a name for the band, Archer finally found the name as we searched in the Birmingham library - 'The Blue Ox Babes'. We were in the very early stages as a band with no manager, only a few songs and only a few solid members - Archer, Leek, Nick Bache and myself. We were focusing on getting a recording contract so that we had funds to develop further. Helen was paid as a session player and after our first demo was recorded Archer gave her an open cheque as an invitation to join the band but she declined. Shortly after Rowland said he was looking at using a violinist and a cello and asked Archer if he could have Helen's number, Archer gave it to Rowland. I'm not sure exactly how much time elapsed but I do remember not seeing Rowland for sometime until I was walking along Broadway near Outlaw Studios, I saw him looking all raggedy and rugged, he looked like he hadn't slept in weeks, dishevelled and unkept. Shortly after this, I can't be sure of the exact order of events, Archer said he had heard 'Come On Eileen' on the Radio. I don't remember being shocked but I remember my stomach feeling twisted and knotted, it sounded so similar to our demos and the build up in the song where it stops and builds was a replica of the one we done in 'What Does Anybody Ever Think About', Archer was in shock, he couldn't believe what he was hearing.

We continued to rehearse as a band, and as 'Come On Eileen' climbed the charts Helen had made the decision to commit herself to Rowland and Dexys, so we had to go about sourcing a new violinist which we did but it turned out to be harder than anticipated. When you have someone as talented and as versatile as Helen Bevington (renamed O'Hara to suit the image of the 'Too-Rye-Ay' period) it becomes a real mission to replace them. We spent a lot of time trying to recruit a new violinist, most of the players were classical in approach and did not have enough edge or that punch in their style of playing to go head on into that raunchy sound that was required for our style of music. I do remember the guys in the band trying to be polite to one classical violinist - "Can you play a bit harder?", "Could you be a bit more aggressive?", "Don't be afraid to give it a bit of punch" in the end through pure frustration Andy Leek's final comment was "Just knock the fuck out of it!" We could not replace Helen which held us up quite a lot and was a cause for concern, as well as the fact that we didn't have a manager and then Andy Leek dropped the bomb shell that he was also leaving to pursue a solo career. This really knocked us around and totally dampened our spirits. I eventually found us a manager called Frank who was an Irish guy working as a hairdresser and had previously managed bands before. By this stage Dexys were already climbing the charts with 'Come On Eileen' at a fast rate. The song was becoming ubiquitous and their image bore a striking resemblance to what we also had in mind. The worst thing about all of this was that we would at times see Rowland, Helen and Billy on the bus as we were all going to rehearsals, none of us would speak to each other. I would have liked answers at this point and felt a little cheated but they would be sitting downstairs and we would go upstairs, there was never any exchange of conversation. I think it was my first real introduction into the world of deception. This was someone I had a huge amount of respect and reverence for. It felt like someone had twisted my insides and turned me inside out. I hated the whole scenario, I wish I could just turn back the clock and none of it had happened.

I was still aching to get out there and introduce The Babes to the world though, but we still had no set, had not played live but had a limited but growing number of songs. We weren't ready, Archer knew this and I felt like he was holding back now. His enthusiasm had dwindled a little, I didn't realise at the time but he had started a slow descent into a dark hole from which he would never return. Archer took the tapes to EMI who said the tapes sounded too similar to Dexys, Archer tried to explain why but no one wanted to listen. Our manager organised a meeting with Stiff Records and Dave Robinson whom we met, played for and they were very interested and wanted to sign us. I was excited, enthusiastic and ready to go, I thought this is it, this is what we have been working towards, and at least we get a chance to put our music forward too now (this is also where we had first contact with Andy McDonald who worked for Stiff and later signed us to Go Discs). But for whatever reasons Archer decided not to take the deal with Stiff Records who had a number of successful acts. I have never really gone into any kind of great details with Archer as to why he turned the Stiff Records deal down. All he said at the time was that with Dexys being so popular with 'Come On Eileen' at Number 1 in the British music charts, considering the uniqueness, individuality and the similarities in our music The Babes would be seen as copycats. I wasn't happy with his decision, it really knocked me about for a while and it caused some friction between us.

Archer began to fall into a further slump as Dexys were hitting the top of the album charts with 'Too-Rye-Ay'. I think he was happy for Rowland on one hand but on the other he had very conflicting feelings, I think if Rowland at any point during his success with the 'Too-Rye-Ay' period had come forward and maybe even quoted Archer or The Babes as having some influence on his music it might have been justified or even understood and we would be seen in a different light, but he never once mentioned Archer or The Babes throughout the entire 'Too-Rye-Ay' period as having any influence or even existence, which was a little inconsiderate considering how much he got out of it, not financially but musical success and admiration of millions for his contribution and ideas during this period.

We went to see Dexys play live in Birmingham, they cleverly performed at a theatre rather than a concert hall where everyone sat down, it was more of a show than a concert which I love, they were once again brilliant live and Dexys blew me away with their intense passion in their performance and music. This time their show was very theatrical, energetic and unique in regards to any other music at the time. They had worked really hard, performed an amazing set and were totally professional, everything was 100% perfect. Rowland was a perfectionist and this was obvious in everything he created and performed. He took what we had and made it a hundred times better, I loved 'Too-Rye-Ay' and listened to it all the time during this period. I still to this day have the original vinyl copy of the album. Again, Dexys music and the lyrics were very special to me. I loved those violins, the purity, strength and passion in their music.

The Blue Ox Babes continued to rehearse without a violinist or a keyboard player until we found Pete Wain. Archer would stay in doors a lot and sit there all day thinking and smoking whilst I went to work. I didn't know it at the time but he was sinking into oblivion. I was very young. I didn't know what to think or do, we argued lots and eventually he asked me to leave him. I left him thinking I did the right thing as he said he couldn't write any more and needed space. I went to college where I took up drama and other subjects as I left school early without qualifications. I threw myself into work, study and theatre. I continued to sing in musical theatre and in a choir, I found the love of my life through acting, even though I was shy I suddenly found an open door which took me to a place I felt comfortable in and able to express myself. Meanwhile times passed and Dexys had received much success with 'Too-Rye-Ay', 'Jackie Wilson Said' etc and touring reviews. I didn't see Archer for some time and Dexys had enjoyed the 'Too-Rye-Ay' period and were also moving on. Rowland wrote 'Because Of You' a song used in a popular TV programme, it did well in the charts and during this period Rowland was friendly and even helped me as a poor student by paying my rent once, he took me to Martin Fry's wedding in Sheffield and introduced me to a man I found to be one of the most interesting men I have ever met which I later discovered was Bernie Rhodes. Rowland also came to see me playing Mrs Alving in Ghost which I was very proud of. I didn't see him again for some time and moved into a new house which by total coincidence (I think) Steve Shaw also moved into a new house. I walked out of my room one day and there was Steve Shaw - "What you doing here?" he said, "I live here, what you doing here?" I responded, "I just moved in" said Steve. I knew Steve had played violin for Dexys but I have never really spoken to him much in the past. This was the start of a friendship I treasured for quite some time.

I visited Archer a few times but he didn't seem interested in seeing me, so I kept my distance for some time then one day he just turned up at my work place. Adamant that he needed to see me. He became pretty obsessive, he was staying at Rowland's flat on Hadley Road at the time, and I went there a few times to visit him. He started displaying very unusual and out of character behaviour. We went through some seriously intense arguments and situations over the next year which caused me a lot of pain and frustration. Eventually Rowland and Archer's family stepped in to help and Archer was diagnosed as schizophrenic. I just thought he had depression and I still think this was the case to this day, but he started taking medication and this eventually further down the line took him to another place.

Meanwhile Steve Shaw who was now also in between bands asked me to join in with some musicians he was involved with (Tony & Vanessa) from a band called 'The Letters', which I did. Again, I was not so comfortable singing in front of others at first but I loved singing so I pushed my feelings of reservation to one side and we started rehearsing in Steve's upstairs room with guitar, violin and two backing singers. We recorded a demo and did the rounds of a few record companies, which resulted in very little interest, what we were doing was nothing new, original or even great but it was a good experience for me. Steve started hanging around with Archer and a mate of mine called Janet. The band with Steve and Tony fell apart. Archer and Steve started seeing each other and Archer recruited Steve Shaw to play the violin for The Babes, he started to put the band back together, they also recruited Janet Harrison to do vocals. Janet didn't work out so Archer went in pursuit of recruiting me again. I initially declined the offer due to the fact that I had won a place and a scholarship to go to drama school in London, also because of past conflicts and incidents between Archer, and I was very dubious with his behaviour towards me. We had many meetings and discussions before coming to an agreement I would make a commitment to The Babes after Archer had firmly promised that the relationship between us would be purely based on me being my own person and had nothing to do with our past personal relationship.

This time around I had more confidence due to working in a theatre company and having performed a lot on stage. I also gained a job at Brum Beat music magazine and international Jazz Festival with Jim Simpson around the same time whose editor Steve Morris was very interested in The Blue Ox Babes music. We rehearsed in Bearwood, pulled more songs together especially now that Steve was in the song writing team. He was the missing link we needed and I was stronger, wiser and older this time around. We now had Ian Pettitt on drums, Pete Wain on keyboards, Steve Wynne on bass, Steve Shaw on violin, me on backing vocals and Archer on vocals and guitar. It was coming together but still a far cry from a full set. I loved those rehearsal days in Bearwood, just up the road from The Little Nibble café, it was a small room above a shop, Ian was so energetic that his drum sticks would always fly out of his hands and thrust themselves into the polystyrene ceiling which resembled a porcupine, the sound was coming together, it was a very energetic and vibrant sound. We played our first gig at Faces at Five Ways in Birmingham which to me was a disaster, it sounded like shit and to be truthful I was ashamed of that first gig. We recruited Pete Rowland (Kevin Rowland's brother; loved this guy) and Geoff Pearce who also managed Ruby Turner and loved Jazz. We needed solid management and Rowland had suggested his brother Pete. We played our first show case for Go Disc's Andy McDonald who remembered us from Stiff Record days, he showed some interest but was not ready to sign us just yet, he wasn't 100%. We played a few more gigs which McDonald attended with Jonah after which he made a firm commitment to the band legally binding us through contracts and fronting money for us to record at Chipping Norton, to record the album 'Apples And Oranges' with Pete Wingfield who was Archer's choice. Management also made a firm commitment, the studio was amazing, it had everything, I couldn't believe it, it felt like after all this time, things were about to fall into place. I wasn't too keen on working in the studio though, again my shyness and inadequate feelings of lack of experience as a musician

---

BLUE OX BABES
COD CLUB at PIRANHA'S
Birmingham

Well I'll bet Ranking P and Kool Moe Dave never thought that synthetic pomp classics would make it onto the Cod listing!

In fact the great swelling sound of the tune you all know well but can never name when it turns up on TV game shows brought the Babes striding purposefully onto the stage where with no ceremony they launched into a well constructed and tight set.

With enough common heritage to make the family tree as easy to follow as ivy on the side of a house the background isn't going to go away, but anyone who finds it reason enough to avoid the Oxes is both missing the point and the fun. Saxophone and violin topping the solid and potent rhythm section add to the heritage and, to drive the point home, I suggest that decorators do a midnight runner. Stick to backcombed hair and twangy guitars huh, those with taste don't care.

There are minus points. Why was Kevin Archer so visibly and dudibly nervous, he can relax it's more than OK. Enjoy yourself Kevin! The visual side needs a little more, shall we say, Charisma. The dervish on backing vocals and tambourine damage arguably detracts from what ought to be the focal point but then again perhaps the enthusiasm will rub off.

At the core of it all is a really great band and a solid future. Blue Ox Babes should be filed under "can't fail".

Support Prehistoric Pets played a fine entertaining set that reminded me of Yachts Softs Boys and others. I couldn't recall. The on going Donny Osmond joke fell flat when "Crazy Horses" turned out to be the highlight.

STEVE MORRIS

surfaced, I much preferred performing live shows. I also went into the whole commitment with a major problem which no one knew about at the time. I suffered from extreme bulimia but hid it well for many years from everyone. It had a grave impact on my voice and vocals and the way I felt and performed, my voice would vacillate in texture and quality all the time, I would even lose my voice at times. I loved the guys in the band though; they were all like brothers to me especially Ian Pettitt, Steve Shaw and Nick Smith who gave me lots of support, strength and belief. They made me laugh and always made me feel comfortable. It was a real experience working with Pete Wingfield and Barry (Engineer) and their perception of what worked and what didn't, their creative input and experience was quite an insight. I regret one thing about this period and that was that I left Chipping Norton Studios early before they started doing some of the final mixing on the tapes, I was stupid and had an argument with Archer over someone who had called me, it was a really stupid argument and in hindsight Archer was right, I should have stayed but I felt claustrophobic, maybe it was the gypsy coming out in me.

Chipping Norton was amazing as was Pete Wingfield and Barry the engineer. Some of the tracks went down really easy like 'No Deceiving You' but others like the 'Ballad Of The Blue Ox Babes' was a struggle. Both Archer and I struggled with our vocals on this track, it didn't help that he was smoking forty cigarettes a day and I was throwing up 2-3 times a day at this point. In hindsight I didn't have a huge contribution in the studio but more to live performances. We went in a couple of times before finishing the first tracks and I have to say listening to the likes of Big Jim Paterson play on our tracks was amazing, Big Jim was truly talented and I was both in awe and a little intimidated by the talents of these guys. I felt privileged to be a part of something which included Jim Paterson, Pete Wingfield and other talents, as I was when I first witnessed Andy Leek playing on our first demos in Outlaw Studios. All the guys in the band were amazing in the studio; Steve Shaw came up with some great impromptu creative violin parts for some of the tracks. I wasn't overly impressed with my vocals but I could see I was improving and loved working with all these guys. Being the non musician I felt like I was an imposter as usual in many ways and that I didn't deserve to be there.

With half of the album 'Apples And Oranges' recorded, the single 'No Deceiving You' was released, it charted and went to about Number 74 I think but that was all, it was a disappointment, but not the end of the world as we were new and it was our first single. The image we decided on was simple, neutral and wasn't meant to make any great statement. I remember when we went in to record the video for 'No Deceiving You' and they put so much make up on me, when the video came out it appeared like my lips were animated! Steve and I laughed so much when we were watching the video as it looked like Pete Wain's silhouette was fucking the piano! We had a lot of fun making the video, Archer laughed lots and I sensed the old Archer coming through during this period, I hadn't seen him laugh so much for a long time, he seemed far more relaxed as we went into rehearsing more and playing more live gigs throughout the UK, which resulted in some very cynical reviews from music journalists listing us as a Dexys mark 2 and I remember one review that said "If you like Bonny Langford on a Saturday, it's alright until the

> **THE BLUE OX BABES: There's No Deceiving You (Go! Discs)**
> A **wild** name that's tagged to the ear of a thoroughly convincing, impressively precise impersonation of Dexy's doing a runner. A neat trick, but how many times dare they pull it before the clouds of self doubt close in on them? Boogie to this bull while you can.

energy runs out, I'm off Eileen", there were constant comparisons which Archer hated, but it was a case of when I see a spade, I call it a spade. Of course we sounded like Dexys, Archer was one of the main writers for Dexys mark 1 and also one of the main instigators of the 'Too-Rye-Ay' period which they were not aware of as nothing was ever revealed by Rowland when 'Come On Eileen' or 'Too-Rye-Ay' was hitting the top of the charts regarding Archers influence in their music. Our first single 'No Deceiving You' was getting some air play on national radio and the video was getting some air play on TV too. Go Discs were very enthusiastic, talking about plans for the future, the enthusiasm was there. They also hooked me up with a singing teacher, Tona De Brett who was Johnny Rotten's singing teacher, I didn't like singing lessons even though she was an amazing teacher, she got me to sing an aria which wasn't really my style, she told amazing stories, she gave me some amazing information on singing and exercises too, but with my illness it didn't really matter how many lessons I had, I had a serious problem that effected my voice at times. I also felt a little shy and embarrassed thinking that the record company thought I need lots of improvement but in actual fact they were just trying to help me. I went for a few lessons in London, she told me some stories about how Johnny Rotten approached his lessons which made me laugh but I didn't want to continue, I should have taken the lessons whilst I had the chance but with my voice constantly changing due to my illness it really wasn't worth it, I needed professional and medical help really.

'No Deceiving You' did OK for our first single but not as well as we expected, as it left the charts we hit the road and started touring with The Proclaimers which was again very daunting but exciting for me. I had the upmost respect for Charlie, Craig and all the musicians in The Proclaimers, they were great guys. I didn't talk to them too much initially but they were so respectful and such talented musicians. I loved watching their set after we had been on as supporting band. I was the only female amongst all these guys and it felt a little intimidating because I was also the only non musician amongst some great musicians. Unlike The Proclaimers who had made it in the music industry we had to pack up our own instruments and instead of staying in a hotel after each gig, to save money we would drive back to Birmingham almost every night. Phil Savage from Outlaw Studios was on the road with us doing the sound and Eddie the Eagle (nick named so, cos he looked just like Eddie the Eagle the skier) was our roadie whom we all helped with piling the instruments back into the van after which we would all pile in. It was a rough ride but lots of fun. We would get home in the early hours of the morning then congregate again at Outlaw Studios to hit the road again the next day for the next concert. Hitting the road with The Proclaimers was the best thing that could have happened to us as far as building a following was concerned, initially we received very mixed reactions from the crowds as no one had heard of us, the audience didn't quite know what to make of us and some saw us as a Dexys mark 2, but after a while as we became tighter musically and more together as a band, we were getting some great reactions from the audience and building up a growing number of fans, it was exciting to get some praise and positive feedback from people in the crowd. I had found my niche on stage and even though I remained reserved about my vocals I knew there was no place I would rather be than on stage singing with The Babes at this point. I loved being on stage with The Babes, Ian Pettitt's energy was amazing, he was like Animal off The Muppets, he had crazy energy on the drums which made me buzz out on stage too. One look at him pounding with his head going ten to the dozen and I was off too... I loved some of the guys dearly, they put commitment and energy into their involvement with The Babes.

Our second choice of single was 'Apples And Oranges' which I loved. It was one of my favourite songs to perform live because of that real energy and raunchy sound it conjured up, real raunchy fiddle with an upbeat to it. I thought this would become a real popular play for the radio, but the feedback we got was "It sounds too much like Dexys, it's already been done," no one on the radio would play it, which was really disheartening. We couldn't get away from the comparisons. There are many varieties of style in soul music, country music etc but because this sound was so unique and apart from Haysi Fantayzee who kind of touched on this style of music at the time it truly was new, original and a unique style of music first time around which replicated stood out as a copy cat band.

During this period I do remember seeing Helen and Rowland at the Town and Country Club but otherwise we didn't see an awful lot of them.

'Walking On The Line' became the choice for third single, I wasn't really happy with this choice and I'm not sure how it was chosen, I wanted 'It Could Have Been Love' or 'She's So Strong'. Archer and I toured the country doing interviews at radio and TV stations. My shyness and insecurity would get the better of me though and I would sometimes come out of an interview feeling like an idiot, in my head I was like "Why the fuck did I say that for?" With three failed singles and finishing the tour which, as I said, really brought

Babes bounce back!

● The Blue Ox Babes — ready at last

IT'S been a long time coming, but The Blue Ox Babes are finally ready to burst on to the pop scene.

The seven-piece Birmingham band, which features two former members of Dexy's Midnight Runners, originally formed in 1984.

After a short spell the group split, eventually reforming two years later. Now after months of rehearsals and line-up changes the Babes, who take their name from a Walt Disney character, have landed a record deal.

They have been signed by Go! Discs, the label of former chart toppers The Housemartins, and their first single "There's No Deceiving You" is released tomorrow.

It is a swinging soul stomper which has more than a hint of the brassy sound Dexy's achieved on hits like "Geno".

The song was written by singer and guitarist Kevin Archer and violinist Steve Shaw, who are both former Dexys. Kevin wrote the Number One "Geno" and "There, There, My Dear" in collaboration with Dexy's lead singer Kevin Rowland.

Babes vocalist and percussion player Yasmin Saleh, who lives in Edgbaston, said: "We are not trying to copy what Dexy's did, I think the music is a natural progression."

The Babes are halfway through recording their debut album and will be playing a series of live dates to promote the single.

in a lot of support from new fans. The final gig was The London Dominion and due to a technical failure there was an embarrassing interlude when all our sound went down and we were face to face with the audience which was totally unrehearsed. It felt like a life time, I was stunned, totally unexpected, no one knew what to do or say, which really frustrated Archer in front of thousands of people. Lots of record company executives and major artists attended this performance, the whole sound just went down and we were left standing there on stage, gobsmacked. It was highly embarrassing, Archer was annoyed and afterwards there was a bit of a clash between us. The comparison in the reviews and even in interviews to Dexys continued on a regular basis which Archer hated and his behaviour towards me started to get a little didactic at times, I realise that he didn't mean to be the way he was at times, it was a result of his illness. I had to spend a lot of time with Archer touring in the band and on the road, for most of the time we worked fairly closely together, there were conflicts and arguments which came to a climax one night when we were in Scotland in a hotel, things between Archer and I became more difficult to handle. I don't think I was committed enough as I should have been at this point in time and I think Archer could see this which was frustrating for him too. Archer's not so respectful ways of approaching me caused me to rebel though; I didn't want to spend time with him and wanted to get away.

I was disheartened about the whole events that occurred and we had a bit of a quiet spell over the Christmas period, not playing any gigs, rehearsing or recording. I went back to working behind bars to make extra cash. It broke my heart when I left The Babes. I didn't really tell anyone apart from Steve Shaw that I was leaving. I wanted to get away, as far away as possible from all the hurt and pain from the past years with Archer and in regards to Dexys. I was too young to cope with everything that had happened, but then again, maybe I was just living out my character as Gypsy Rose Lee nomad lifestyle again. I left The Babes and Archer, I had my reservations as I boarded the plane for Australia to join my then boyfriend.

I never really found the strength or confidence to get up again on stage and even though I have no solid regrets I wish I had taken up my position at drama school, I tried getting back into theatre but it was never at the same professional level and I just kept getting pulled back. In reflection dancing and singing was the love of my life and I never really realised that until I left and discovered dancing and acting again recently, I just never found the confidence to get up and do it again. I sing all the time and people constantly say to me, you should be singing but I always find excuses because underneath I still suffer with fear of having to get up in front of people, funny thing is though that once I'm up I'm OK, it's just the fear of getting up in the first place.

After I left The Babes I really didn't think they would split, I honestly thought I was doing the best thing possible as far as Archer was concerned, I thought, "I'm just a backing vocalist they will get someone else in who could sing much better than me and who Archer would be able to have a professional relationship with." To me The Babes were literally his baby and he could continue to grow with it, from this point on I just kept running. Running to Australia, around the world and I have now ended up in New Zealand. Steve did mention prior to my departure that he was offered some work with

The Proclaimers and he went on to play on their next album 'Sunshine On Leith' which was released in 1988 and then continued to tour with them. I felt bad for Archer but for me personally there was no way to continue with The Babes at this point.

Archer did come to Australia at one point but I didn't have the strength or courage to catch up with him, it wasn't until sometime later that I heard The Proclaimers were playing in Australia, I contacted the promoter and reconnected with Steve Shaw. He filled me in on everything that had happened in my absence after I had left the band, and my heart dropped as I really thought they would go on and create more music, to hear that Go Disc's did not re-sign them broke my heart. I never told anyone about my past history in the UK, set about my travels in Australia and the world but years later in 2001 I think, when The Proclaimers played Auckland in New Zealand they told me that there were many interesting sites dedicated to Dexys and The Babes and that Rowland had finally admitted to his plagiarism of Archer's ideas and music and given him some of the credit and royalties to 'Too-Rye-Ay' which were due to him. Archer was finally credited with his input to the 'Too-Rye-Ay' period where as previously he had been totally overlooked while 'Come On Eileen' and 'Too-Rye-Ay' were hitting Number 1 spots around the world. I was so happy to see this, better late then never, at least Rowland, someone I respected and admire was doing the right thing. I had always maintained my respect for Rowland. I was blown away with the information I found on The Babes on the internet, I thought we were dead and buried and here it was in writing. A Big Thanks to some of the fans that have persisted with their dedication to both bands and created sites to keep The Babes alive too. I also think that through Rowland, The Babes were also kept alive and kicking. I met a guy called John through the internet after leaving a comment on his page, who I am deeply indebted to for his input on writing The Babes sites and his dedication to the band, it was through John that I reconnected with Pete Williams and Rowland. Apparently Rowland was doing an interview at a radio station with someone he knew and he had asked John if he could have my telephone number in New Zealand, he rang me one day in New Zealand and apologised for something, I won't go into it but just to say that it wasn't what I was expecting. I did visit Rowland in Brighton but he asked me to leave after a day, not sure why. It all seemed very strange.

I reconnected with Archer and went to visit him. He told me about his story about Germany and how he had become a tramp, how his mother had brought him back to England and how Rowland had finally admitted plagiarism of his ideas and how his writing and ideas had a huge influence on the 'Too-Rye-Ay' period. Archer's story is heartbreaking, the way he fell deeper and deeper into a dark hole. Over the next couple of years I visited Archer whenever I returned to the UK with my son. He gave me some tapes of some of the songs he had recorded with another female and Pete Wain after I had left entitled 'Last 13 Songs', which I still have, they were the last thirteen songs Archer wrote. I have them on tape and did send a copy to John who I previously mentioned as building websites in remembrance of The Babes, I really liked the songs but Archer once again struggled to get a record contract with these songs. Archer and I still talk over the phone from time to time, Archer also sent me some money for my son as he knew I was a single Mom. He also paid for us to fly back to the UK to do some interviews when Cherry Red first offered to release 'Apples And Oranges', which I did but felt the interviewer put Archer in a bad light making it seem like he was very money orientated, which he isn't, he's generous and kind but at times because of his illness he says things in response to questions without thinking too much. He has been very good to me and as I said he paid for me and my son to visit family in the UK, otherwise I would not have been able to come back. I was shocked when Cherry Red emailed me contracts through for the release of 'Apples And Oranges' and really happy that finally it was getting released. It had been sitting there shelfed for so long. It's not climbing the charts but it got released, I was up for doing some stage work but Archer is so far beyond doing any gigs, performing or singing now. It's sad as we couldn't even really promote the release of the CD. I've just received a new contract from John Reed at Cherry Red who will continue to print more copies of the CD which I am very happy about and grateful for. I stay in touch with Archer and very rarely Steve Shaw and I visit them when I am in the UK, but due to being so far away and travelling costs I only see them about once every five years.

I have to say that regardless of any plagiarism, conflict or arguments along the way in reflection being part of The Babes was a real ride and it was one of the best times in my life. I loved all the guys in The Blue Ox Babes especially Ian Pettitt, and I would say this was the closest I ever came to realising my dreams and feeling connected to my souls purpose. I felt privileged to be able to share these times with such talented, dedicated and creative musicians. It was a real experience in life for me, one that I will never forget. Being on stage was like finding a home, a place to belong. I got a real buzz out of it and despite my nerves and fears once Ian hit his drums and the energy started pumping, there was no place I would rather be, I felt invigorated and alive.

My thoughts for the people we lost along the way are also still alive. Pete Rowland who was such a gentleman, kind and humane person. I still see him smiling to this day, standing there in his grey suit and his cheeky face.

Paul Burton who was funny, warm and a real Geordie character.

My favourite track from The Babes collection of songs is 'She's So Strong'.

Yasmin Saleh, December 2013

THE BLUE OX BABES

There's No Deceiving You/The Last Detail (GOBOB1) 7"
There's No Deceiving You/The Last Detail/Take Me To The River (GOBOB112) 12" *(Released 7th March 1988)*

Apples And Oranges (The International Hope Campaign)/Pray Lucky (GOBOB2) 7"
Apples And Oranges (The International Hope Campaign)/Pray Lucky/Yes Let's/Russia In Winter (GOBOB212) 12" *(Released 20th June 1988)*

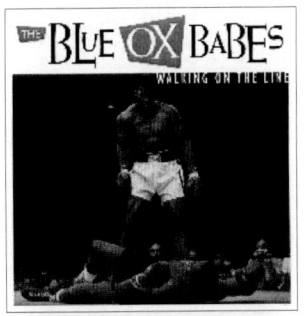

Walking On The Line/Four Golden Tongues Talk (GOBOB3) 7"
Walking On The Line/Four Golden Tongues Talk/What Does Anybody Ever Think About/Thought As Much (GOBOB312) 12" *(Released 31st October 1988)*

Apples And Oranges. Originally unreleased album in 1988. Released on CD 18th May 2009 with bonus tracks (CDMRED401)

Dexys SHOW TIMES 2012/13

2012
Saturday 28th April Berns Salonger, Stockholm, Sweden
Monday 30th April Pustervik, Gothenburg, Sweden
Friday 4th May Park & Dare Theatre, Treorchy, UK
Sunday 6th May Cottier Theatre, Glasgow, UK
Monday 7th May Playhouse, Whitley Bay, UK
Tuesday 8th May 02 Shepherd's Bush Empire, London, UK
Monday 28th May Berns Salonger, Stockholm, Sweden
Wednesday 30th May Pustervik, Gothenburg, Sweden
Saturday 23rd June Luften Festival, Frankfurt, Germany
Saturday 7th July Lounge On The Farm Festival, Merton Farm, Canterbury, UK
Friday 17th August – Sunday 19th August Green Man Festival, Abergavenny, UK
Sunday 9th September Colchester Arts Centre, Colchester, UK
Tuesday 11th September Corn Exchange, Cambridge, UK
Wednesday 12th September Symphony Hall, Birmingham, UK
Thursday 13th September Guildhall, Southampton, UK
Sunday 16th September Barbican Centre, London, UK
Monday 17th September The Sage, Gateshead, UK
Tuesday 18th September The Queen's Hall, Edinburgh, UK
Thursday 20th September Brighton Dome, Brighton, UK
Friday 21st September The Bridgewater Hall, Manchester, UK
Saturday 22nd September Colston Hall, Bristol, UK
Monday 24th September Liverpool Philharmonic Hall, Liverpool, UK
Tuesday 25th September New Theatre, Oxford, UK
Saturday 10th November Harvest Festival, Melbourne, Australia
Monday 12th November Astor Theatre, Perth, Australia
Thursday 15th November Enmore Theatre, Sydney, Australia
Saturday 17th November Harvest Festival, Sydney, Australia
Sunday 18th November Harvest Festival, Brisbane, Australia

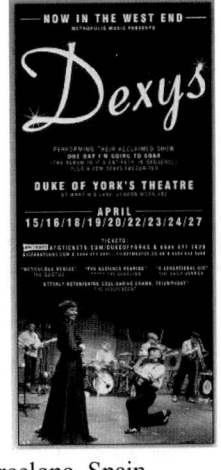

2013
Wednesday 10th April Komedia, Bath, UK
Saturday 13th April Guildhall, Gloucester, UK
Monday 15th April Duke Of York's Theatre, London, UK
Tuesday 16th April Duke Of York's Theatre, London, UK
Thursday 18th April Duke Of York's Theatre, London, UK
Friday 19th April Duke Of York's Theatre, London, UK
Saturday 20th April Duke Of York's Theatre, London, UK
Monday 22nd April Duke Of York's Theatre, London, UK
Tuesday 23rd April Duke Of York's Theatre, London, UK
Wednesday 24th April Duke Of York's Theatre, London, UK
Saturday 27th April Duke Of York's Theatre, London, UK
Thursday 2nd May Olympia Theatre, Dublin, Ireland
Friday 3rd May Cathedral Quarter Arts, Belfast, UK
Saturday 4th May Anglican Cathedral, Liverpool, UK
Saturday 25th May Primavera Sound Festival, Parc del Forum, Barcelona, Spain
Sunday 30th June Parkpop Festival, Den Haag, Netherlands
Monday 1st July Melkweg, Amsterdam, Netherlands
Sunday 28th July Stockton Weekender Festival, Stockton, UK
Sunday 8th September Bestival Festival, Arreton, Isle Of Wight, UK

Show photos by Andy Purcell. Fan photos: Above left – Ann-Marie McKenzie with Kevin Rowland, bottom left – Andy Purcell with Lucy Morgan. Right – Nic Miller with Kevin Rowland.

Dexys

"The power of Dexys is undiminished"
- The Observer

"The soul album of the century and a live show to match"
- The Independent

Photos by Clive Gray

THE LONG AWAITED NEW
ALBUM FROM DEXYS

Includes

SHE GOT A WIGGLE
INCAPABLE OF LOVE
NOWHERE IS HOME

ONE DAY I'M GOING TO SOAR

OUT 4TH JUNE

BMG

hmv
hmv.com

That's about the size of it...